From EVEREST *to* Enlightenment

Alan Hobson

Mount Everest Climber and Summiteer

From EVEREST *to* Enlightenment

An Adventure of the Soul

Alan Hobson

Mount Everest Climber and Summiteer

Inner Everests Inc.

Published by: Inner Everests Inc.
#5 – 100 Prospect Heights
Canmore, Alberta, Canada
T1W 2X8
Tel: (403) 609-9939
Fax: (403) 609-2818
E-mail: info@alanhobson.com
Web: www.alanhobson.com

Canadian Cataloguing in Publication Data

Hobson, Alan, 1958-
From Everest to enlightenment

ISBN 0-9685263-0-6

1. Success.   2. Mountaineering — Everest, Mount (China and Nepal)
— Psychological aspects.   3. Mountaineers — Canada — Biography.
4. Hobson, Alan, 1958-   I. Title.
GV199.44.E85H62 1999   158.1   C99-910458-6

Printed and bound in Canada by Friesens, Altona, Manitoba
Fifth Printing, 2003

ACKNOWLEDGMENTS

This is my fifth published book. Like all the previous ones, it was like an expedition for me, filled with fun, challenges and long, long hours.

Every time I write a book, I'm convinced it will be my last, in much the same way I'm always sure I'll never go back to another high mountain. I think I'll form a support group called *"Authors Anonymous"* and every time I think of writing another book, I'll call up one of my colleagues and they'll convince me otherwise. But write I must, even more than I must adventure, for it is an integral part of me. I must share.

Books are huge personal undertakings. This one was no different. I am grateful, first and foremost, to all those who made the Colliers Lotus Notes Everest Expedition possible. Without them, there would be no story.

Although it is impossible to mention all of them here, I would graciously request forgiveness in advance should I inadvertently miss someone.

Colliers International:
John McLernon, CEO; Jim Bowles; Michael Dingle;
Hilary Horlock; Jamie Horne; David Weinkauf

Lotus Development Corporation:
Jeff Papows, CEO; Gloria Simpson; Michael Cetaruk;
Jane Eisenberg; Steve Sayre; Cyril Spratt

Great Escapes Kathmandu:
Sonam Gyalpo Lama; Ang Jambu Sherpa;
Kiran Manandhar; Ram Bomjam

The Expedition Team
Steve Matous, Expedition Organizer (Great Escapes USA)
North American Climbing Team
Jamie Clarke, Co-Business Manager, Climber;
Jason Edwards, Expedition Leader, Climber;
Jeff Rhoads, Deputy Leader, Climber;
Dr. Doug Rovira, Team Physician, Climber

Nepalese Climbing Team
Ang Temba, Sirdar (Head Sherpa)
Climbing Sherpas: Mingma Dorjee; Gyalbu; Nurbu; Pema
Temba; Kami Tshering; Lhakpa Tshering; Tashi Tsering

North American Support Team
Bruce Kirkby, Telecommunications Coordinator;
Dave Rodney, Communications Coordinator

Nepalese Support Team
Buddhinath "Booty" Bhattarai, Liaison Officer, Nepalese
Department of Tourism; Pemba Jeba Bhote, Base Camp
Cook; Ang Dawa, Mail Runner and Assistant to Pemba
Jeba Bhote; Padam Bahadur Limbu, Assistant to Pemba
Jeba Bhote; Shyam Prasad Pun, Advanced Base Camp Cook

The Odyssey Adventure Society
Leigh Clarke; Aaron Engen; Tom Valentine;
Sandy Pearson

The Everest Effort Inc.
Karen Harris; Mary Ross

I would also like to thank:

Friends
Rob Aikens; John Amatt; Shawn Biggings; Milan Hudec;
Hal Kuntze; Bill March; Patti Mayer; Grant Molyneux;
Karl Nagy; Barb Neumann; Valerie Simonson;
Laurie Skreslet; Sharon Wood; Cal Zaryski; Diane; Julie

Book Production Team
Vincanne Adams, Consultant; Brian Chu, Designer;
Dale Ens, Proofreader; Friesens Corporation, Printers;
Leslie Johnson, Substantive and Primary Editor; John King,
Copy Editor and Production Manager; Wayne Logan,
Counsel; Ingrid Meger, Research; Cecilia Rau, Production
Coordinator; Tracy Wuth, Coordinator

Family
Isabel and Peter Hobson; Dan Hobson; Eric Hobson;
James Hobson

Supreme Overseer
"Baba" (The Father)

TABLE OF CONTENTS

Introduction

*Though the search for simplicity is, at any time,
a difficult journey through a wilderness, we can
learn from guides ancient and modern.*

— MARTIN MARTY

NESTLED HIGH in the rarefied air of the Himalayas, amid the towering ramparts of the tallest summits on Earth, lives a people unlike any other in the world. Adapted over the centuries to life at extreme altitudes, they go about their lives today much as they have since migrating here from ancient Tibet centuries ago. They tend to high-altitude yaks, hardy goats and specially bred oxen, till the thin mountain soil growing potatoes, barley and wheat, and move about toting back-breaking loads over steep mountain footpaths in the cold, thin air.

These are the Sherpas of Nepal, the "Tigers of the Snow." No longer exclusively porters or mountain guides, they have evolved into the world's finest high-altitude climbers, bar none. More Nepalese Sherpas have been to the summit of Mount Everest than from any other nation on Earth — at the time of this writing, about 100 of the 700 or so climbers who have touched the top of the world. The Sherpas have also experienced the greatest number of deaths, 134 (on all parts of the mountain), according to Vincanne Adams, an anthropologist at Princeton University and author of *Tigers of the Snow*.

It is impossible to imagine the raw power and speed of a Sherpa until one actually sees one move with a load. Using a wide banded tump-line of cloth across their foreheads and around the back of packs, they move with astonishing ease under burdens of up to 150 pounds. Some lowland porters (not to be confused with high-altitude climbing Sherpas) can carry loads up to 250 pounds — about the weight of your average refrigerator. But above 17,000 feet, the base of Everest, the strength and courage of the Sherpas is unequaled. Born and genetically adapted to life at 13,000 feet and above, they are as at home in Everest's rarefied air as most Westerners are in their living rooms. One Sherpa, Ang Rita, has been to the top 10 times. Another, Kaji, holds a world ascent speed record from the south side of the mountain in Nepal — an astonishing 20 and a half hours. Hans Kammerlander, of Italy, holds the current world record for the fastest ascent to date from the northern side of the mountain in Tibet — an amazing 16 hours, 45 minutes.

But to marvel only at their astonishing physical powers is to miss the true strength of these quiet, humble people. Isolated from the outside world, without the "luxuries" of automobiles, roads, bicycles, telephones, radios, televisions, microwave ovens, central heating, air conditioning, plumbing, running water, computers, or the Internet, the Sherpas live in a world richly steeped in Buddhist culture. They have strong spiritual values and a sense of community all but absent in much of our "civilized" world. In the Khumbu region from which they hail, several hundred miles northeast of the Nepalese capital of Kathmandu, human beings are solitary figures against the vastness of nature's awe-inspiring backdrop. The landscape is not only breathtaking and the climate hostile; the region is also forbidding and empty. The unrelenting solitude can be as much of a challenge as the thin air. What brings color to this world of rock, snow and ice is the Sherpa culture and especially Sherpa compassion. The only way the several thousand of these resilient beings survive is by sticking together.

I met my first Sherpa in 1991 at the offices of "Tiger Mountain," a large trekking, mountaineering and expedition firm in Kathmandu, at the base of the mighty Himalayas, north of India. I had heard of them through books, photographs, magazine articles, and film documentaries. These painted them as superheroes of the snows, beings capable of colossal feats of strength and endurance. Imagine my surprise when the first Sherpa I met appeared in a baseball hat and jeans, weighing at most 120 pounds ringing wet. He stood a little over 5 feet 2 inches tall. Physically, he looked no stronger than my grandmother.

"How in heaven's name," I thought, "could such an apparently diminutive and self-effacing human being ever carry twice his body weight?" The idea seemed absurd.

I came face to face with the error in my thinking one crisp morning a little over a month later. As the mid-morning sun cast its warming rays across Tibet at about 23,000 feet, I found myself face first in the snow on all fours, panting uncontrollably and on the verge of vomiting.

As my heart raced at over 170 beats a minute, the massive North Col ("Col" is French for "mountain pass") slope of Mount Everest loomed around me. Below, it fell 2,000 feet to the East Rongbuk Glacier. Above, massive ice blocks the size of six-story apartment buildings teetered on the edge of reality. They clung to the face, threatening at any moment to "calve off" and crush me.

Despite years of heavy training, which included climbing more than 230 stories at a time in the stairwell of a Canadian office tower with my friend, Jamie Clarke, I had believed, erroneously, that I was ready for Everest. We had carried 85-pound packs for a mind-numbing three hours at a time up and down the tower's 29 stories. I had supplemented this training with marathon runs of up to 26 miles long.

That morning on Everest was a rude awakening. First, I hauled myself up from the snow. Then, I squeezed out two or three excruciatingly difficult steps. Next, I crouched down on all fours again and came face to face with the cold reality of my own inadequacy. Between hurried breaths, I tried to hollow out a breathing hole in the snow with my hands.

Suddenly, my panting was interrupted:

"Good morning Alan!" came a cheerful voice from behind me. "Are you okay?"

Like a scared rabbit with its head buried in a hole, I peered out between my legs. I was amazed to see "my grandmother" strolling up the slope below me like he was at a Sunday school picnic. The diminutive figure I'd seen in Kathmandu was, in fact, Da Nuru Sherpa, who at 30 was one of the strongest Sherpas with whom I would ever climb.

"Yeah ... (breath) ... yeah ... (breath)," I struggled to say.

"Good," he replied.

In the next moment, he and his four Sherpa companions blasted effortlessly by me. Without missing a step, they dispensed with the traditional "jumar" braking devices usually used to move safely up anchored rope. Instead, they "batmanned" flawlessly hand-over-hand up the line like so many kids pulling in perch on fishing filament. The damage to my ego was severe. What made it worse was when I realized moments later that the Sherpas were carrying packs more than twice the weight of mine. I did eventually make it to the top of the slope, but not until hours after the Sherpas had not only reached the spot, but already returned to the camp below.

Looks can be deceiving, especially when it comes to the Sherpas. This was the first of many lessons they would teach me. Over the next six years or so, the Sherpas of Nepal would so change the way I looked at myself and my world as to inexorably alter my very outlook on life — how I viewed success and failure, what I knew of teamwork and commitment, and my whole concept of effort and achievement. Silently and almost imperceptibly, these gentle men stole their way into my heart and shook the foundation of who I was. They guided me in a completely new type of adventure — one deeper into my soul.

"The Sherpas do with a lot less than we do and they think about the greater interaction with society versus just a 'me' approach," says Jason Edwards, climbing leader of the Colliers Lotus Notes Everest Expedition. "If something bad happens to you while they're around, they think it's their fault. Every day is Sunday for them. Religion and spirituality is a way of life."

I wrote of some of my experiences with the Sherpas in my last book, *The Power of Passion — Achieve Your Own Everests*, which I co-wrote with Jamie Clarke. *The Power of Passion* was the story of our first two expeditions to Everest in 1991 and 1994 and some of the lessons of life we learned along the way. It became a national bestseller. This book is the story of our third Everest expedition in 1997, the further lessons I learned and, most importantly, how I changed as a person in the process. The expedition became more of an inner Everest than an outer expedition.

During my three Everest expeditions, besides the constants of Jamie and "Chomolungma" (Mother Goddess of the World), as the locals refer to Everest, there were dozens of Sherpas on our trips. Some worked as cooks, others as mail runners and trekking assistants. Most helped carry me — or more accurately, my equipment — to and from the top of the world. Amid my struggle against Everest's adversity, there was their ever-present loyalty, inestimable strength and limitless spiritual resilience. I could not possibly have climbed Everest without them.

The most well known Sherpa is Tenzing Norgay. On May 29, 1953, at the age of 39 (the same age at which I summited), he stood on Everest's summit with Sir Edmund Hillary of New Zealand. Together, they became the first people to successfully reach the top of the world and return alive. The book of Tenzing's life, *Man of Everest*, by James Ramsey Ullman, tells the stirring tale of Tenzing's life, his struggles against Everest and his even-greater struggles to come to grips with his personal transition from a once humble load-carrier to an equally humble international celebrity.

At the time of Hillary and Norgay's historic ascent, there was considerable debate about who had reached the top first, even though both were roped together and as such, it is really an irrelevant question. The uninitiated came to know Tenzing simply as "the other guy," perhaps because, as Buddhists, the Sherpas believe one should suppress the ego, not flaunt it to the world.

One member of our 1997 expedition, Dr. Doug Rovira, has his own theory:

"I have little doubt Tenzing Norgay arrived on the summit of Everest on that blustery day in 1953 a full hour ahead of Sir Edmund, had a hot pot of tea waiting, and lightened his load for the trip down."

While Sir Edmund has explained that, at the time, he just happened to be leading the rope to the top, anyone who has witnessed the strength and speed of a Sherpa knows that if you happen to be tied to one, you'd better be ready to run uphill. Blind patriotism and egos aside, in sheer numbers, the Sherpas stand alone at the apex of the world high altitude climbing community.

I wrote most of this book many months before I was given a copy of *Man of Everest*. But in reading Tenzing's story, I came to see many dramatic parallels with my Everest experience. I have, therefore, included many quotations from *Man of Everest* here with the goal of re-inforcing some of the key lessons the Sherpas have taught me.

A Sherpa's idea of success, for example, is very different from ours. It relates more to an individual's ability to put key values into action in their lives — values like compassion, humility, a lack of ego, and being true to your own path in life. These are just some of the lessons I have learned from the Sherpas. Although I am a long way from rising to the peak of these ideals, I aspire to them much as I aspired to climb Everest. Ironically, the achievement of that goal has led me to a whole new understanding of true greatness and it has nothing to do with physical achievement, the "conquering" of mountains, or the "victory" of human beings over nature.

You have to be born a Sherpa. You cannot "become" one. Yet in many ways, the Sherpas differ little from any of us. They desire to live a quiet and happy life, one as free as possible from disease, strife and heartache. But that's where the similarities end and the differences begin.

"They [the Sherpas] wouldn't write about greatness," says Steve Matous, the organizer of our Colliers Lotus Notes

Everest Expedition and a man who has been in business with the Sherpas for five years. "They're too humble. They'd push others to the front.... They summit Everest four, five and six times and then laugh all the way down the trail. The wives and mothers would be the heroes. Women hold the family together."

The ultimate goal of a Sherpa is to pass into the next life having made the lives of as many others around them as rich as possible. The virtue to which they most aspire is not financial wealth, material possession, position, power, or fame. It is compassion for all living things. In that sense, although we can never become Sherpas in the literal sense, we can still aspire to some of their more admirable personal and social qualities, while understanding that they are just as human as the rest of us. They too have their faults.

"Westerners are lulled into ascribing an egalitarian ideology to the Sherpas that simplifies, if it does not downright distort, the ethnographic facts," writes James Fisher in *Sherpas: Reflections on Change in Himalayan Nepal*. He explains that in many ways the Western romantic myth about Sherpa society is an image of how Westerners would like to be themselves. We seem to ignore that Sherpas are equally prone to such vices as alcoholism, drug abuse, crime, violence, and sexual promiscuity.

In spite of these short-comings, I still believe there is much we can learn from the Sherpas, if not how to better program a computer or run a company, certainly how to better program ourselves and run some aspects of our lives. A case in point:

A few days after I dragged my sorry butt to the top of the North Col slope that morning in 1991, I managed to corner one of the Sherpas, Ang Temba. He had summited Everest the previous spring as part of the first all-Sherpa expedition to the mountain. I asked him why it had taken his people almost 40 years after Tenzing's ascent in 1953 to finally launch an Everest expedition as a tribe. Everest was, after all, the world's tallest mountain and it was literally in their backyard.

"We didn't need to climb Everest," Ang Temba explained quietly.

"Why not?" I asked. "It's right here. You're right here. All you had to do was climb her."

He looked back at me like I didn't know anything (which, of course, I didn't). Then he paused and smiled.

"Everest is beautiful and it's there. What more do you need?"

These and other "whacks upside the head" have helped me to understand that there is far more depth and breadth to the Sherpas than their climbing ability. The only reason any Sherpa Everest expedition had apparently been staged was because a few supporters in the West (one of whom was Steve Matous) arranged financing for the expedition. Were it not for this injection of foreign capital, the Sherpas might still not have climbed Everest as a group. In their isolated world of solitude and silence, the land of the Yeti, of savage winds and colossal snows, they have managed not only to carve out a unique existence, but they have also gained a truly unique understanding of life.

I believe we are all Sherpas carrying loads of one sort or another. And, we find ourselves struggling up our own mountains — whether they be professional, personal, marital, emotional, interpersonal, parental, medical, or financial. At times, some of us cannot seem to find the strength to bear our burdens. The path we're on seems brutally steep and unrelenting. Sometimes, "we just can't take it any more." We sit exhausted and disillusioned by the side of the trail and hope that somehow the crushing weight on our shoulders will magically be lifted, or at least lightened. Our hearts are heavy, as are our souls.

We are all Sherpas carrying loads of one sort or another.

Whatever path we have chosen in life, climb we must, for to do otherwise is to relinquish our own self-respect and give in to our frailties and fear. This is the story of my own climb as a white-faced "Sherpa," one against the weight of my own personal fears, insecurities, and self-doubts, past the pain of my past and upwards to a true personal triumph. Were it not for the Sherpas, not only would I have not have made it safely to and from the summit of Everest, but I could not possibly have been able to see what I did from that vantagepoint. It was a new view of myself and our world, of the price of success and the true value of people in our lives. The Sherpas helped point the way to a new life path for me, and perhaps for you. The expedition became far more than a physical ascent of Everest. It became a spiritual journey and awakening, an adventure of the soul.

So now, let us climb together not only to the highest point on the planet, but to the depth of ourselves, into the dark crevasses of our own inner Everests, past our deepest fears and out into the searing sunshine and breathtaking view at 29,028 feet. This is a story not just about climbing a mountain, but about the mountains we are all climbing in life.

> *Never bear more than one kind of trouble at a time.*
> *Some people bear three — all they have had, all they*
> *have now, and all they expect to have.*
>
> — EDWARD EVERELL HALE
> (1822–1909)

This is a story not just about climbing a mountain, but about the mountains we are all climbing in life.

Back to Everest

*Failure is the opportunity to begin again
more intelligently.*

— HENRY FORD

2:35 A.M., MAY 23, 1997 — I don't know what's happening to
me. I can't seem to keep up. Amid the wild gusts of wind and
spindrift snow, by the eerie light of the moon, I see Jamie and
the Sherpas disappearing from sight. For a second, they ghost
into view. Then ... a moment later ... they vanish.

What's going on? Where did they go? Did they fall?

Why can't I get enough air?

I feel like I'm suffocating. Every breath is a battle. I look at
my altimeter. It reads 27,600 feet. Camp 4 is a long way below
me. If I fall here, I'm history. I'll slide all the way into the
South Col and maybe 4,000 feet down the Lhotse Face too.
Everest, in all its massiveness, will consume me like a crumb.

If I could just get to the ridge. If I could somehow just get
there. Maybe we'd stand a chance. Are we off route? Why can't
I keep up?

A second later, I get my answer. A powerful gust of wind hits
me like a battering ram. With it comes yet another swirling
cloud of spindrift snow. It hammers straight into my hood,
goes around several times and straight down my back. I become
an instant icicle.

I start to shiver.

"K-K-Kami," I say to the Sherpa I am with as my teeth start to chatter. "We need to go down."

He acts like he doesn't hear me.

Seconds pass. I feel the cold penetrating to my core. It stabs like a driven nail. I am succumbing to hypothermia, a potentially lethal condition in which the body's inner temperature drops. If it falls by just a few degrees, the victim very soon becomes incapable of moving. Death can come soon after.

I begin to panic. I know what will happen to me if we don't get out of here fast. I will freeze to death — my worst nightmare, cold, afraid and freezing near the summit of Everest. What a way to go. So close, and yet so far.

"No damn way!" I tell myself. "I'm not going to die here. No damn way. Not here, not anywhere — not if I can still do something about it."

"Kami," I say again, this time yelling at him through the howling wind. "Kami! We need to go down *now!*"

He doesn't hear me. He doesn't even respond.

I feel alone and very, very afraid.

* * *

Technique and ability alone do not get you to the top —
it is the willpower that is the most important.
This willpower you cannot buy with money or be
given by others — it rises from your heart.

— JUNKO TABEI, of Japan,
after becoming the first woman
to climb Everest, in 1975

Almost as soon as the snow had melted from our crampons after saving John McIsaac's life during the 1994 Emergo Mount Everest Expedition, and as we had after our first "unsuccessful" expedition to the mountain in 1991, Jamie and I began to orchestrate our return to Everest for Round Three. When John had come within just 162 vertical meters of the top before succumbing to the effects of high-altitude sickness and eventually having to be rescued, we couldn't just walk away from our dream. Our expedition had come within a couple of city blocks of our goal. Jamie and I both knew neither of us would rest until we had either closed the gap, or come to the realization that neither one of us ever would. One way or the other, we wanted to know the answer to Everest's ultimate question: Could we do it?

> *"I am sick at heart," Dr. Chevalley wrote in his diary as he thought about our second failure; and we all felt much the same. But mixed with our sadness, I think, was also a certain quiet pride, for we knew that in the conditions we had faced no men could have done more than we did. If Everest was still my dream, it was only a bad one.* — TENZING NORGAY, *Man of Everest*

As human beings, we are conditioned from an early age to believe that failure is bad. It is not only to be feared, we are taught. It is to be avoided at all cost. We are punished for failing — by being benched, held back a year, scolded, fired, ignored, ostracized, shunned or just plain rejected. No one enjoys it.

In the eyes of the world to which we returned after our '94 expedition, a trip that had seen us raise close to a half a million dollars, move five tons of gear and six North American climbers half way around the world, to the top of the world and back again safely, we had failed because we had failed to reach the summit. In our view, however, we had not failed. We had saved John's life and that had been a huge victory. It had taken us a grueling 33 hours and pushed every member of the rescue team further than they had ever been pushed before. Most importantly, we had certainly not failed to learn from our experience. We now knew, or more importantly, we believed we knew, how to get safely to and from the top of Everest.

The first step was to forgive ourselves for coming up short. If we failed to do that, we knew, we would never be able to return to Everest. Without this forgiveness, our "failure" would

As human beings, we are conditioned from an early age to believe that failure is bad.

remain so — at least in the eyes of those around us. I found great solace in knowing that if John had decided to continue climbing from his high point rather than descending as he had, he would likely have made it to the top, but he would most certainly have perished on the descent. Would that have made our expedition a success? I didn't think so. Sometimes, we have such a skewed view of "success," especially in contrast with what the Sherpas believe. Compassion counts in our culture, but not, it would seem, as much as the achievement of the goal.

Forgiveness can be difficult to achieve — especially self-forgiveness. To re-program an ingrained response than has been with us since birth can be very, very difficult. But when forgiveness is combined with proper analysis of our mistakes and we change our behavior based on what we have learned, the results can be amazing. Thus, there is success in failure, but only if we know how and where to find it.

> *Forgiveness can be difficult to achieve — especially self-forgiveness.*

The end of the 1994 Emergo Mount Everest Expedition was a sad time for me. As with every major expedition, I went through a type of post-partum depression. For the second time, we had not achieved our goal of making it to the top. Once again, a part of the dream was dead. I experienced depression, emptiness, a sense of deep loss, and an inability to focus.

> *We had given all we had, and it was not enough.*
> *We turned without speaking. We descended without*
> *speaking. Down the long ridge, past the high camp,*
> *along the ridge again, along the snow slope.*
> *Slowly — slowly. Down — down — down.*
>
> —Tenzing Norgay,
> *Man of Everest,*
> on reaching 28,250 feet [only 778 vertical feet from the top]
> with Raymond Lambert during the Swiss Expedition, spring, 1952

The way I cope with this depression is to be with the pain and emptiness for a period, usually two or three difficult months. During this time, I often find myself asking if there is something wrong with me. Where did I go wrong? What could I have done better? What could *we* have done better?

On Everest, it is such an effort just to breathe, let alone take a step, that the mountain kicks our butt every time we face her. I like to think of her as the ultimate extractor. She extracts from us in all ways — physically, financially, mentally, emotionally and spiritually. One of my mentors, the late Bill March, who was the leader of the first Canadian expedition to Everest in 1982, once said that climbing Everest is like growing old very fast — you don't eat well, you don't sleep well and you don't feel well. Yes, the mountain can fill us up and enrich us with her energy and our experiences, but mostly, she empties us. She drains us of our resolve and saps us of our motivation. She is like the swift hand of God when we misbehave. She puts us in our place, at the bottom of nature's order, not at the top of the food chain as we erroneously believe.

Key to my adjustment in 1994 was my girlfriend at the time, whom I will call "Julie" to protect her privacy. I had met Julie through one of our expedition suppliers a few months before leaving for the mountain. She proved to be an invaluable emotional support during and after the expedition. When I came off Everest, she floored me by asking me to move in with her.

I loved Julie very deeply. Like most women with whom I have had relationships, I was passionately committed to her. I loved her energy and grace. She had a wonderfully gentle way about her, a captivating laugh and a warm smile. She worked as a freelance clothing designer, but her passion was the art of high fashion embroidery common in the designer boutiques and fashion show runways of Paris and New York. Although we moved in diametrically opposite worlds, I in the adventure world and she in the fashion world, we shared a common love for creativity — I through my writing and expedition-making and she through her design. She was a stunningly beautiful woman physically, but that is not why I loved her. I loved her poise.

It was so reassuring to come home to Julie. After months in a cold tent, her apartment was both a sanctuary and a place of solitude. She was also nurturing. She took care of me. We all need tender loving care and I am no exception, especially after an expedition. I rebuilt myself with her.

Over time, my strength returned, and I began to more seriously anchor myself in the next goal. This is part of the reason why Everest has been so important to me. It has been such a difficult goal, such a massive undertaking, that it has virtually consumed me for the better part of the last 10 years.

The winding down of the Emergo Mount Everest Expedition in the summer of 1994 was like the winding down of The Climb for Hope Expedition in the fall and winter of 1991 and 1992. There were outstanding obligations to sponsors and suppliers, banners to return, photos to be processed and speaking presentations to be made. And always, there was that explaining, explaining what had happened, why we hadn't made it to the summit, and how, thank goodness, we had all come back alive. It was that telling and re-telling, however, that I now see was so important to the future of Jamie and me on Everest. It galvanized a depth of motivation and commitment in us that is difficult to describe. It became our foundation for the future.

After a few months of telling our story, we became more determined than ever to see our Everest dream through. Our passion and focus bordered on obsession, but thankfully, never became it. Passion, as Jamie has said, is powerful. Obsession is destructive.

Passion, as Jamie has said, is powerful. Obsession is destructive.

> *It was a sad disappointment for Mr. Gibson, who had tried so long and so hard to climb this mountain. Yet he made no complaints. A fellow-climber had been in trouble; he had felt himself the proper one to help him; and by doing so he missed the great chance at his goal. That is the mountain way — the mountaineer's way.*

> —TENZING NORGAY,
> *Man of Everest,*
> on the attempt on Mt. Bandar Punch, 1950

The first person we contacted when we came back from Everest in 1994 was Steve Matous, of Boulder, Colorado. We had met Steve during our 1994 trip, during which time he had been guiding paying clients on Everest's north side. Both Jamie and I were so impressed with his interpersonal ability, his affable personality, his professionalism, and his attentiveness to detail that we knew we wanted him involved in our next Everest effort, not as a guide, but as a professional expedition organizer. We had learned from our 1994 trip that we couldn't be involved in the fundraising and organizing of an expedition, physical training, shipping and transportation logistics, load carrying once on Everest, media relations and team leadership, and still hope to climb the mountain. We needed to focus our energies exclusively on climbing the peak. That meant we had to find others to organize the trip, lead it, and report back to the world about it. Jamie and I hoped Steve could fulfill at least two of these key roles — as expedition organizer and leader. On our behalf, he agreed to start the application process with the government of Nepal to secure a permit to climb Everest from its southern, Nepalese side.

"I was extremely excited," Steve remembers. "I thought, 'Okay! This is a good project with good guys.'"

This time, we would approach Everest through the land of the Sherpas, the Khumbu valley. After two expeditions to the north side of Everest, Jamie and I had had it with the Tibetan side. In 1991, we'd gone to Everest because we'd been part of an expedition organized largely by Dr. Peter Austen of Prince George, British Columbia, several hundred miles northeast of Vancouver, Canada. We'd gone back to the north side three years later, in 1994, because we then had had experience on that side of the mountain.

Our experience in Tibet had borne out one cold reality — that the routes on the north side were long, their approaches lengthy and the wind and cold there severe. We felt we needed to get up and down the peak as quickly as Everest would permit. We needed to find a route that offered the shortest distance to our goal. The more direct, South Col route through Nepal, the one originally used by Sir Edmund Hillary and Tenzing Norgay during the first successful ascent of the mountain in 1953, offered what we believed would be our best chance. It was about one-quarter the length of the north ridge route. That also meant it was steeper, but we saw that as an asset. We could go up and down "quickly." After having been on two previous expeditions that hadn't reached the top, I felt the time had come to use all our learning, all our experience and every dime we had or could raise to make one more stab at the peak. To do so, we would literally follow in the footsteps of Hillary and Tenzing.

I knew this would definitely be my last Everest expedition. At 36, I was 10 years older than Jamie and in the words of my brother, Eric, I'd been doing "the full court press" 10 years longer. I'd spent 10 years working as a full-time freelance writer for such long hours and so little pay that it had taken a toll on my motivation. I wanted to either make it to the top of Everest and come back down safely, or at least know that I had given it everything I had, short of my life. That way, I hoped, regardless of the outcome of the expedition, I would be able to come away from Everest with a sense of positive closure with the mountain. I wanted to be able to turn a page in my life, close a chapter, and get on with living the rest of my life — enjoying the second half of it under far less personally imposed pressure than I had the first half of it. The way I saw it, I didn't want to turn 40 still pushing my way upwards trying to prove something to myself. I needed to come to terms with my past disappointments as an author and as a gymnast when I'd lost the U.S. national gymnastics championships by five one-hundredths of a point. One way or another, I wanted a victory, and I was willing to do almost anything to get it.

To achieve this goal, I first had to improve my friendship with myself. I hoped, naively, that Everest would help. My relationship with Julie took me only part way to the base of my real mountain — the struggle for self-acceptance, and the ever-elusive personal peace that comes from fulfillment, in whatever form. I had to forgive myself for what I perceived as my past failures. That, it would turn out, would be an order taller than Everest.

The organizational mountain was easier to ascend. I knew where to start. Once we'd contacted Steve Matous and got him rolling on the permit application process, Jamie and I went back to my main external wellspring, Mr. Laurie Skreslet, the first Canadian to climb Everest. Laurie had summited on October 5, 1982, after four members of his expedition had died and six others had decided to leave amid gut-wrenching disappointment and highly publicized controversy. That expedition, which had been led by Bill March, had become something of a phoenix that had risen from the ashes of accusations and acrimony. Then, I had hung on every word of news that had come back to Canada on the expedition and I had been well positioned to do so too. At the time, I was working as a cub reporter at *The Ottawa Citizen*, one of the five biggest daily newspapers in Canada and the newspaper of Canada's capital.

When news came back of Laurie's summit, he became an instant hero to me. He and his teammates had overcome deaths, despondency, potential dishonor, howling winds, freezing cold, rarefied air and searing ultraviolet rays. In my books, they became elevated almost to the status of gods.

Heroes are important to all of us. Although I now regard people like Mother Teresa (unfortunately no longer with us in body) and Nelson Mandela as greater heroes than almost any on the planet because of their contribution to the world as a whole, when I was a boy, I had the usual boyhood heroes — football and hockey players. As I got older, however, I discovered a whole new breed of heroic figures. They were tougher, more determined and more driven than professional athletes. You rarely read about them in the newspapers, you almost never saw them interviewed on television, and they didn't get paid a dime.

After retiring from competitive gymnastics in 1981, I discovered "the mountaineers." For me, they completely redefined courage, determination, and nobility. It was like you took the hockey player, put a heavy pack on his back, cut his oxygen in half, pitched his ice on a 45- to 60-degree angle and extended it thousands of feet high. Then you turned off all the lights in the arena, removed the television cameras, the cheering fans, the salaries, and the press and replaced them with 50-mile-an-hour winds, freezing cold, and total anonymity. Finally, you added the possibility of serious injury or death.

Here was a game with *real* consequences. Here was a game that demanded the utmost in self-control, commitment, and courage. Mother Nature did not tolerate temper tantrums or the pitching of tennis racquets at referees. She didn't allow fistfights or bench-clearing brawls. If you engaged in this kind of behavior in the mountains, the result was the loss of the one thing that was keeping you alive — your own energy, whether physical or emotional.

I'd met Laurie Skreslet years earlier in the process of writing *One Step Beyond — Rediscovering the Adventure Attitude* with John Amatt, another hero of mine who was a climber on and the business manager of the 1982 Canadian Everest Expedition. The book consisted of five personality profiles of top adventure achievers. Its goal was to pinpoint what successful people had in common. In reality, it wasn't a book about adventure at all. It was a book about life, and the adventure and sometimes misadventure we are all on.

Of the five fascinating individuals I profiled in *One Step Beyond*, I probably got to know Laurie Skreslet best. He is an intense character. The first time I met him, I knew he was special. His facial muscles stood out like they had been sculpted by the wind and his tanned but weathered skin showed clear evidence of years of battling the natural elements. He spoke clearly and pointedly and when he got rolling on stories about climbing, his stare became so sharp you felt like it could stab through you. Within minutes, his lips became taught, straight and thin — like elastic bands. His jaw set back with equal tension and the entire picture created a combined sense of intimidation and awe.

But he was not a fierce individual at home. In his living room in Calgary, Canada, he laughed easily and often. He delighted in poking fun at me for whatever he could, and he had a youthful exuberance about him I truly loved.

For me, Laurie is the quintessential mountaineer. After a few years traveling the world as a merchant seaman and at one point selling his own blood for money to keep moving, he had joined the ranks of the now-famous outdoor organization, Outward Bound. There, he had quickly distinguished himself as an instructor reliable in a crisis. He was tough, passionate, but likable. I was drawn to him not only because of what he had done, but because of who he was. I entitled my profile of him, "The Warrior Soul." I liked his brutal honesty, his directness and his drive. He had a certain nobility about him, like the Knights of the Round Table I had worshipped as a kid. I could visualize him in the heat of battle, ice ax raised against the spindrift snow and howling wind, tilting against the mountain. He had real personal power. We became fast friends.

When Jamie and I arrived on Laurie's doorstep that morning in the fall of 1994, it didn't take long for Laurie to set us straight about the South Col route on Everest, the route he had climbed 12 years earlier.

"If I had one piece of advice to give both of you about that route," he said as his brow furrowed and his stare took on its characteristic intensity, "… it would be to go through the Icefall only two times — once on your way to the summit and once on your way down."

Jamie and I looked at each other like we'd been presented with one of the tablets of the Ten Commandments. If we had had any misconceptions about the South Col being the "regular" route up Everest, they instantly evaporated. The sober reality of Everest once again spoke to us, this time literally from the mouth of one of the mountain's disciples.

The Icefall, or Khumbu Icefall as it is known, is a hideous cataract of moving ice that descends to the base of Everest. It is a glacier that is squeezed between Everest and its sister peak, Mount Nuptse. In its journey slowly downwards under the force of gravity, it tumbles 2,000 feet over a rock ledge and in the process splits into ice blocks the size of apartment buildings. Crevasses can be more than 15 stories deep and 50 feet wide. The whole terrifying mess moves up to three feet a day. It is a cemetery in the snow, a slow-moving avalanche of ice. In 1982, it had consumed four members of Laurie's expedition — one whose body has yet to be recovered. Three of the four had been Sherpas.

Jamie and I left our meeting with Laurie somewhat subdued. Before we departed, however, my hero left us with a few final words of wisdom:

"We could not have done what we did in '82 without the Sherpas," he said emphatically. "They respect and honor the power of the mountains. In the early days, they used to wash the blood off the newborn baby in a freezing-cold mountain stream. If it survived, great. If it didn't, it wouldn't have survived anyway.

"The Sherpas teach us to leave our arrogance at home and show respect for the mountains that are more powerful than we'll ever be. In a sense, they are the mountains. There's something undying about them. There's a sense of history of time that goes far beyond ours."

Laurie went on to tell the story of Sungdare Sherpa, who had climbed to the summit with him. One day in the Icefall, he explained, rather than make two trips through the danger, Sungdare had carried two packs at once, a back-breaking load of close to 100 pounds at 19,000 feet!

"He didn't draw any particular attention to it," Laurie remembered. "It was just his way of being safer."

All this seemed to reaffirm our plan to have Steve assemble the strongest Sherpa team we could. But what Laurie said next did not affirm anything in me. It shook me.

"Before you leave for Everest," he said as he looked me straight in the eye, "make sure your emotional house is in order. You don't need to have any more weight in your back pack than you'll already be carrying."

Perhaps he knew something about Julie or another I did not yet know.

Jamie and I had hoped the south side of the mountain through Nepal would be more forgiving than its northern equivalent. Obviously, we were wrong. The Icefall was clearly a major threat. Even with the strongest Sherpas in the world to help carry loads through it, it was obviously a place we should avoid, if we could.

When we got back to our office, Jamie and I quickly pulled out a topographical map of the Everest region. Were there peaks in the vicinity that could afford us the opportunity to acclimatize and train for Everest without having to actually set foot in the Icefall before we were ready for our summit attempt? Sadly, the answer was no. In a telephone call to Steve Matous later that day, that fact was reinforced.

No, if we were going to climb Everest from Nepal, we were going to have to make many trips through the Icefall, like playing many rounds of Russian roulette. Laurie's words came back to me over and over again in the months that followed. Much as I tried to put them from my mind, they haunted me. Would we too become corpses in the Khumbu?

On the other side of fear is freedom.

It was a thing not of the eye or body, but of the mind — a cloud of fear. — TENZING NORGAY, *Man of Everest,* on deaths during an expedition to Mt. Nanga Parbat

In climbing, and in life, we are often faced with fears like this, fears of the unknown. How we manage them, however, is our choice. I believe that on the other side of fear is freedom. The key to unlocking the door to that freedom is courage. Nine times out of 10, the disasters we imagine never occur. Yet we expend huge amounts of time and energy worrying about them.

So there we were. We didn't even have a permit to climb Everest and already we were afraid. Could we pull off a third trip to the mountain? Could we actually survive the Icefall? Where could we find the Sherpas who could help us? The only way to remove the doubt was to go find out.

What I wanted was to see for myself; find out for myself. This was the dream I have had as long as I can remember. There they stood above me, the great mountains. And above them all Chomolungma — Everest. 'No bird can fly over it,' said the story.

But what could a man do? A man with a dream?

— Tenzing Norgay,
Man of Everest

**The only way
to remove the
doubt is to
go find out.**

Climbing the Mountain
of Money

*Every worthwhile accomplishment, big or
little, has its stages of drudgery and triumph;
a beginning, a struggle and a victory.*

— ANONYMOUS

BEFORE WE GOT THE ANSWER to the Icefall, I was faced with another mountain. Just a few months after I moved in with Julie, she began to become unhappy in our relationship. The turning point came when a friend of hers called from New York to say she was getting married. Julie hung up the phone and looked strangely sad.

"What's wrong?" I inquired.

She paused a long while. Then, she started to cry.

"I'm really happy for her," Julie said as the tears streamed down her face, "but I'm sad for us. I can't see us ever getting married."

Affairs of the heart are the most difficult mountains to climb in life. Mine have always made Everest look like a tea party. They tear at my soul, force me to look more closely at myself and inevitably cause me to ask the most frightening and potentially dangerous question of all: Is there something wrong with me?

I could speculate as to why it wasn't working. Maybe it was my speaking schedule, or religious differences (Julie came from devout parents, while mine were basically agnostic), or business stresses (I came home from Everest to a tax audit which

Affairs of the heart are the most difficult mountains to climb in life.

concluded months later without a dime of tax owing, but with me emotionally drained and angry), or lifestyles that weren't necessarily compatible, or, or, or … maybe there really was something wrong with me. I asked Julie why, but all she said was she just couldn't see it working long-term. I knew that was just a polite way of saying I'd been rejected for reasons which she probably knew, but either couldn't completely articulate or didn't choose to for fear of hurting me.

Looking back on it now, I find it amazing that I can't even remember any specific incidents from that painful time. It's funny how your mind blocks them out. All I can recall is a gradual but inexorable distance developing between us, like she was on the deck of a ship pulling away from shore and all I could do was stand on the pier and cry out after her. I wanted to dive into the ever-increasingly frigid waters and swim out, but I knew her ship was moving too fast. She'd already set sail for somewhere, and someone, else.

Given a choice between an intimate relationship and Everest, I would choose Everest. Perhaps this is why my intimate relationships frequently fail. Everest, I find, is more predictable. Yes, her moods change. Yes, she can become so angry she can kill you. But I must only react to her. I would never be so arrogant as to believe she reacts to me. Therein lies the challenge of an intimate relationship — the mystery of how your partner chooses to react to you. The wonderful thing about Everest is she just sits there. It's up to us as climbers to interpret what she's saying, and she is always speaking, if only in a whisper. Sometimes, we're not listening and at other times, we choose not to hear. That's when we can get into trouble.

The week before Christmas, at Julie's request, I moved out of her apartment and into my own. It was hard, especially because it was Christmas. Everyone else was celebrating the arrival of the holidays. I just felt sick emotionally. There was nothing "holiday" about it. It hurt.

Julie helped me with the move and for that I was grateful. She said she still wanted to continue with our relationship, but

I know now she was just moving me to a safe place until she could find someone else. When she really ended our relationship the following April, it was swift and sudden. She found another partner and, within only a month, she was engaged.

I remember calling Jamie on the phone to tell him and being so choked up I could hardly breathe. I've never had an anxiety attack in my life, but maybe I had one then. It was awful. The words came out in spurts, haltingly, like a dam bursting for a moment and then suddenly being plugged. Then the tears came, a few at first, then a full flow. Emotionally, I bled. Julie, like an avalanche, swept into my past. With the exception of a few faxes and the odd telephone message over the weeks that followed, she vanished from my life. In fact, I deliberately pushed her out of it. The pain, however, persisted for months and to some extent, still does. I felt like I'd been swept under a rug, discarded as unacceptable.

The Sherpas teach that "it will be okay." Our society says, "time heals all wounds." Personally, I wish I could be more like the Sherpas and not get so emotionally involved in the first place. They don't seem to get upset about anything. They seem to understand at some deep level that whatever is happening is supposed to happen and that there is no sense in tearing ourselves apart or beating ourselves up about our past. It took me a long time to understand this, and I have to keep reminding myself of it today. If I could take one thing forward from my Everest experiences, it would be the Sherpas' ability to live in the present, to understand that each moment *is* a present and that we are given it, in fact, *gifted* it. I did not see that time as a gift for me. I saw it as a burden. I bore my load as best I could, but I weaved under the weight.

Fortunately, Everest was calling me. I say fortunately because I needed to ground myself in something just then and at least *she* was there. Everest has always been there.

When Julie and I split up, I poured myself into my mountain mistress — that black, frigid woman who had attracted me since I was a boy. Cold, aloof, and untouchable on the other side of the world, I let her seduce me. She was, and still

Each moment is a present. We are given it, in fact, gifted it.

remains, the grandest adventure, the ultimate allure. To touch her hand is to touch the love of God and the fear of the devil at the same time. She is, after all, Mother Nature. For me, she is the embodiment of mystery and power.

That power, that draw, became immediately apparent a short time after that fateful meeting with Laurie Skreslet in 1994. In January, 1995, a month after I had moved into my own apartment, Steve Matous called to say our permit to climb Everest in the spring of 1997 had been approved by the Department of Tourism of the Nepalese government.

That was the good news. The bad news was, we had to come up with $50,000 to secure the permit within a little over two months. Even with an $8,000 "re-issuing" fee Steve somehow got to a government official on the inside, we couldn't "buy" any more time. If we didn't come up with the money, we would lose both the "re-issuing fee" and the permit to the next expedition in line. Because there were dozens of other expeditions from around the world vying for the permit, we knew we had to act quickly.

Fifty thousand dollars may not be a lot of money to some big corporations, but Jamie and I are not a big corporation. Yes, our public-speaking business was thriving, but no, we didn't have that kind of cash just sitting around in the corporate coffers waiting for a worthwhile use for it. Nor did we have anything even close to a nest egg of that size in our personal savings either.

Using an impressive piece of negotiating, Steve got the Nepalese to agree to a deposit of $25,000 by mid-April with the balance due October 1. Jamie and I breathed a sigh of temporary relief, rather like having your medical condition downgraded from critical to good. We immediately flew off to speak to General Motors in eastern Canada and Enrich International, a multi-level herb marketing company, in Orem, Utah. Our hope was to "pitch" them well enough to get them interested in becoming involved in our expedition.

Whenever possible, Jamie and I try to piggyback our fundraising efforts on the back of our public-speaking presentations. We tell the story of our Everest experiences and then conclude by talking about our next adventure. Because our audiences often include members of upper management from the organizations to whom we speak, companies like Kodak, General Motors, Price-Waterhouse Coopers, Merrill Lynch, Morgan Stanley Dean Witter, J.P. Morgan, Mobil Oil, Johnson & Johnson and many others worldwide, if an organization is interested in becoming involved with us, our Everest story often gets the ball rolling on future sponsorship negotiations. Sponsors provide the capital that helps create adventures, and adventure experiences help create speaking presentations. In this way, Jamie and I have become professional adventurers. Our speaking is the key that unlocks the door to a world of possibilities.

As exciting as this may sound, the reality of our lives is that we are almost perpetually on the road, living in hotels, traveling on aircraft and raising money. This creates something of a nomadic existence that often leaves me with a feeling I don't really have any permanence in my life. And, it can be lonely. On one hand, I thrive on constant change, but on the other, I don't have much of a life outside of my work. All I seem to do is change planes, cities, presentations, "pitches," and hotels. I often don't see much of a city aside from the inside of the hotel room in which I present, and no sooner am I finished with one presentation than I must often travel on to the next one.

As anyone who travels a lot on business will tell you, after a short while, all the hotel rooms begin to look the same. So, in fact, do most cities. Most hotels try to impress you with their lobbies, but the reality is that most hotel rooms aren't impressive. And, here's the key — none of them are home.

Still, there is a tremendous amount for which to be grateful in my life. The upside of this itinerant lifestyle is all the people Jamie and I are able to positively affect through our speaking, if not for a lifetime, then at least for the time we are on stage. That is what makes the journey worthwhile — making a difference to others. There is nothing more thrilling for me than to receive a letter from an audience member months or years after a presentation explaining how they took an idea from what we said and applied it in their personal or professional lives. In so doing, they either changed the direction of their lives or substantially improved it. I have accumulated many such letters over the years, and they are priceless to me. If we can make a difference to others in life, if even for a short while, I believe we have achieved a high degree of success.

Our "pitches" to General Motors and Enrich, unfortunately, fell on deaf ears. Rejection is part of life, and we were not about to be deterred. Besides, we had no time to be. With less than five weeks to go to our April 12 deadline, Jamie and I began to panic just a little. We needed ideas — fast. So, we arranged a brainstorming meeting with my brother, Eric, and his business partner and friend, my cousin, Bob. They had built a series of successful energy companies and had recently sold them to the large North American pipeline organization, TransCanada Pipelines.

If we can make a difference to others in life, if even for a short while, we have achieved a high degree of success.

We met for lunch on March 9, 1995. Jamie and I came armed with a rough sponsorship proposal and some background on our expedition. Our hope was that Eric and Bob might have some suggestions on who we might be able to present them to.

We were very pleasantly surprised. In a matter of minutes, both men understood the urgency of our need and, perhaps more importantly, saw how our expedition could be used by a corporation for its benefit.

"What about TransCanada?" Bob inquired. "Eric and I have a meeting with the company CEO this afternoon."

Bob called me after lunch to say that, in a one-hour meeting, they had spent half the time talking about Everest.

"The last I saw of George [George Watson, CEO of TransCanada]," Bob said, "he was marching your media kit and proposal down the hall to the vice president of government and public affairs."

The next day, I arranged a meeting with TransCanada. We knew that the number of organizations who could part quickly with $50,000 was exceptionally small. We needed the inside track and thankfully, it seemed we had it. Now, however, we had to close the deal. The meeting was set for just two weeks before our Nepalese deadline.

On March 27, Jamie and I "pitched" TransCanada with everything we had. We requested the money within 10 days — a potentially dangerous maneuver we knew might easily be perceived as bordering on arrogant, but we felt now was not the time to be coy. Sooner or later in life, you just have to ask for what you want.

A week later, TransCanada called to say they were interested. Two days after that, with just six days to our deadline, we did the deal. We received a fax from TransCanada that will forever be known as "the $50,000 fax." On April 7, 1995, the money was received.

Jamie and I skipped around our office with the check like a couple of schoolboys passing around an ice cream cone. Within hours, we arranged for the money to be wired to Kathmandu.

For a moment, albeit a brief one, the pain of having lost Julie was temporarily subdued. I went for a walk and savored the victory of our efforts. While the love of my life had chosen to leave, my mountain mistress had once again returned to me.

We had taken our first big step back toward Everest.

Nothing happens unless first a dream.

— CARL SANDBURG

Sooner or later in life, we just have to ask for what we want.

The Big Pitch

*Bear in mind, if you are going to amount to anything,
that your success does not depend upon the brilliancy
and the impetuosity with which you take hold, but
upon the ever lasting and sanctified bull-doggedness
with which you hang on after you have taken hold.*

— DR. A. B. MELDRUM

HAVING CLEARED THE FIRST financial hurdle en route to the mountain, it wasn't long before the next one appeared. This one was a true Everest. We needed a mountain of money, about half a million U.S. dollars. Given our previous experience, that's what we believed we needed to do the job right — for our sponsors and for ourselves.

Our strategy for our third expedition to the mountain was simple: focus, focus, focus. First, we needed to raise sufficient capital. Second, we needed to train like we'd never trained before, and third, we needed to climb the mountain and return safely. We decided that for three years, we would do nothing else but focus on those three things. Every time the telephone rang and someone asked us to do something, we would ask ourselves: If we do what is being asked of us, is it going to get us closer to the summit? If the answer was "no," we didn't do it. This required a singleness of purpose that sometimes bordered on militancy. Some of our friends and associates did not understand. They were personally offended.

Although this kind of focus is often regarded as a good thing in the West, the Sherpas, although ultimate financial beneficiaries of our fundraising, would not likely have approved of our methods. In their world, it is the charitable, mild, and tolerant person who is most admired. Their ideal is not the forceful, focused and driven individual, but the wise, restrained, and mild-mannered human being who always has time for others and who values compassion above all else. Unfortunately, Sherpas were not in control of the government in Nepal, nor of the airlines that would get us there, the manufacturers who would supply us with our tents and other supplies, nor the telecommunications companies who would be happy to handle our long distance telephone charges from 29,000 feet on the side of the world's tallest peak — for a price.

Our focus extended through everything we did. We didn't want to expend months and years of precious energy arranging to obtain tents, sleeping bags, food, clothing, and other equipment from manufacturers in return for benefits we could offer them. So, we decided to go after enough cash to buy whatever we needed. Cash sponsors of this type, we knew, would be difficult to find, but if our strategy worked, we believed we would be left with more energy to climb the mountain.

Our plan was to delegate everything that did not fit our focus, even if we had to pay someone to help ensure they would commit to the task at a level commensurate with the Everest challenge. That meant we had to find others to handle everything from organizing the trip to leading it, communicating from the mountain, and ensuring that the tons of equipment the expedition needed actually got to the proper place on the mountain at the proper time. We did this by developing specialty teams, not unlike a football team that has an offensive and defensive team, a punt return team and a kickoff team, among others.

Our teams were:
1. Fundraising team — Jamie and myself
2. Organizing and leadership team — Steve Matous
3. Route-fixing team — Nepalese Sherpas and some North American climbers
4. Communications team — to be named
5. Summit team — to be named

In return for finding sponsors for the expedition to underwrite its entire cost, Jamie and I hoped that, weather and our personal health permitting, we would have the option of forming the first summit team.

Others didn't necessarily agree. News that we had acquired our third permit to attempt Everest was met with skepticism in the local climbing community. Just as we had been in 1991 and 1994, we were met with charges that we were incapable of climbing the mountain, that we had insufficient experience or skill, and that we were just a couple of opportunists blinded by our own ambition. We would die on Everest, some maintained.

This argument had no basis in fact. This was my tenth expedition to high altitude and my third trip to Everest. I had already climbed the highest peaks in both North and South America, been twice to the Andes and slogged up three high-altitude peaks in Mexico. I'd been training long and hard for years and had somehow managed to transform myself from a gymnast into a capable aerobic athlete.

Skeptics, I have learned, never seem to allow the facts to get in the way of their opinion. They are not interested in the facts. They are interested, I believe, in trying to make others look bad and themselves look better.

The best way of dealing with skeptics is to ignore them. Jamie and I believe we cannot achieve anything of significance in life without acquiring at least a few critics. They serve an important purpose — to keep us focused on what we need to do. If we allow them to anger us and divert our focus and energies onto them, they can control us.

After such a successful experience with TransCanada, Jamie and I went right back to George Watson's colleagues in the hope of securing the rest of the money we needed to stage our expedition. Unfortunately, they declined. At the same time, Steve Matous began, rightly, to request at least some kind of financial compensation for the work to secure our climbing permit. Again, we found ourselves walking a fine financial line. We sent him some money we had in savings to buy us some time. We hoped we could come up with more money from somewhere the next time he asked.

Skeptics never seem to allow the facts to get in the way of their opinion. The best way of dealing with them is to ignore them.

To find that "somewhere" we knew, would actually mean finding and getting ourselves in front of someone — a CEO to be specific. Many CEOs, we have learned, are not necessarily risk-takers. Nor are they all visionaries. Many have significant legal or financial education and are trained to think carefully about the "what ifs" and "debit" and "credit" sides of an idea's ledger. Many lawyers, in fact, are actually paid pessimists. In considering becoming a sponsor of an Everest expedition, it takes no time at all to reject it as an "unsafe" special event because of its inherently high risks. After all, people die on Everest. Who would want to be associated with that?

We weren't looking for pessimists. We were looking for a leader, a real one — someone with vision and courage.

One day at the office while I was reading up on some of the organizations I thought might be headed by such a CEO, my telephone rang. It was David Weinkauf, one of Jamie's friends. David worked as a commercial real estate broker for the Calgary office of Colliers Macaulay Nicolls Inc., a very large international commercial real estate firm. David explained that he thought Colliers might potentially be interested in becoming involved in our expedition.

There Is no such thing as coincidence.

To be embarrassingly honest, I didn't think much of David's suggestion. I thought it was probably just the local office wanting to contribute $1,000 or so to our climb. While I was grateful for that, we needed more than 500 times that amount. I thanked David for his interest and foolishly put my nose back into my information.

Anyone who has read *The Celestine Prophecy*, by James Redfield, understands that things in life happen for a reason. There is no such thing as coincidence. While you would have had a hard time convincing me of that when I was in my 20s, the older I get, the more I believe it. There actually is some higher power controlling some of what goes on in our lives. That is not to say we should sit back and wait for things to happen. Quite the contrary. What I mean is that if we passionately believe in something, if we patiently acquire the necessary skill level to make it a reality, and if we work hard at achieving our dreams, we will get exactly what we need exactly when we need it. Providence will appear as if by magic. Suddenly, it will contribute its wonderfully mystical spell. *But* we have to want our dreams so badly we can taste them. And, we have to be willing to work and sweat and cry for them. Only then will Providence appear. In a way, we summon Providence to appear. In fact, I believe, She, He, It, Whomever, or Whatever we believe has actually been watching the whole time and when She's seen us invest enough time, energy and money, when our commitment is clear, that's when She does her stuff.

The Sherpas have known this for a very long time. In Buddhism, there is something called "dharma" — the path (it is also translated as "religion"). They believe that our role in the world, the reason we are all here, is to find our path. We begin our journey of self-discovery on a path of learning and gradually, if we're really listening, we find our way to our true path. Having found it, we are to pursue it with all our heart. It is where we should be, where we need to be, and where we will be happiest, most fulfilled, and at peace.

There are as many different paths as there are people — through business, art, science, industry, adventure, recreation, parenting, education, academics, physical activity, community work, volunteerism, charitable activities, and on and on. The key is to find the path that is right for us, one that will not only benefit ourselves, but others as well. As long as what we do supports nature and does not detract from it, nature will support us.

But how do we know when we are on our path? More to the point, how do we get there? Does someone post a sign? In a way, the Sherpas believe, someone does. When we are on our path, "coincidences" happen naturally because when we do life-supporting things, things that support our pre-determined mission in life, nature supports us. The key to finding our path is to follow our heart and intuition. As long as we do this, we will live a fulfilled and peaceful life, not just one in which we exist by eating, sleeping, working, and struggling to pay bills.

If we passionately believe in something, and if we work hard at achieving our dreams, we will get exactly what we need exactly when we need it.

FROM EVEREST TO ENLIGHTENMENT

The Sherpas see the world as a complex interwoven balance of karma (action and re-action) and natural energy flow. But it is not the flow of physical energy. It is the flow of metaphysical energy, the kind I believe is undeniably present on Everest. The overall flow of metaphysical energy is "controlled," if you will, by Mother Divine (it is no coincidence the locals call Everest "Mother Goddess of the World"). It is our actions, or inactions, which determine whether nature works for us or against us. Thus the intangible becomes tangible.

If all this sounds too far outside the box to be plausible to you, that's perfectly fine. I respect your opinion. I can assure you, however, that I am as pragmatic and realistic as you are, and, as a trained journalist, probably even more skeptical. If you think what I'm saying is hogwash, try something. For the next week, watch for "signs," and "coincidences" of the direction you are or should be taking, all around you, in all forms, whether seen, heard, touched, smelled, tasted, or felt. Take note of them. Write them down. At the end of the week, ask yourself what conclusions might be drawn from the information you have gathered. If you conclude nothing, that's fine. But if you conclude something else, could this help you on your path?

The problem I have faced in my life is that often, I either get off my path, or I just can't seem to find it at all. The path I'm on seems more like a rush-hour freeway than a smooth interchange. I feel like I'm playing in traffic, or as one author, Harvey Mackay, put it, I'm "swimming with the sharks" — and getting eaten alive.

A sign I was on the right path came a few weeks later when out of the blue, I received another phone call from David Weinkauf.

"Alan, I think Colliers would be interested in becoming involved in your expedition."

"Why?" I inquired.

"I don't know," David said. "I just think it would. Besides, what have you got to lose?"

"Well, a lot of time for starters Dave," I replied skeptically. "We're looking for big dollars, by our standards."

"What if I told you I could get you a meeting with the international CEO of Colliers, John McLernon, would that interest you?"

"Of course," I said. "Absolutely. But how are you going to do that?"

"I'll call you back," David said.

He hung up.

"After speaking with Alan and getting the cold shoulder," David remembers, "I knew I could put the meeting together and I would, just to prove it … so, I called John. He was hilarious … [he] immediately blew the idea off. I would not get off the phone though until he promised to take 20 minutes when he was in town for unrelated business. I knew he couldn't say no, and so did he. He knew I would keep hounding him. So, he reluctantly agreed, but not before he attempted to verbally offer a donation to the expedition in lieu of the meeting."

"Despite giving David a tough time, I had every intention of meeting with Alan," McLernon recalls. "I make it a point of answering my own phone and meeting with the many callers who want to see me about a job, a product, or an idea. If you aren't curious, you might miss a great opportunity."

Back at our office in Calgary, I too was skeptical. "Dave's living in a dream world," I thought. "He's lost touch with reality." I went back to more "productive" things.

Stupid, very stupid.

Twenty minutes later, my phone rang again.

"Hobson, Weinkauf. I got you your meeting."

I almost dropped the phone.

"What the hell are you talking about David? You got me a meeting with whom? No, no, wait, I'll tell you, you got me a meeting with the assistant to the assistant to the assistant of the CEO."

The tone of David's voice changed suddenly.

"No Alan, I got you a meeting with the international CEO, John McLernon, of Vancouver, just like I said I would. He's flying in Friday and he'll meet with you then."

It was Wednesday.

> *"If you aren't curious, you might miss a great opportunity."*
>
> – JOHN MCLERNON, CEO, COLLIERS INTERNATIONAL

Frantic preparations followed. I wasn't sure if I'd just been given my Christmas gift seven months early or if I'd just been sandbagged. So, I called David back half an hour later, this time with a whole list of questions about Colliers. He answered all the ones he could. The rest of the answers he faxed to me the following day. Clearly, he wasn't bluffing. He was serious. It was clear I'd better get serious too — fast!

Together with my associate, Karen Harris, who handled the bookings for our public-speaking business, I went into a frenzy to prepare a customized proposal for Colliers.

Friday came quickly. I loaded one of those suitcases on rollers with a slide projector, some Everest slides, and the proposals and walked a few blocks into Bankers Hall, the very same building where Jamie and I had met with Fred Balm, the chairman of Emergo, to talk about sponsorship in 1994. There was something uncanny about Bankers Hall, even just to look at it. For starters, it was the only building in downtown Calgary with an actual pointed roof on it. It was like a summit I thought. Then there was that vertical pane of continuous glass that extended down from the top several stories. It looked a bit like the Great Couloir on the north face of Everest.

It sounds silly, but looking back on it now, I believe that building has special significance for me. I used to think only natural features were "power places," places from which I drew energy, but I was wrong. Laurie Skreslet used to say Mount Yamnuska, just west of Calgary, was one of his. I never thought a human-made structure could have that kind of power. The building is made of concrete, steel and glass after all. It doesn't make sense, except when you remember that all those things come from nature. So, in fact, does everything around us — everything we can see anyway.

I walked over to Bankers Hall, into the Colliers offices, and set up my slide projector. The head of the office, Larry Mason, his property management manager, Dan Doherty, and David Weinkauf were there. After exchanging a few pleasantries, we waited for John McLernon.

The moment he set foot in the room, I knew I'd only get this one chance. He marched in like a drill sergeant, and in a deep, raspy voice declared something about being behind schedule and needing to keep this thing brief. We shook hands firmly and he took his seat at the end of the boardroom table. Then he looked at me over his reading glasses, and with a piercing stare, his brow furrowed deeply, and he said crisply: "Okay. Let's get on with it."

I felt like I'd been given my marching orders.

I swallowed hard and began talking as fast as I could. I hammered through the Everest slides in about five minutes and then moved straight into overhead transparencies of my proposal pages. I'd been careful not to give anyone present a copy of them yet (Rule #1 of pitching — never let them see where you're taking them).

No matter how fast I rattled along, McLernon kept nodding his head. I wasn't sure if he was agreeing with me or ushering me to get it over with. Whatever the case, I felt the adrenaline rush I always get when I'm asking for money, especially big money — like the next sentence that comes out of my mouth could change my life forever. I just love face-to-face fundraising with a potential sponsor. I don't know what it is exactly, but it seems to bring out the best in me. I love walking the fine line between the possibility of disaster and the potential for success. I love having to spontaneously respond to objections, and I love talking about my passions and my dreams. Nothing gives me a more concentrated rush. But it is not all adrenaline. It is the fire I feel inside me when I am pursuing my passion and sharing it with others.

I wrapped up the "formal" part of my presentation, then opened things up for questions. The first thing McLernon wanted to see was the financials. He says he thought the whole idea was ludicrously expensive.

I must have done something right. He said he was interested. Nine times out of 10, they just tell you "they'll get back to you." Of course, they don't, or if they do, it's to tell you to take a hike — which in our case was precisely what the whole exercise was about anyway. But no, McLernon said he was interested. Although I'd just met him, there was a sense about him — that he was a straight shooter. The meeting adjourned 45 minutes after it had begun, and he never told me he had no money. I thought that was a good sign. I packed my suitcase, left the office and skipped down the street back to our office. I would be thrilled if our idea went somewhere, but whatever the outcome, I had sure enjoyed the journey.

"Alan's presentation was passionate and well prepared," McLernon says. "The concept was interesting, although I had not immediately worked out how best to consider it."

"Alan is the kind of guy who is hugely competitive without advertising it," David says. "That's because he competes with himself. He knew what he wanted, he prepared for it and now he was making his kill —not with ego, or flash, or jazz, but with knowledge, a focused goal and an understanding of people. John was impressed as well."

I fired off a quick "thank-you" fax to John. I was delighted and very surprised when he responded the same day — at 6 p.m. Vancouver time. I still have the fax:

Dear Alan:

Thanks for your quick fax. Your presentation was crisp, to the point, well prepared and focused on our needs. You got my attention.

However, I was daydreaming on how to sell you on a career in commercial real estate. Just kidding! I will call you next week.

Best regards,

John R. McLernon,
Chairman and Chief Executive Officer

Holy shoot! The CEO responded — personally! Jamie and I did a little dance. We were nowhere near a sale, but, by God, John had actually responded. I was blown away. That had never happened to either of us in five years of fundraising together.

Apparently, John had got back on the plane to fly home to Vancouver and started doing a little math. He took a look at the size of Colliers, about 195 offices in 35 countries with some 4,400 employees at the time, pulled out his calculator and figured out how much half a million U.S. actually translated to per office. It turned out to be peanuts by corporate standards.

"I do some of my best thinking on planes," McLernon says. "I have lots of opportunity as I fly some 200,000 miles plus a year. On the way home from Calgary, I began to think about Everest as a symbol for our emerging international organization and to think about how the funding could be shared throughout our worldwide organization."

That's exactly the way I'd pitched it, but usually, that's not how sponsors see it. Most see only the total cost and not the cost-effectiveness. They see the number, but they don't see the number of possibilities. Many decision-makers are fascinated by Everest, but when push comes to shove, their imaginations are not captured by the potential for success, but by the possibility of disaster. They quickly become overwhelmed by fear — of death, negative publicity, team conflicts, controversy, environmental issues, commercialization, and so on. As human beings, when confronted with the unknown, we are much more inclined to predict catastrophe than victory.

McLernon, Jamie and I were to learn, wasn't one of "them." He was a maverick. He'd helped build the company. He'd peer at you over his reading glasses, smile and tell you straight exactly what he thought. Yet he was careful never to offend, or get himself cornered into a spot he couldn't get himself out of. He was clever, like a fox. He was exactly the kind of guy we were looking for. He was a leader.

"By the time I returned to Vancouver, I was really excited," McLernon says. "So, I went to dinner with a great friend who was president of a significant Vancouver-based business. He told me I was crazy — that it had been done before, the risks were too high, etc. This made me even more determined.

"The evening went on too late and when I got home, I remembered the video Alan had given me and I slipped it into

> **When confronted with the unknown, we are much more inclined to predict catastrophe than victory.**

the machine. What an experience! I was immediately transported to the mountain and into the life and death situation of the rescue on the second climb. I was transfixed. Not only was this a great story, but Alan and Jamie communicated it at a very polished and professional level. Twice denied, I felt there was no way these guys would not succeed a third time."

Things happened fast from that point on. Three weeks later, I found myself flying to Budapest, Hungary, of all places, to gain more buy-in at an international level within Colliers. The organization was having a world meeting there and I was to present to its executive committee.

Heavily jet-lagged, I dragged myself off the plane some 16 hours of travel time and nine hours out of sync with Calgary. I tried my best to put on a brave face at a reception hosted by Colliers in one of the downtown hotels. It felt bizarre being there, like being caught up in a whirlwind. I was completely disoriented. I wasn't sure what day it was, what time it was, or even what continent I was on. To make matters more challenging, my arrival in Europe had been less than smooth. First, my flight into Frankfurt had been late arriving and I had missed my connection to Budapest. This wouldn't have been so bad except that it also meant I had missed the one meeting I had traveled almost halfway around the world to attend. Fortunately, I discovered after a few frantic phone calls that for reasons that had nothing to do with my travel challenges, the meeting had already been re-scheduled for the next day. Coincidence?

Next, the airline I had flown on from Canada had only checked my luggage as far as Frankfurt. It was only after two hours of waiting at four check-in counters that I managed to re-locate it and send it on to Budapest with me.

Needless to say, I was stressed, frustrated, and in serious need of some sleep. That trip was an exciting moment in my life. Here I was, transplanted by jet to Europe, hot on the trail of a major international corporate sponsor of my greatest lifelong dream. I was in one of the most beautiful cities in the world, surrounded by Colliers people who were, for the most part, exactly like me — between 30 and 40 and hustling hard to make things happen. They were energetic, assertive, and fun.

I was greatly reassured when the friendly face of McLernon appeared. He welcomed me to Budapest and promptly made fun of my pale face, blood-shot eyes and foggy mental state. This whole thing had been his idea, after all. John led from the front, I was to learn, but he never did it unilaterally. If he liked an idea, he didn't try to jam it down the throats of others in his organization. He wanted them to accept the project as their own. Obviously, he was interested in our Everest idea, but I still had to get his troops on side, in part, so they didn't resent him for being selfishly bull-headed enough to like the idea. He wasn't about to risk his own professional reputation for the sake of our dream. The ball was firmly in my court to help him sell the idea to his team, and I was damned if I was going to drop the ball. Jamie was counting on me.

I managed to stay standing until well past midnight that night. After joining John for dinner with two dozen or so of his colleagues at a local restaurant, we got together at the bar in the hotel for a nightcap.

That's when things really got interesting. John told me he was looking forward to my slide show and story.

"What do you mean?" I asked, not quite believing what he'd said.

"I mean we're really looking forward to hearing the story of your two previous expeditions. I've told everyone on the executive committee. They can't wait to see your Everest slides."

I felt like someone had dropped me out of that 747 I'd taken over the Atlantic. I'd prepared for a sponsorship "pitch" just like the one I'd made to John in Calgary earlier that month. I wasn't the least bit prepared for a motivational public-speaking presentation such as the one John was describing. I didn't even have my slides with me. They were on the other side of the ocean in North America.

My stomach started to churn. Visions of my big dream slipping away from me danced immediately in my head.

"But I don't have my slides," I said, perhaps foolishly.

"What do you mean?" John asked, clearly disappointed.

Immediately, I excused myself, left John to his cognac, and went straight to my room. There, I called Karen in Canada and thank God, she answered. I asked her to fax me a photocopy of our slides so I'd at least have something from which to work. Unfortunately, due to technical difficulties, she wasn't able to.

"I guess Alan and I had not fully communicated on what was needed for our international meeting," McLernon says. "I wanted a mini-presentation of the video I had seen, and Alan was there to pitch for dollars.

"For the presentation, I invited not only the international delegates, but also their spouses, as I wanted to gauge how the presentation and story would be accepted by a mixed multi-national group."

So, there I was, on the eve of perhaps the single most important pitch of my life and I had no slides, no backup and no time to rectify the situation. International couriers, I knew, would take at least three days to get something to me from Canada. I was flying solo, if I was flying at all. I could go down in flames and our dream would disappear in a puff of smoke. I wished Jamie were there to help me, if only to provide moral support.

Then the strangest thing happened. Suddenly, I became absolutely calm, like I was being grounded by or to something very powerful. It was like the aura of Everest came to visit me then. It would again many times in the future.

I realized I could make the presentation without slides. I'd told the story hundreds of times. I didn't need anything except myself. Jamie and Karen were half a world away. Everything I needed I had within me. All I needed was to believe that.

At 1:30 a.m., after 36 hours without sleep, I tried to put the whole problem out of my mind. I closed my eyes and imagined strength coming up within me. The next morning, after six hours sleep, I took out a dozen sheets of blank white paper and from memory, drew thumbnail sketches of all of the 80 or so slides in our show. Later that day, I walked into the presentation room and laid them all out on a table in front of me. Then I told our story before the 20 or so assembled members of the executive committee and their spouses with all the passion, clarity and focus I could muster. When I finished, you could have heard a pin drop in the room.

I think John was impressed.

"Despite Alan's anxiety, he was terrific," McLernon recalls. "He knew his subject well, was passionate and articulate and moved many to tears."

Whatever the executive committee decided, I concluded, it was out of my hands now. I'd given it everything I had.

The next day, I boarded the plane home and awaited the decision from Colliers in peace.

In the end, win or lose, I think that's all any of us can ask for in life.

Satisfaction lies in the effort, not in the attainment.
Full effort is full victory. — MOHANDAS GANDHI

No More Games

When the pursuit of natural harmony is a
shared journey, great heights can be attained.

— LYNN HILL,
leading American climber

IT WAS ABOUT 10 DAYS before I heard from McLernon again. He called to say Budapest had been a huge success. He'd got no "nos" from the international executive committee. Now, he thought he could get the United States on side as well.

A part of me celebrated, but that celebration was short. I'd already got what I needed from my European experience. I had the satisfaction of knowing I'd done my best.

The process of bringing on Colliers as a sponsor, Jamie and I were to discover, was to be a long one — much longer than either one of us could have imagined. It would be a full and frustrating year before we actually signed them as co-sponsors with Lotus Development Corporation, of Cambridge, the distributor of Lotus Notes and Lotus 1-2-3. Lotus had sold Lotus Notes to Colliers as its worldwide communications platform and the company wanted to continue to build its relationship with the commercial real estate giant. It also wanted to continue to demonstrate the ubiquitous nature of Notes — that it was being used everywhere, even on Everest. If all worked out well, our expedition was to use Notes to communicate from the mountain back to the world via our satellite telecommunications uplink.

First, however, we had to strike a deal. It wasn't easy. With each new negotiation hurdle cleared, another appeared. It seemed like we would never actually finalize an agreement. There was always one more segment of the organizations to bring on side, or one more outstanding issue, objection or concern. The process put such a strain on my relationship with Jamie and that it almost destroyed it. We frequently butted heads on how best to handle negotiations and, indeed, ourselves.

"Although Alan and Jamie had some misgivings about how we were going to get there, I never wavered," McLernon recalls. "Jamie Horne, president of our Canadian company, offered complete support and offered to backstop the project if we had difficulty raising the funds from other Colliers entities … but we also did not want other Colliers partners or the climbers to know it could be backstopped as this would have taken the pressure off and our funding goals would not have been attained."

Colliers was a fascinating and dynamic organization, but the very reason they were interested in our expedition was the same reason they needed our expedition — they were big. There is a huge push for organizations and, indeed, individuals, to operate in the global marketplace. The advent of the Internet, e-mail and other global communication devices has virtually eliminated international borders and brought us all closer together as inhabitants of Earth.

One of the most notable exceptions to this is the Sherpas. Virtually cut off from the outside world except through mail they receive during sporadic forays to Kathmandu, they still enjoy a measure of mountain peace virtually unequalled anywhere in the world. While many might regard this form of isolation as backward and primitive, it is the very attribute that every year draws thousands of trekkers and climbers to the Khumbu region. As James Fisher wrote in, *Sherpas: Reflections on Change in Himalayan Nepal*, "Having discovered that technology enables us to control nature without enhancing our experience of it or ourselves, we retreat to the high Himalayas to intensify our sense of both. Khumbu offers tourists the rare opportunity to experience culture and nature, and their combination — high human adventure — at the top of the world."

At the top of the corporate world, however, the game is entirely different. What Jamie and I have observed is that, as organizations move into the global marketplace, as they are being forced to do to compete, they run the risk of fragmenting. They risk losing their common sense of corporate culture, direction, goals, and, in fact, their very identity.

This was precisely the challenge Colliers appeared to be facing. Unlike the strongly centered and geographically isolated Sherpa community, Colliers had begun as clusters of independently owned commercial real estate companies spread out around the world and gradually, over time, these agencies had come together under the Colliers International banner. The problem, as we saw it, was that some parts of the organization were still working and interacting as independent offices. What McLernon saw was that they had a need to pull together, to work as a team. In short, they had to become Sherpas.

"Colliers at that time was a global partnership, patterned off the majority of international accounting firms," McLernon says. "Although there had been some consolidation, there were still many separate entities bound together.... There was a strong need to continue to bind the organization in a unified vision, a common set of core values, and an emphasis on communication throughout the world. I thought that if Colliers had a strong and recognizable icon (symbol) for these issues, it would pull the organization together quicker than it was moving.

"I knew that it would be difficult, but not impossible, and we would have to knock off the obstacles one by one. The key was to win grass roots support that would push various global executives, some of whom are generally reluctant to take a risk or spend discretionary money, to get on the bandwagon."

John knew he needed to bring his group together, not only under one banner, but as much as possible, as one mind. What he needed, and what he apparently saw in our expedition, was the ultimate common corporate rallying point — the summit of Everest. He also saw that the metaphors and values of mountaineering — teamwork, communication, goal-setting, overcoming obstacles, dealing with setbacks, and trusting each other with our lives, were exactly the corporate values he wanted to continue to instill in his people. Our public speaking, and more specifically Jamie and I, we deduced, could provide the critically important human link between those values and his people. Because we were both communicators as well as climbers, we could translate the experience of Everest into lessons applicable in the world of commercial real estate.

Early in our sponsorship deliberations, John began to refer to Jamie and me as "Everest Icons." Although both of us were and remain singularly uncomfortable with this designation (anyone who knows us can talk at length about our faults), we could see the basis of John's thinking. He wasn't the least bit interested in any external promotional value or exposure the climb might be able to provide. We were relieved to hear that because it took a huge amount of pressure off us to contact the media and the public at large. He was, however, very interested in the benefits the expedition, together with Jamie and me, could provide internally to Colliers worldwide.

The relationship Jamie and I and Colliers had was not without its challenges, however.

"Early in the expedition, we had communication problems," McLernon remembers. "In previous expeditions, they [Jamie and me] had had an executive presentation and had realized the money without significant corporate involvement. They had not been involved in marketing within the organization to help secure funding. These strains were ultimately talked through and also resulted in some personnel changes on both sides to smooth the communications. Alan and Jamie were professional athletes with all the ego, stature and presence that goes with the title. It took us a while to recognize them as such and not just as a project. Alan and Jamie, on the other hand, had to learn to work with a global sales organization with many jurisdictions and demands. Ultimately, we got it together."

So there we were — we needed Colliers and they needed us. Once again, Providence had appeared exactly when we both needed her. In business they call that good timing. I call it yet another example of synchronicity or coincidence created by commitment and dharma.

One afternoon, Jamie, John and I met in Vancouver to begin to negotiate a deal. There, John invited us to lunch. We walked across the street to the Waterfront Center Hotel. He surprised us by inquiring if we had a boiler plate contract we used with sponsors or whether we normally used a letter of intent. He said Canada was in for half of the money we needed, but the U.S. CEO still needed to be reached for his commitment. Unfortunately, he was on vacation. John said he'd fax us a letter of confirmation or rejection by the end of the week.

A few days later, in true McLernon style, our fax machine surged to life:

"Our commitment is based upon successfully working out a three-year plan with you that meets both our needs," John's letter said. "This is essential for ongoing education and experiences. It is also subject to developing a contract we are both comfortable with.... We are very excited about working with both of you and attaining all our goals. It is imperative that we develop a slogan along the lines of the past climb — The Achievement is in the Effort."

At first, I didn't feel anything. We had a commitment, and yet we didn't. The commitment came with two strings attached: that a mutually acceptable plan be developed and that an acceptable contract follow. As a final caveat, in instructing us to develop a special slogan for the climb, Colliers clearly wanted to detract attention away from summiting and focus instead on the process and effort of mounting the expedition. Jamie and I celebrated this because we knew it would again take pressure off us individually to reach the summit. On the other hand, it also made us both wonder if Colliers really thought we could climb Everest.

But that was the future. The point of the present was they were committing, with a few strings attached, to sponsoring our expedition in large part. We had taken a huge leap closer to our goal.

I fired off a quick fax to John confirming receipt and acceptance of his terms. I felt like we were at the South Col at 26,000 feet on Everest and that the clouds on our dream had started to clear. Suddenly, the summit was a lot more visible.

The Clincher

Play for more than you can afford to lose,
then you will learn the game.

— WINSTON CHURCHILL

ABOUT TWO WEEKS AFTER McLernon's fax, my relationship with Jamie hit a new low. The combined strain of on-going negotiations with Colliers and the interpersonal challenges we had had during our two previous Everest expeditions continued to take its toll. Both of us realized we had to do something.

It's hard to run a business, speak all over the world, travel at least half the year, train physically every day, raise half a million dollars and not expect to have challenges somewhere along the way. The human component is the most delicate one in almost any achievement and Jamie and I are no exception. People were often surprised to hear that after they watched how well we worked together on stage, but it is considerably more difficult to run a high performance partnership through three Everest expeditions over six or so years than it is to speak from separate sides of a stage for an hour.

Realizing Jamie and I were out of balance, I wrote him a note. In it, I outlined a few things I thought each of us could do to improve the quality of our relationship. My list included:

- improve my relationship with myself by taking a self-improvement course
- take a course in anger management (I was still bitter about my break-up with Julie)
- find a wife

In preparing this list, my thinking was that if I could improve my relationship with myself, I would naturally improve my relationship with Jamie. He did not have an equivalent list, as this is not his style, but I felt it was important for me to have one and to share it with him. He was still making a concerted effort and he was committed to making things work between us. He suggested we seek professional help with a counselor.

As Bill March, my friend and mentor once said, "We come into this world alone and we die alone. There's nothing we can do about that. That's how life is. But between birth and death, there are people. They help make our lives worth living."

Jamie and I continued to struggle. Since our second expedition to Everest in 1994, I have had to come to terms with the fact that our friendship will probably never be what it once was. That has been deeply disappointing for me and in some ways tragic. Jamie has other close friends and he has chosen to spend more time with them. Our friendship has evolved into strictly a business partnership. We still respect each other and value each other's strengths, but Jamie no longer confides in me. He is distant, more private than ever, and often aloof. I find out about things happening in his life after the fact. That is disappointing, but I have had to learn to accept it.

As we had in the past when we hit rough spots in our relationship, Jamie and I headed back into counseling. Our counselor determined we were experiencing a breakdown in our decision-making and conflict resolution methods, particularly as they pertained to Colliers. When we came upon a problem, each of us would decide very quickly what to do. If we both agreed on the solution, things were great. If we didn't, that's when we got into trouble. Each of us would polarize into our respective positions and when lobbied by the other to soften our stance, we simply dug our heels in deeper. Result — more distance than ever and a deeper rift in our relationship.

The Sherpas would not approve of this kind of ego-driven behavior. In their world, the more "ego-less" you are, the better. The Sherpas believe that the key to success in life (and, more to the point, the next life) is gentle thoughts, non-violence and good deeds. That is not to say that they never lose their temper. They can, and do, sometimes violently. But in comparison to our society, they are a peaceful people. Religion and spirituality is a daily, if not hourly, practice. It is not uncommon to pass by a Sherpa and find him quietly uttering his mantra. The goal of a Sherpa is to seek internal enlightenment, not external "success." Quarrelling is taboo.

By that standard, Jamie and I were failing miserably. The oxygen issue quickly became a point of heated contention. Jamie wanted to climb Everest with the use of bottled oxygen. He said he wanted to return some thanks to his family for everything they had done for him to help get him to that point. He also wanted to ensure he fulfilled his commitments to sponsors. As part of my commitment to myself to give the effort everything I had, I wanted to see if I could climb without the use of bottled oxygen. Jamie said he felt my decision could potentially affect his safety and summit chances as well as those of the entire team. I felt that criticism infringed on my independence.

We agreed that each of us should have the right to climb the mountain in our own way. This would mean, however, that we would have to climb as separate summit teams. The question then became: who would get the first shot at the summit? If one of us went first, perhaps there wouldn't be enough time, energy, supplies or support for a second summit attempt. How would the other guy feel if he'd agreed to go second and only the first guy summited? All the attention would go to the first guy and the second guy would be forgotten. This could create lasting resentment.

Could we both go at the same time then? What if one of us got into trouble? Would that mean the other guy would have to forfeit his summit chances and save him? How would that affect our relationship long-term?

Obviously, there was no easy answer — except if we both agreed to try with bottled oxygen, or both without. Unfortunately, neither one of us wanted to do that.

Jamie and I were once again forced to look inside ourselves to answer the question of whether attempting Everest was really worth our lives, let alone our relationship. The answer, of course, was "no," but at the same time, we both understood it would take a willingness to die for our dream if we ever hoped to achieve it. If that sounds like a contradiction, it is. To make it to the summit, you have to be willing to die trying, but you have to be ready to give everything you have to keep from dying.

> *I was lonely and sorry for myself, away from my own people, and often, out in the jungle alone, I would sit down beneath a tree and weep. Already I was learning that dreams and reality are not quite the same thing.*

> —TENZING NORGAY,
> *Man of Everest,*
> recalling his first expedition at age 18

Life is risk. Where there is no risk, there is no life.

To answer these and other questions I am faced with in my life, I always return to this base: Life is risk. Where there is no risk, there is no life. Exploration and adventure, I believe, is the essence of living. Without adventure, there cannot be life, at least not the way I define life — whether that's the adventure of running a business, or the adventure of a quiet afternoon walk along the sea shore. I was born to reach, risk and realize whatever it is I must realize — whether it is that I have failed at something and must therefore try again more intelligently, or that I have succeeded and must therefore reach, risk and realize again in a new way. I do not want simply to exist. I want to live.

A few difficult weeks later, I was snapped from my introspection by another telephone message from McLernon:

"Hobson!" he said in his classically direct style. "I'm sending you a faxed copy of what I'll be presenting to the company this week."

Our fax machine in Calgary proceeded to spit out 25 pages of what amounted to a state of the union address from John to Colliers worldwide. It read like "The Battle Cry of the Republic," springing off the page, exciting and igniting me like nothing had in months. After pages of description of Colliers' state of affairs, four letters galvanized on the page:

B.H.A.G.

We need a "Big, Hairy, Audacious Goal" (B.H.A.G.) around which to unite and on top of which to piggyback our own corporate goals, he wrote. He had apparently read about B.H.A.G.s in James C. Collins and Jerry I. Porras's, *Built to Last*, and had completely adopted the concept. John went on to explain how he believed our Everest expedition offered just such a goal.

McLernon's document was circulated throughout Colliers. It helped set the stage for the next important step in bringing them on as a sponsor, an international meeting in Denver the following week. Our task was clear — to light the fuse and really get our rocket rolling. We had to continue to build a ground swell of support.

Many books have been written about climbing Everest. Most focus almost exclusively on the climb. The reality today is that raising the capital to climb Everest is at least three-quarters of the challenge in scaling the mountain. To skip this process is to leave out, if you will, three-quarters of the story. Fundraising is not glamorous stuff. It does not necessarily make for the most exciting reading. But it is necessary because it is an integral part of the story.

I will greatly foreshorten the description of how Jamie and I finally made it to the summit of the most difficult mountain of all, the mountain of money. Suffice to say it was more like an iceberg. What you have read and will read here is but the tip of the huge, unseen challenge with which Jamie and I wrestled, sometimes together, sometimes apart, sometimes with each other. It was the hardest part of the climb — not the most dramatic, not the most dangerous, but unquestionably, the longest and most difficult.

On September 9, 1995, after three hours sleep en route from another speaking presentation in central Canada, Jamie and I flew into Denver and rushed to set-up in the main ballroom of the Hyatt Regency Hotel downtown. We were to speak to 500 Colliers brokers from all over the world, most of whom were from the United States. If the U.S. did not come on to our idea here and now, the deal would die and we would lose Colliers as a sponsor. It was make or break.

Steve Matous was in the audience. Like most of the people there, this was the first time he'd seen Jamie and me speak.

Despite lack of sleep, Jamie rose to the occasion. He was the funniest I'd seen him in months. Together, we were able to bring the crowd to its feet. We got a thunderous standing ovation.

McLernon followed. In the days leading up to the conference, he'd somehow broken one of the arms on his reading glasses. So there he was, glasses at an obtuse angle on his face, looking drawn and pale from pressing the flesh with his troops until 3 or 4 a.m. He had this elaborately prepared speech, complete with overheads, but he cancelled it moments before going on stage and instead carried a tattered piece of yellow paper to the podium. With the aid of only a few hand-written notes, McLernon delivered a stirring speech that would have rung out with as much power if he'd been standing on the summit of Everest herself. His passion and vision jumped through the microphone. Even with busted glasses, he made his point clear — this was the direction this organization needed to take — upwards, as a team. When he was done 10 minutes later, I felt like I had just heard J.F.K.'s commitment to Congress to put the first man on the moon. There was more thunderous applause.

The next morning, John summoned us to his hotel room.

"The States are in!" he told us triumphantly.

Jamie and I were overjoyed, even more so when John asked for a draft contract and a pre-planned public speaking program that would see us visit all of Colliers' key offices worldwide before and after the expedition. He also wanted to start the cash flowing as soon as possible so we could back Steve's organizational effort as well. It seemed almost too good to be true.

The meeting lasted only 15 minutes. It felt very much like the one Jamie and I had had with Fred Balm on Nov. 25, 1992 when he'd committed to sponsoring our '94 expedition in five minutes. It all happened so fast we didn't quite believe it. "It takes 20 years to become an overnight success," Eddie Cantor, an American entertainer once said.

As we had done following the meeting with Mr. Balm, Jamie and I got on the elevator after the meeting with McLernon feeling like we were flying at 29,000 feet.

"12th floor, going down," the computer synthesized voice said as we got on.

"Hell no!" I said. "We're going up!"

Jamie and I double high-fived.

"Now it's serious," I said.

"It's always been serious," Jamie replied.

> *"It takes 20 years to become an overnight success."*
>
> – EDDIE CANTOR, AMERICAN ENTERTAINER

Rifts and Resolutions

Whatever you can do, or dream you can do,
begin it. Boldness has genius, power and
magic in it.
— GOETHE

THE MINUTE WE GOT OFF the elevator, we went straight to the phone to arrange a celebration dinner with Steve in nearby Boulder, Colorado, that evening. He was thrilled with the news and we immediately began planning in earnest for Everest.

The following day, I joined Steve for a hike up Mount Lady Washington, 13,200 feet, just outside Boulder. It was a beautiful fall day. The sun was shining and there was a warm breeze cresting off nearby Long's Peak.

Our spirits were buoyed by the news of the previous day, and we pounded like madmen to the summit, a vertical gain of almost 4,000 feet. There, it was blowing about 55 miles an hour and hailstones tore against our faces.

"You're strong enough to make it up Everest," Steve remarked, looking at his watch and calculating our ascent time at two and a half hours. This was great news to me. I had really only just begun training for Everest in a serious way and already, Steve thought I had the jam. I imagined what I could do with a year and a half of training still ahead of me. Perhaps I might even be able to keep up with the Sherpas for a few minutes.

That trip to Denver was a summit for Jamie and me, and a huge breakthrough. It was so wonderful to finally see all our hopes and plans coming to fruition. It felt marvelous, even amid the challenges we were having interpersonally.

But no one can stay on top, at least not for long. A week later, we were back in Colliers' offices in Vancouver, this time to begin to hammer out the specifics of our sponsorship contract.

Much like the meeting weeks earlier when we'd sat in that very boardroom to cut our initial deal, this meeting started badly too. John floored both of us by iterating that Colliers had only committed to part of the money. He said he was very serious about raising the balance, but could offer no guarantees. We felt a bit like the wind had been taken out of our sails. We still required a sizable amount of cash and without it, we couldn't stage an expedition according to our plan. Jamie and I knew that if we were under-capitalized, our chances of safely making it to and from the summit could be in jeopardy.

Jamie and I adjourned to another room. There, tensions between us boiled over.

"I say we sign these guys right now for what they've committed to and lock them in," I said. "The way things are going, if they don't raise the balance, they might just back out of the whole deal and we'll be left without a dime. Now's the time to close them."

"I disagree," Jamie said. "We need to go with the flow. We need to give them some breathing space, you know, take the pressure off them a bit. Obviously, they're nervous."

"That's my point exactly," I countered. "They're nervous. Nervous people can turn tail and run at any moment. They function out of fear. If they do run, where will that leave us? We're only 18 months away from departure and Matous needs cash to get rolling on this thing. Do you honestly think we can find another major sponsor, pitch them, negotiate them, sign them, and get things rolling with only a year and a half left? I say not likely. We can't afford to play Mr. Nice Guys here. This is business. I say we get them to sign a contract for what they've committed to right now and see about the rest later. A bird in the hand is worth two in the bush."

This discussion went on for about 10 minutes. It became more and more heated. We totally forgot the conflict resolution and group decision-making process we'd spent so much time and money working on with our counselor. We fell apart in the heat of the moment and reverted back to our old ways. We hadn't yet learned the lesson. The Sherpas would not have been impressed.

Fortunately, before we could come to blows, we ran out of time. We had to go back into a second negotiating session with the Colliers team. There, we discussed methods of raising the balance of the money. After that meeting, Jamie, Karen Harris, and I adjourned to the boardroom again to discuss the polarization of our personal positions behind closed doors. That's when things really got ugly.

Again, I asserted my desire to get Colliers pinned down to something. Again, Jamie pushed to give them more time. He was fighting mad. Fortunately, rather than belt me, he elected to leave the room. Karen followed shortly after.

I turned swiftly and looked out the window. All of a sudden, Vancouver in sunshine seemed cloudy.

"What a mess," I thought to myself. "What a God damn mess! We get these guys so close and Jamie and I can't even get consensus. Some partnership we've got. How in hell's name are we ever going to survive Everest if we can't even agree on what to do with a sponsor?"

It was awful. I just stood there, boiling, looking at the view, trying to come to grips with the whole senseless scene. Thank God Colliers didn't know what was going on between the two of us — or at least I hoped they didn't. One whiff of it and they'd be gone.

About 10 minutes later, Jamie came back into the room. He said we should think about terminating our partnership.

There was a knock at the door. It was Hilary Horlock, Colliers' communications manager. She had some ideas from the other camp down the hall. She wanted to know what we thought about them.

"My God," I thought. "They're still negotiating. They think this thing is just another business deal. Jamie and I are talking about separating and they're still talking about money."

I felt like I was in two worlds at once. One was drawing us closer to Everest. The other was pulling Jamie and me apart. It was like climbing up a steep ice face. If you looked down, you were staring into the icy abyss. If you looked up, you saw the rest of the frozen route above you. Depending on where you put your feet, things could go either way. It was a very fine line.

Neither one of us wanted to tell Colliers what kind of an interpersonal crisis we were in. So, we played along as best we could until it was time for them to go home for the day.

That night, Jamie and I stayed with separate friends. I gave things a few hours to settle, then I called Jamie and arranged to meet him for breakfast the next day to discuss our next move.

I didn't sleep well. I'm sure Jamie didn't either. Both of us were trying to broker the biggest business deal of our lives and we were in real trouble interpersonally. I don't think Colliers ever dreamed how bad things were between us. Sometimes we're able to put up a strong common front. We don't air our dirty laundry in front of a sponsor.

Thankfully, the Sherpas rarely have to deal with these kinds of big-league financial issues. Perhaps that's a blessing, and to us, a curse. Were it not for the salesmanship of Steve Matous and other Westerners in raising money for the 1991 Sherpa expedition, in fact, the Sherpas might not yet have climbed Everest. Why? Because they saw no benefit in it, and certainly no financial benefit. That's the only reason they'd subject themselves to such risk — to feed their families by serving others. In their eyes, there is no other reason to climb Everest. The Sherpas only climb for the money generated in the service to others. Beyond that, they see no point in it. They certainly wouldn't do it just to be able to say they had, or to write a book about it. Climbing Everest, they know only too well, is difficult, it's dangerous and it can keep them away from home up to 10 months of the year on expeditions and treks. But in a country with an average annual per capita income of just over $1,200, they can earn as much as $5,000 or more on a two-month climb.

If Jamie and I hoped to climb Everest, we needed Sherpas, which meant we needed money to pay them. So, the next morning, we met for breakfast in a restaurant across the street from Colliers' offices.

That meeting was one of the most important of our lives. It was the urban equivalent of our "little" set-to on the moraine in Advanced Base Camp in 1991 when we were trying to decide who would climb higher and who would descend. Then, Jamie had compromised and let me go on.

This time, neither one of us compromised. And that, oddly enough, was the key. Within minutes, we'd established at least one area of common ground — neither one of us was willing to give up Everest. We discussed the possibility of splitting any money we raised and forming separate expeditions, but we quickly saw the lunacy in that. Colliers would realize something was seriously wrong and then they might really run. No, if we wanted to go to Everest, we had to work things through. We only had one option. As tough as it was, as angry as each of us was with the other guy, we'd have to continue. Really, we'd come too far to turn back now. We were already committed, if not contractually to our sponsor on paper, at least psychologically to our goal. We'd been that way since we'd returned to base camp after our team had missed the top in 1994. That was what made the difference. Neither one of us was willing to quit.

By 9 a.m., we were back in that boardroom together, face to face with John and Hilary. Negotiations continued until we had come to an agreement on a few things. Then Jamie and I got back on a plane to Calgary. We went to see our counselor a short while later.

During these counseling sessions, Jamie and I articulated our respective positions on the issues of the moment and tried to come to some resolution. I rarely felt we adequately did, but what we did do was help get things out in the open. This helped to slow the ticking on the time bomb of our deteriorating friendship, but it did not defuse it. Negotiation challenges with Colliers aside, I tried to explain why I wanted to go to Everest. Without a better relationship with myself, I explained, I could not hope to have a better relationship with Jamie. This I believe Jamie misinterpreted as Everest being more important to me than him or our friendship. What I was trying to explain was that my relationship with myself was more important than my relationship with anything or anyone else. While some may accuse me of being selfish for saying this, I believe no one can hope to be in harmony with others unless they are first in harmony with themselves.

My harmony with others took a significant step closer a short while later when I met Cal Zaryski and Grant Molyneux, of Calgary. They were exercise physiologists who had heard of our upcoming expedition and offered their services at no charge. Cal was a national-level triathlete. He and Grant had completed dozens of triathlons. Cal had even survived the grueling Ironman triathlon (2.4 mile swim, 112 mile bike, and 26.2 mile run). They ran a company in Calgary called The Coaches Inc. It specialized in weight loss, personal coaching and fitness training for everyone from homemakers and corporate executives to Olympic athletes. We arranged a meeting.

Cal and Grant concluded that I had been over-training. Instead of training at maximum intensity for short time periods, they said I needed to train for longer time periods, but less intensely. It was no good being fit if you weren't also healthy, they said. Because I knew personal health was the number one thing that determined success on Everest, aside from weather and team dynamics, my ears perked up when Cal and Grant spoke. What they said made sense to me. If I was to get up Everest, I needed not only to be well trained, but well rested, happy, and healthy. So, I bought myself a heart rate monitor and began to follow their guidelines religiously.

It worked. Cal and Grant helped get me into the best physical shape of my life, times 10. But the biggest benefit I received was a friendship, especially with Cal. He regularly accompanied me on long training hikes and back country ski and snowshoe tours of 14 to 16 hours long. During these often-grueling sessions, he always maintained an optimistic attitude. He was a joy to be with.

On one such winter training session, Cal and I headed into the Rockies to snowshoe over Corey Mountain Pass just outside the town of Banff, about an hour's drive west of Calgary. Our plan was to be out no more than 10 hours, but because of unexpectedly challenging snow and ice conditions, we were substantially delayed. With darkness fast approaching, we found ourselves frantically thrashing around in the woods on the other side of the pass trying to determine the right way back to my truck. In summer, navigation in the mountains can sometimes be challenging, but in winter, with the trail under several feet of snow, it can be especially difficult.

That day, there were no tracks to follow and cloud cover made navigation challenging. When compass bearings to nearby peaks and some serious map-reading failed to adequately tell us which of two merging river drainages we needed to follow, we split up to try and find the "trail." Soon after, I crashed through the ice of a swiftly flowing stream. Were it not for some fast footwork and a little luck, I might have gone in over my head and succumbed to hypothermia, but I managed to quickly haul myself out with only a wet foot.

Just as it was getting dark and I was feeling like we might have to overnight, Cal cried out: "I found a sign!"

I headed after him. To my amazement, in the gathering darkness, Cal had literally found a Parks Canada sign at his feet, almost completely buried under the snow. I turned my headlamp on and low and behold, it pointed us in the right direction. Relieved, we began the long plod back to my truck, still several miles away, but soon after that, I ran out of food and water. When that happens, especially during what has already been a long day of heavy physical exertion, I quickly run out of energy. Athletes call this "bonking" and that's exactly what happened to me. Cal saved the day with some extra food and together, several hours after dark, we returned to my truck. There, we were greeted by a Parks Canada official who'd already been dispatched to look for our vehicle. Before leaving in the morning, we'd left word with a friend in Calgary that if she hadn't heard from us within 12 hours of our departure, she should let the authorities know. She had done just that.

So ended one little adventure. There were others. On another occasion, after crawling on our bellies in the snow to keep from being blown off a nearby peak in extreme winds, we'd managed to climb close to the summit, only to be greeted by the sound of a disconcerting "hum" in the air. Suspecting an impending lightning strike, I took off my hat and asked Cal, "Is my hair standing on end?"

He looked at me strangely and said, "Well … yes … as a matter of fact, it IS!" At that point, I declared an immediate "about face" and we marched swiftly down the mountain. A severe storm broke minutes later, but we missed the worst of it.

From all these adventures, and near misadventures, we returned safe and sound. No one came close to dying, of course. Yet the incidents were another reminder of how easily things can go awry in the mountains, especially in winter. While I am accustomed to such "mini-epics" as part of life in the mountains, I'm sure Cal will remember them for the rest of his life. These are the kind of experiences that build friendships.

Cal and another friend of mine, Milan Hudec, became my primary training partners when I was in town. During the winter, we would rise at 4:30 or 5 a.m. and head out into the darkness of the frozen Rockies to slog around for hours through the snow. Neither one of them ever complained, except the odd time when Cal became uncomfortable with the height exposure common in the Rockies, and they were always keen for more.

Toward the end of my two years of formal physical training, I had scheduled a 20-hour training day. Milan joined me for the last 10 hours of it, from 5 p.m. to 3:30 a.m. In the wee small hours of the morning, we returned to our vehicles ahead of schedule, so we decided to continue hiking along the nearby highway. Our level of fatigue was such that I found myself falling asleep as we trudged along, our way lit only by a veiled moon. The most dangerous part of the evening came when we tried to drive back to a nearby motel. The trip, less than 30 miles long, took well over an hour because we kept falling asleep at the wheel. Each of us took turns watching the other guy's vehicle cross the centerline and stray dangerously close to the ditch. It was one of the more foolish things I have done in my life, but it helped get me accustomed to the level of fatigue I would encounter on Everest.

In my relationship with Cal and Milan, I found a lot of what I had lost in Jamie. Prior to our first expedition to Everest in 1991, Jamie and I had started as training partners and became friends. Every once in a while, in spite of our trials, the magic of that special friendship would resurface as we moved toward 1997:

"Alan, as the day has left us both with little energy for much more, I will be brief...." Jamie wrote to me in an e-mail late one night. "It has become more and more clear to me that our goal of 'Hobson and Clarke, or Hobson or Clarke' on the summit is no longer acceptable to me. My goal is solely: Hobson AND Clarke. The victory for me will be hollow if I stand, or mostly kneel, on top of the world and you are not at my side.

"For me, there is no other option. If we do not together realize this dream, the climb will be a failure to me.... The true victory is for us to both know the summit."

> *Dearest of all things in my heart would have been ...*
> *to climb high into the sky again with my friend*
> *Lambert, and this time, perhaps, to reach our goal.*
>
> — TENZING NORGAY,
> *Man of Everest*

I replied:

"I feel the same way you do, except that alas, as we both know only too well, The Mother Goddess [Everest] and our own personal health may have final say over our dream....

"... despite the considerable mistakes I have made in the past in our relationship, and fresh ones I make on a regular basis, one thing remains clear — when the chips are down, we still deliver. This I can say of no other person I have met in my life. There have been fellow gymnasts with whom I shared struggle [in elementary school, high school and at university], but none whom I can say I have trusted with my life. This, more than anything, will get us to the top, provided we never forget the one fundamental truth that has got us this far: for you and me, Jamie, one plus one does not equal two. It equals four. That is not just synergy. It is something else."

On April 24, 1996, Jamie, myself, Jamie's brother, Leigh, (our lawyer) and representatives from Colliers and Lotus gathered in a hotel room in San Francisco to hammer out and sign a final sponsorship agreement. Almost a year after deliberations began, our agreement with Colliers and Lotus was finally inked.

We hugged Leigh, thanked him deeply for his efforts in saving the deal and our collective dream, and jumped into a cab for the airport.

Jamie and I sat there silently looking out the windows of the taxi. There was emptiness in our hearts. The whole negotiating process had left us frustrated and disillusioned. A part of me wondered whether we'd sold ourselves out just so we could get the money to do the dream. Another part of me wondered if I'd regret it for the rest of my life. The financial business of climbing Everest had tainted the purity of the adventure. At that moment, we momentarily lost the power of our passion and fell into an abyss.

Two days later, after our return to Calgary, Jamie departed to climb North America's highest peak, Mount McKinley, in Alaska, with his girlfriend, Barbara Neumann. She was to prove to be a superb climbing partner. Because I had climbed McKinley several years earlier and was not keen to return there, I continued to move things forward back at the office.

The day Jamie left for Alaska, we received our first check from Colliers. Together with our office manager, Mary Ross, I held it up to the fluorescent lights and said a sincere thanks. I should have been overjoyed, but I wasn't. I still felt empty. It seemed so lifeless — the way summits so often do. Money really can't buy happiness.

Even with the check in hand, however, we were to discover that the deal was far from secure.

Reality Hits

There are no shortcuts to any place worth going.

— BEVERLY SILLS

THE INK OF LEIGH'S SIGNATURE had barely dried on our contract with Colliers and Lotus when news came of a disaster on Everest. Within weeks, in May, 1996, 12 people had died on Everest, including seven from two commercially guided trips — the worst single mountaineering disaster in Everest's history. Because two of those seven were Americans, including the renowned climber and mountain guide, Scott Fischer, who led one of the trips, the U.S.-based news media had a field day. The story became front-page news in daily newspapers worldwide and the likes of *Life, Newsweek, Men's Journal, Vanity Fair, Outside,* and a plethora of other print and electronic media, including all the major television networks, raced to explain the unexplainable — how so many people could have perished. Climber and writer, Jon Krakauer, of *Outside,* himself an American and a member of one of the expeditions on which four people died, became a household name for his role in the drama. His subsequent book, *Into Thin Air,* became an instant bestseller.

This disaster sent our newly formed expedition into a tailspin at a moment when it was highly vulnerable. Some of our sponsors and suppliers became very concerned. Colliers questioned whether their participation could adversely affect their market share, the way some sponsors of the 1996 South African expedition apparently had when one of the members of that expedition, Bruce Herrod, had died.

"I only had one serious moment of concern over the three-year relationship," McLernon remembers, "and that was following the unfortunate deaths in May 1996. Any other Board [of Directors] would have had some pretty strong statements and possibly decided to bail out of our project. Our Board was different. I had done some homework. I understood as much as I could about the situation, including a two-and-a-half hour meeting in Seattle with Ed Viesturs, one of the world's most accomplished mountain climbers [after Ed had returned home from Everest]. We analyzed what had happened and why, and had a long discussion about our climbers — their attitudes, experiences and skills. Based on these discussions and further input from Alan and Jamie, I felt that the risk we assumed at the beginning of the project had not changed and our Board unanimously endorsed the continuation of the project. At that time, we also agreed to formally drive the project with emphasis on internalizing communication rather than marketing it to the world."

Lotus, which had previously spoken of a high profile advertising campaign, announced they had decided to re-evaluate their position. They would also use the expedition internally instead. In the end, this turned out to be a blessing because it took a lot of external pressure off Jamie and me to reach the summit. With two previous expeditions behind us, we had enough self-imposed pressure. We didn't need any more added from the outside.

Jamie and I moved swiftly to try to control the damage. This would have been challenging under the best of circumstances, but Jamie was fresh off achieving the summit of Mount McKinley. Together with Barb, they had somehow endured nine days in a snow cave at 17,000 feet while winds outside their snow hole raged at over 60 miles an hour and temperatures plummeted to 60 degrees below zero. After three unsuccessful attempts to push through the freezing gale, they finally stood on top of North America on their fourth try. To sustain themselves during the long wait for a summit window, they had had to scrounge food from other expeditions leaving the mountain — yet another illustration of Jamie's dogged tenacity and determination.

Needless to say, by the time Jamie returned to Calgary, he looked exhausted. But Everest is totally indifferent to challenges elsewhere in our lives. She needed our full attention at that moment; in fact, she demanded it.

The last thing sponsors wanted to be associated with was death. Our fear was that the deaths on Everest would cause our sponsors and suppliers to back out, pulling their money and products with them. Using the height of his considerable interpersonal and diplomatic skills, over the next several months, Jamie contacted as many of our sponsors and suppliers as he could. I did my best to plug the holes too. It became a small-scale investor relations campaign.

Together, we prepared a memo to be sent to Colliers and Lotus:

"The climbing community is a very close knit one and we were all shaken by the recent deaths on Everest. Climbing Everest, like taking on any big goal, has big rewards. It also has big risks.

… If climbing Everest were easy, everyone would do it. The fact that it's difficult makes it worth doing. If Everest were without risk, it would not be worth doing at all. It is in facing risk that we grow…. We feel the rewards of Everest greatly outweigh the risks….

Everest is difficult. Everest is dangerous. To deny it is to escape the obvious. What is not so obvious is that to rise to this challenge, as it is to rise to a common corporate point or to rise above something else, we must not give in to fear. We can be afraid, but we must not turn away. We must buoy up our courage and go forward with hope, strength, and determination. Nothing of any significance in life was ever achieved any other way.

> *To rise to a challenge, we must not give in to fear. We can be afraid, but we must not turn away.*

... To succeed on Everest, we must become Everest — solid, defiant and absolutely unshakable.

In the words of T. S. Eliot:

'Only those who risk going too far can possibly find out how far they can go.'"

This memo was only the beginning of our effort to renew confidence in our expedition. By the time of its writing, I had already begun work on *The Power of Passion*, our first book and the predecessor to this one. I was up to my eyeballs in writing and production deadlines aimed at getting the book finished before we left for the mountain. After much consultation, we decided Jamie would be the best person to act as the primary point man during the crisis. He was more patient than I was and far more diplomatic. Once again, we used the strength of our partnership to put our strongest foot forward.

Unfortunately, Jamie did not really want to fulfill this role. We both knew it could lead to him helping organize the expedition and this could seriously jeopardize his summit chances. In the end, that's exactly what happened because, from that point on, when sponsors had a question or problem, they called Jamie. As always, however, he ultimately surmounted this challenge and still made it safely to and from the summit.

To make matters worse, however, because of his commitment to sponsors, Jamie could not devote enough time to his contribution to the book, and he felt insufficiently included in it. The result was a double dose of more bad blood between us. He reluctantly consented to liaising with our sponsors, for the good of the team, but he would much rather have been quietly writing the book than dealing with the constant ringing of phones.

Jamie met face to face with many of our key sponsors, especially Colliers and Lotus. Between Jamie and me, we somehow managed to keep everyone on board. Nevertheless, considerable pressure came to bear on our partnership.

If there is one thing that has impressed me about Jamie, at least so far in our relationship, it has been his persistence.

"Only those who risk going too far can possibly find out how far they can go."

— T. S. Eliot

Unlike many other people I have met in my life with whom I have become close, he consistently demonstrates a commitment to work things through. He does not give up easily — at anything.

In my own naive way, I wish more people were this way. If they were, there would be far less broken business partnerships, relationships, friendships, and marriages. There's something very rare about being able to say, "Ya know, I think we're starting to get into trouble, or we're already in trouble, and we need to get out of trouble." It's easier to walk away and say, "That's it. I give up."

Almost half of all marriages today end in divorce, and, while that may seem totally unrelated to Everest, I believe the two have a lot in common. Both require a life commitment — in Everest's case, a commitment to stay alive and, in the case of marriage, a commitment for life. Like many things in our world today, commitment has become temporary.

On Everest, we have confused commitment with money. Today it is possible to get on Everest by hiring a guide for tens of thousands of dollars. Many of those who died on Everest in 1996 were clients and guides involved in commercial trips. The primary weakness of a commercial trip, as I see it, is that you do not know the level of commitment or experience of your fellow "team" members.

Like many things in our world today, commitment has become temporary.

Our 1997 expedition was different. We had sponsors and suppliers, but there were no guides or clients. Jamie and I handpicked a team of highly compatible and experienced mountaineers, all but one of whom had been to Everest at least twice before. In the old style of mountaineering, we sought to challenge Everest backed by corporations that saw a fit between our goals and theirs.

"Many people asked me about how we assessed the risk of a disaster and did we have a disaster plan should anything untoward happen," McLernon says. "The truth is, we never thought that much about it. We had two professionals [Jamie and me] who had been to Everest twice before and who seemed to understand and respect the mountain and its potentials. Their motto, 'Victory is in the Effort' showed a respect for participating, but a sense that life was worth protecting. Finally, meeting regularly with Alan and Jamie gave us confidence that we had picked some very sensible partners. Although reaching the peak was obviously the goal; it was not the goal at any risk.

"Our involvement would have been satisfied with a tremendous effort to the highest realistic point that lives were not unduly risked. We never put that to Alan and Jamie, however. We believed that that was their objective also. If the Gods were with them, of course they would reach the summit."

We will never know what happened on Everest during those terrible hours and days in May, 1996. Jamie and I were not there. None of us were. We were all half a world away, some of us safely asleep in the comfort of our beds.

"Nobody can speak for the leaders of the two guided groups involved," wrote Jon Krakauer in *Into Thin Air*, "because both men are dead."

As climbers, Jamie and I are frequently asked to comment on the disaster. Some people, amazingly, still confuse our 1997 expedition with what happened in 1996. The reality is, no one, not even Jon Krakauer himself, will ever know exactly what happened on Everest in the spring of 1996. Only Everest, and the Supreme, know. We can only speculate and speculation, as I've said, is inconclusive.

Having now been to 26,000 feet and above, I believe no 26,000-foot mountain can be safely guided over an extended period of time. We may get away with it a few times, but not repeatedly without some kind of incident. At those altitudes, there is only enough partial pressure of oxygen for individual climbers to sustain themselves. Every ounce of energy you have is being expended just trying to keep yourself alive. If you try to give some of that energy away to others, you both risk dying. This *appears* to be what *may* have happened in 1996 — but again, that is speculation. The climbers on Everest in 1996, Krakauer says, were oxygen-deprived and could not think clearly. We will never know much beyond that.

> **No one, not even Jon Krakauer himself, will ever know exactly what happened on Everest in the spring of 1996.**

We are in the age of instant information, an era in which information from Everest can be transmitted in an instant to the Internet and, in 60 seconds, hundreds of millions of people can read it. While that's exciting, it's also frightening. Now, billions of people around the world can form opinions about incidents in which they were not involved. While that is the nature of news, and has been for decades, on Everest it has a different connotation. It is difficult, if not impossible, for some to imagine, let alone understand, how challenging it can be just to take a single step at 28,000 feet.

One thing we can all say emphatically is that what happened in 1996 was tragic. Many died. Every year, more do. Many of them are Sherpas. As they spend the most time on the mountain, it makes sense that, statistically, they would be the ones most exposed to the hazards. They don't like that, but they accept it as a necessary part of the job — and that is exactly what it is — a job.

A few miles from base camp, just below the Sherpa village of Loboche at 16,000 feet, there is a cemetery of sorts overlooking a valley below. Although no Sherpas are actually buried there because the Sherpas believe in cremation, there are innumerable stone memorials, or chortens. These stand like rock sentinels against the sky, gray and bleak against the frequent clouds of the backdrop behind. They are a constant reminder to mountaineers of the price you can pay when you tackle Everest. The Sherpas have paid a very heavy price indeed. Two died in the spring of 1996.

What happened on Everest in 1996 deeply disturbed me. But it was not the fact that climbers perished that affected me the most. That is one of the risks of high-altitude climbing. What unsettled me, and what continues to frustrate me every time I speak in public or am interviewed by media, is the damage the disaster did to the sport of mountaineering as a whole and to Jamie and me as ambassadors of the benefits of living your dreams. We have spent the better part of the last 10 years of our lives committed to demonstrating the positive aspects of risktaking. A disaster like the '96 one put us back many, many years. Hardly a day goes by when either Jamie or I are not asked to answer to the consequences of the '96 disaster, commercialism on the mountain, reports about overcrowding, inadequately prepared clients and environmental concerns on Everest, specifically the accumulation of garbage. Most of these issues had nothing to do with our Everest experiences in '91, '94 or '97. Yet we are still asked to speak to them. We do, to the best of our ability, and although we completely acknowledge the terrible tragedy of what happened and the unimaginable grief suffered, we would prefer to speak about the more positive applicability of Everest's lessons to everyday life.

So, what did we learn from the Everest disaster? I learned that we must play by nature's rules, or risk incurring nature's wrath.

We must play by nature's rules, or risk incurring nature's wrath.

There has been a lot of controversy lately about the commercialization of Everest, that people are paying large sums of money, up to $60,000 at the time of this writing, to be guided up Everest. What many people do not understand is the forces that have driven this to occur.

In 1982, when Canadians first climbed Everest from Nepal, the cost of the permit to scale the mountain was $1,200. Then, the government of Nepal suddenly announced it was raising the permit fee to $50,000 — an increase of over 40 times! That's just the cost of the 8-inch by 11-inch piece of paper that says you and four other non-Nepalese climbers can take a stab at the mountain in a specific year and season on a specific route. It includes nothing else — no airfare, no food, no climbing or communications equipment, no oxygen and no Sherpas. Once you've acquired a permit, you still have to shell out $150,000 to $5 million (depending on how you decide to climb the mountain) to actually stage an expedition. The bottom line is that an expedition to Everest today costs in the neighborhood of $250,000. One can be staged for far less money, but you risk sacrificing safety and efficiency.

Not surprisingly, most of us who are not independently wealthy (Jamie and I included), do not have the financial resources at our fingertips to bankroll an entire expedition. We don't even have the capital for a permit. But, a small number of wealthy or determined individuals working together can each shoulder a portion of the cost. The result has been the evolution of commercially guided expeditions. On these trips, entrepreneurial climbers-*cum*-guides raise the money needed to climb Everest by approaching individuals with the dream of climbing Everest and asking each of them for $20,000 to $60,000 (again depending on whether they want a "Ford" guided trip or a "Cadillac" version). With four to 12 of such "clients," guides are able to raise the money needed. If the operators are frugal, which climbers usually are, they can even realize a profit and return year after year.

All of this works in theory except when the clients are not ready for Everest. In 1994, I remember queuing up at the bottom of a very steep section of the North Col slope in Tibet waiting for climbers above me to descend the anchored rope. The temperature was about 15 degrees below zero. After about 30 minutes of waiting, I began to become very cold. Finally, just as my fingers were starting to go numb, two climbers appeared from above — a guide and his client.

"Sorry," the guide declared matter-of-factly. "My client has never rappelled (the process by which climbers lower themselves safely down a rope) before."

I was aghast, and more than a little irritated. I felt like my life had been put in potential danger because someone else had enough money to buy their way onto Everest.

Most of the climbers who show up on Everest have a lot of high-altitude climbing experience, even most of the clients who are paying large dollars to be guided up the peak. A small minority are inadequately prepared and unfortunately, they can put their own lives, and the lives of the rest of the climbers on the mountain, at risk.

Since the spring of 1996, commercial operators are now much more careful in their selection of clients and guides. Books like *Into Thin Air*, the ABC-TV made-for-television movie of the same name, other books like *The Climb*, and many magazine articles have made the hazards of commercialization and group leadership on Everest household news. Nevertheless, with only a limited number of people with the desire and financial capability of shelling out the kind of money necessary to get on a commercial trip, the danger that clients will be insufficiently skilled or guides questionable in their decisions remains.

It is for this reason and many others that Jamie and I have chosen to stage our Everest expeditions using the "old" style of expeditioning — finding corporate sponsors from the business sector. This is a more difficult way to raise money because corporations today are deluged with people asking them for money. Hence, the competition for the corporate dollar is heated. There are tens of thousands of worthwhile charities, for example, who actively approach and recruit corporate sponsors looking for donations. Some have full-time staff dedicated exclusively to the challenge.

Jamie and I do not operate a charity. We are full-time adventurers and speakers. Thus, we spend a great deal of our fundraising efforts showing our corporate sponsors we are business partners who can deliver real benefits, not only to their employees, but hopefully also to their bottom lines. We do not approach potential sponsors asking for donations. We approach them as joint venture business partners looking to invest in us and our project as members of our business team. We offer them tangible and intangible benefits for their involvement and a measurable return on their investment, just like any investment.

By securing corporate funding, rather than recruiting individual clients, we can handpick our team. Clients who pay their way onto commercial trips usually find themselves climbing with virtual strangers. They have no way of knowing how their fellow climbers are likely to perform under the stress of weeks of intense exertion at high altitude, how they'll react to sleeping, eating and working in extreme conditions, not to mention how they'll deal with the colossal emotional challenges of isolation, danger and interpersonal conflicts that are commonplace on Everest. Nor do they necessarily know what it will be like to work with the commercial guide or guides.

I believe there are three major reasons why Everest expeditions fail. One is weather, another is personal health, and a third is conflict between team members. We choose our climbing team very carefully based on compatibility first (usually based on experience with them in the past or solid referrals from other climbers we respect) and experience second. Commercial operators may have some idea of how experienced their team is, but they have no way of knowing how it will perform under pressure. This is precisely the reason many "dream teams," no matter what their field, fail. On Everest, as in life, the most important component, and the one most difficult to manage, is the human one. No family can succeed if its members do not get along.

The most important component, and the one most difficult to manage, is the human one. No family can succeed if its members do not get along.

Every year, hundreds of people show up on the north and south sides of the mountain with the dream of climbing Everest. Statistics show that only about one in 10 ever reaches the summit. There are places on the mountain when the number of climbers can become a safety concern, and bottlenecks and excessive delays have occurred. This, of course, was one of the factors that appears to have contributed to the 1996 disasters. However, in my three expeditions to Everest, there was only one day when I felt overcrowding might have been a safety concern. Fortunately, that day was not summit day. It was on my way from Camp 3 to Camp 4 prior to my summit bid when many loads of equipment were being moved by other teams so summit bids could begin from the South Col two days later. The majority of these people descended back to Camp 3 or lower that day. There were no serious consequences.

On my summit day, some 20 people made it to the top, but they were spread out over the route, not because of good planning and communication between teams, but because that's how things worked out that day. It is difficult to plan for summit day. There are too many variables — health, strength, snow conditions, wind conditions, weather conditions, Sherpa support, supplies of oxygen, and on and on. In cases in which the "weather window" only opens for a day or two, you really have to be in the right place (the South Col if you're climbing on the south side of Everest) at the right time (the day before the weather window opens). Either way, calculated decision-making, experience, guesswork, luck, fate, "coincidence" or Providence must play a role. The mountain must give you permission. If you are "meant" to make it to the summit, you will — if it's your turn, your time, your path and your dharma. If it isn't, it isn't, and there is nothing you can do about it. To believe we can attain the summit without the blessing of "Chomolungma" is folly. To impose our insignificant, egotistical ambitions on nature is to invite disaster.

The issue of environmental concerns, I am happy to say, is finally being addressed on Everest. Expeditions must now weigh in and weigh out before and after each expedition to ensure they are bringing out as much or more equipment and refuse as they went in with. If they do not, they are fined by the government of Nepal. The removal of human waste from the mountain is also closely monitored by Nepalese government officials in base camp. They are quick to hand out stiff fines when they see infractions and non-compliance. Unfortunately, because Nepal is a developing country, they do not have modern waste disposal systems and although human feces and urine are removed from base camp in thick plastic drums, it is stockpiled a few miles away and, to the best of my knowledge, is never treated and properly disposed.

The only place where I found an inordinate amount of discarded gear and equipment on Everest was at the South Col camp at 26,000 feet. There, the camping spot is festooned with empty oxygen tanks, spent gas canisters from stoves, the tattered remains of old tents from years gone by and pieces of shredded rope. The reality is that by the time teams have made their summit attempts, they have precious little human energy left to clean up after themselves, let alone clean up the Col.

This raises the larger question — if that's the price we have to pay to climb Everest, then maybe we shouldn't be there. I think that's a legitimate question, and I'm not sure I have an answer for it except to say that in this day and age especially, it is incumbent upon anyone, anywhere, doing anything in the

To impose our insignificant, egotistical ambitions on nature is to invite disaster.

outdoors to make sure they leave nothing behind but footprints and take nothing away but memories.

Due to exhaustion, during our 1997 trip, we did have to leave behind some empty oxygen tanks above 26,000 feet. We knew that carrying them, at about 12 pounds each, could potentially threaten our lives. If you're struggling to take a single six-inch step and your oxygen tank is empty, you have a decision. You can continue to climb with the tank and risk dying, or you can replace the empty tank with a full one and leave the old one behind. Most people choose to climb with a new tank and pick up the spent one on the descent for later refilling and eventual re-sale in Kathmandu after the expedition. However, as I know from personal experience, because of fatigue, climbers are not always able to retrieve these tanks. The good news is, however, that the Nepalese government is now levying fines for unreturned oxygen tanks as well.

By and large, the rest of Everest is reasonably clean. Considering the mountain was first attempted in the 1920s and hundreds of expeditions have made attempts since then, I find it surprising there is not more rubbish lying around. Remember that Everest is the only place in the world where the jet stream winds touch down, and thus much of anything left behind on the mountain's upper reaches is ripped off the mountain. That does not mean, of course, that it disappears. It is just displaced elsewhere. Rubbish left lower on Everest can still accumulate without being blown off because the jet stream generally only scours the top 3,000 or so feet of the mountain.

* * *

While Jamie and I were trying to control the damage of the '96 disaster on Everest, my personal life took a major upswing. That spring, while on a speaking presentation in, of all places, the flats of the Canadian prairie, I met a woman named Diane. Along with many others who had taken the time to come up and personally thank us after our presentation, she had ordered a copy of my book, *One Step Beyond — Rediscovering the*

Adventure Attitude. Her order, however, somehow became lost, so one day she sent me a very diplomatically worded reminder note in the mail.

For some reason, as soon as I opened the note, I knew exactly who it was from. Jamie and I meet literally thousands of new people every year through our speaking presentations, and we receive a substantial amount of mail from audience members. Yet for reasons I still do not understand, I clearly remembered Diane. She was a very attractive, physically fit school teacher and somehow, she had made a distinct impression on me in the few short minutes I spoke with her. I can still remember her walking up to me after the presentation and shaking my hand. I can even remember the dress she was wearing. She had a glow about her that immediately set her apart. My heart fluttered the first time we spoke. There was something special about her.

We spoke very briefly. I remember the client, who happened to be one of Diane's friends, remarking: "You know Alan, she's single."

"You're kidding me," I said. "That's a crime. Are all the men here dead or asleep? Has she ever been married?"

"Yes," the client said. "She has three children."

"That woman is a mother of three?" I asked admiring her trim figure.

"Yes," she replied. "She runs marathons."

"Her ex-husband either needs a lobotomy or has had one," I said.

I thought nothing more of Diane until her note arrived about a month later. When it did, my intuition told me it was a message to take action. What made this reaction so unusual for me was the impracticality of the situation. She obviously lived in another city and she had three children. I had to that point in my life had no desire whatsoever to have children of my own, but something inside me said it was okay to contact her. In fact, my intuition told me I had to contact her. So, I pulled out my speaking calendar and, lo and behold, I just happened to be scheduled for a speaking presentation in her city that very weekend. I called her and arranged to hand-deliver her book to her. She agreed to meet my flight.

Within five minutes of meeting Diane that day, May 25, 1996, I knew I would one day propose to her. I felt an immediate ease with her, a sense that this was right. Diane is a kind, compassionate woman and an attentive listener.

"We went for a walk beside a lake and he told me about his dreams and goals," Diane remembers. "I told him about mine. We sat by the lake surrounded by a huge cloud of mosquitoes, but it didn't seem to bother either of us."

For me, there was a strange sense of sanctuary with her, like coming home. I felt safe.

"In the months that followed, our relationship developed," says Diane. "At least once a month, he would fly in to spend time with me and my kids. I was touched."

The first time I visited Diane's home, I was greeted by the cutest Cocker Spaniel I have ever seen. The moment I set eyes on her, I had a strange sense of the preordained.

"You would have to have a Cocker Spaniel now wouldn't you Diane," I remarked. "Of course you have a Cocker Spaniel. You're supposed to have one."

Diane looked back at me incredulously.

"Be careful what you wish for ..." I thought.

Since my divorce, I had always wanted to buy a dog — either a Golden Labrador, or a Cocker Spaniel. Some might have called it coincidence that she had one, but other signals pointed strongly to something deeper. For starters, Diane was very physically active, something that was important to me, she was a vegetarian and her ex-husband was an Ironman triathlete. Thus, she was accustomed to the demands of big physical efforts. It seemed like a good potential fit.

"My relationship with Alan would turn into one of the most meaningful ones of my life," she recalls. "It would also become one of the most challenging. For starters, there was the distance. We lived hundreds of miles apart. Then, there were my three teenagers. For a guy who had never wanted to have children, I think the prospect of being even a part-time stepparent scared him more than Everest. But he grew to enjoy it. My children liked him almost right away."

My relationship with Diane and her children took time to develop, but I soon felt at home in her home, like it was my home too. There, I could escape from Calgary, where I had to uphold an image of being "this Everest guy." With her, I could just be me.

Diane and her children would form an important part of my extended team back home. But to succeed on Everest, I knew, I also needed a climbing team, and a good one. Our next step was to begin to bring that team together.

Confirming the Team

> *When men climb on a great mountain together, the rope between them is more than a mere physical aid to the ascent; it is a symbol of the spirit of the enterprise. It is a symbol of men banded together in a common effort of will and strength against their only true enemies: inertia, cowardice, greed, ignorance and all weaknesses of the spirit.*
>
> — CHARLES HOUSTON

THE HUMAN COMPOSITION of a team is perhaps the most important decision any organization can make — whether it's a climbing organization, a business organization, or a family. On Everest, you must be a family. Yes, there are and always will be disagreements, often heated ones. That is the nature of high-performance teams, especially those that must operate in stressful environments. But the essential elements of a good team are compatibility, commitment, candor, conflict-resolution skills, mutual respect, individual and team goal alignment, and experience.

Compatibility is critical on Everest. Everyone on a handpicked, non-guided team, such as the ones on which we have gone to the mountain, can tie the knots. Everyone can climb. But can they get along, especially under intense physical, psychological, and emotional stress?

The ultimate test of a team is how it performs in a crisis. Crisis creates chaos, but then, it creates clarity. If a person is diagnosed with a terminal illness such as an inoperable and

The essential elements of a good team are compatibility, commitment, candor, conflict-resolution skills, mutual respect, individual and team goal alignment, and experience.

malignant brain tumor, for example, at first, there is the confusion and frustration. "Why?" we ask, and "why me?" Then, however, we usually take action of some kind. While it may or may not be clear medically what can be done, if anything, usually it's clearer what we can do personally. We decide to spend more time with loved ones, do what we love doing, or take that dream vacation.

The same occurs in a collective crisis, such as might occur for a mountaineering team. If an avalanche buries a camp, pandemonium prevails as everyone races around trying to rescue others and assess the damage. Eventually, however, the team may decide to rebuild the camp, relocate it elsewhere, or dispense with it altogether. The faster a team moves from chaos to clarity in a crisis, the higher performing the team. Similarly, the faster a person moves from chaos to clarity in a crisis, the higher performing the individual — providing, of course, the right course of action is taken in either case.

Crisis creates chaos, but then, it creates clarity.

But what is the *right* course of action? That's not always clear and therein lies the difference between a good team and a great one.

We wanted a great team. We had had one in 1994, and we knew the power of team members who enjoyed each other's company and who could work together under stress. We wanted that again. So, Steve had gone in search of climbers he knew well, those he'd climbed with before in extreme conditions and whom he could trust with absolute confidence.

We also wanted a team compatible with our goal. In 1994, Jamie and I had made the mistake of inadequately clarifying our objective on the expedition. Jamie thought it was to put someone on top. I thought it was to put either Jamie, or myself, or, ideally, both of us, on top. The result was that neither one of us made it to the summit and our relationship suffered terribly in the process.

We didn't want that to happen again. We didn't want to do all the groundwork, put forth all the years of fundraising, organizational work, and a lot of the on-mountain leadership only to watch someone else summit and lose our friendship.

That just didn't make sense to me. I'd already been to Everest twice. Now, having raised the money with Jamie, I felt we'd earned a chance to have the first shot at the top. I felt we'd paid our dues. To be brutally honest, that meant I wanted to be one of only two Canadian climbers on the team. The other would be Jamie. If we made it, I wanted us to get the credit as Canadians. I thought that was just. Others called it selfish and egocentric. In my mind, the 1997 expedition had nothing to do with external perceptions of Jamie and me. For me, it had everything to do with my relationship with myself. It was also about not making the same mistake twice with Jamie. If Jamie and I let someone else go for the top before us because we realized we couldn't make it ourselves, that was fine. But together with Jamie, I wanted to have the first kick at the cat. That way, if I didn't make it to the top, I knew I'd be able to come away from the mountain with some degree of personal peace. My real mountain was struggling to come to terms with my "inner Everests" — my two previous "failures" to reach the summit in 1991 and 1994 and my past personal disappointments in my relationships, as a gymnast, a husband, and an author earlier in my life. I had a lot to prove to myself.

A colleague of ours summarized it best:

"Alan is in it [the expedition] for his relationship with himself. Jamie is in it for his relationships with others."

For me, the 1997 expedition was about my own sense of self-acceptance and personal peace. Summit or no summit, I wanted to conclude the Everest chapter of my life, turn the page and move on to other things. I'd had enough of beating my head against Everest.

In addition to the compatibility of team members, especially under stress, commitment was also critically important. Our challenge was to find others willing to share that commitment with us. So, we went out in search of others who understood our history on the mountain and who were willing to give us the first shot at the top — provided they also had a shot, even a simultaneous one. This required that Jamie and I communicate our objectives clearly, consistently, and openly from the beginning. We could not afford to have any hidden agendas.

Candor - completely open communication — is vital. We made it clear that views and opinions different from our own were perfectly acceptable, and we encouraged the voicing of them. If there were conflicts, we would resolve them to the best of our ability. We were careful to ensure each expedition member's individual goal was aligned with the overall team goal — to put Jamie and I on top, and to hopefully put other team members on top at the same time.

I was also especially careful to ensure everyone knew my personal goal was to see if I could climb the mountain without the use of bottled oxygen. Canadians had never climbed Everest without bottled oxygen, and I wondered if I could be the first. Jamie wanted to use oxygen. We were determined not to make the same mistake we had made in 1994. We both knew what our goals were this time. Ironically, even with that level of awareness, there were still problems.

Candor — completely open communication — is vital.

On Steve's personal recommendation, which we valued highly, Jamie and I were referred to a small number of potential team members during the summer of 1996, less than a year before expedition departure. All had extensive high-altitude climbing and outdoor experience and each candidate commanded immediate respect. After a 22-and-a-half-hour flight from a speaking engagement in Barbados, Jamie and I met with Steve in Boulder. There, we met Jeff Rhoads, himself fresh (or rather not so fresh) off a 23-hour day in Los Angeles working on the rigging for the movie, "Batman." He'd had three hours sleep. After we were rained off a local rock climb, we convened at a local restaurant for dinner to get to know Jeff better.

He was impressive. His résumé of outdoor adventure experience was four pages long and it covered everything from climbing to fishing and river guiding. He had extensive high-altitude mountaineering experience, including two previous expeditions to Everest. In the fall of 1994, Jeff and a small team of other climbers had struggled to climb one of Everest's most difficult routes, the infamous "White Limbo" line straight up the north face. His team had made it to 28,000 feet before being driven back by high winds and extreme cold.

"I want to summit more than anybody," Jeff said. "Three time's a charm."

In Jeff, we knew we had a man of tremendous experience and reliability. He was obviously tough, and he had climbed with some of the finest high-altitude mountaineers in the world. They included Peter Hillary, the son of Sir Edmund himself, and Alan and Adrian Burgess, British-born twins who were considered amongst the world's elite.

Jeff had an easy-going way about him. I immediately dubbed him "the easy-goin', free-flowin' Idahoan," the state from which he hailed. He was a wonderful combination of determination and fluidity, a powerful mix in any mountaineer. He knew when to shut down his own ambitions and when to listen to nature. This is the essence of all great climbers. No amount of will, ambition, experience or determination will get you up a peak unless the mountain gives you permission to do so. That is truer on Everest than perhaps on any other mountain on Earth, and I sensed right away that Jeff knew where the line of demarcation was. He radiated an easy confidence, tempered with care. I liked him right away, as did Jamie.

"I was kind of out of it because I'd had so little sleep," Jeff recalls of that first meeting, "but Alan and Jamie were flexible. I was positive about the expedition. I thought, 'I'll be able to work in this situation.'"

That dinner meeting in Boulder had a certain magic about it. Just as we had with our team members in 1994, we went around the table and asked each potential team member to talk about his strengths, weaknesses, and fears — something that would require him to demonstrate candor and vulnerability.

Jeff started first. He said he was not the world's greatest organizer and that he would often wing it rather than spend a lot of time in detailed preparation. Although we were considering him for the position of deputy leader of the expedition, we felt comfortable with his admission because we knew we already had a superb leader/organizer in Steve Matous.

Jeff went on to explain that if he was selected as deputy leader, he knew he would carry a huge responsibility for everyone's safety on the mountain. He freely admitted that concerned him. He said he did not intend to take it lightly. He also said he got cold easily and that he was not a morning person. He listed his strengths as optimism, composure under pressure, and a deep sense of intuition that told him when to back off a route just because it didn't feel right.

"In the mountains and in life," he said, "I believe things work out when they need to."

Jamie went next. He listed his fears as his relationship with me, something that did not surprise me. We had been in counseling for months working things through about 1991 and 1994 and preparing for 1997. We both knew that it would be a challenge for our friendship to survive a third expedition. I appreciated his frankness, as I always do, and it was useful for Steve and Jeff to know that things between Jamie and I were good, but not great. It seemed to be a risk everyone was willing to live with, as Jamie and I obviously were, and that fact alone probably reassured them.

Jamie said he was concerned about his health on the mountain. In 1994, a sinus infection had almost cost him his life when he'd had an acute allergic reaction to an antibiotic our team doctor had administered to him for it. We promised to determine exactly which drugs he was allergic to and strictly avoid them.

Because Jamie had taken up the liaison role between Steve and our sponsors on this trip while I focused on writing the book of our 1991 and 1994 trips, he admitted he was under the organizational gun.

"I am afraid we may not be able to deliver to our sponsors the kind of benefit they demand," Jamie said. "That is one of my fears."

Jamie is a man of strict integrity and when he says he's going to do something, it is as if it is etched into his forehead for the entire world to see. He carries that commitment everywhere he goes. He becomes unsettled when he thinks he may be coming up short, and he will not rest until he has not only fulfilled those commitments, but far exceeded them. This "over the top"

> "In the mountains and in life, I believe things work out when they need to."
>
> — Jeff Rhoads

modus operandi sometimes leaves him exhausted and susceptible to sickness. Thus, his commitment is both a strength and a weakness.

Like Jamie, Steve also said he was a man of conviction. He said he performed at his best when the situation was at its worst.

"I'm also good at making molehills out of mountains," he joked. "I'm the best friend you'll ever have, but I can also be your worst enemy."

Steve said his biggest fear was being unable to meet his responsibilities to his new son, Cooper-Tashi, then 18 months old, and Connie, his wife. This would eventually create a dramatic change in the makeup of our expedition just before departure.

As the expedition's leader and organizer, Steve's other fears included an inability to control all the variables, most notably the unpredictability of the Icefall. Given the long hours of work required for him to shoulder his considerable organizational load, he was also afraid he might not be physically fit enough to perform well on the mountain.

I was last to speak. It has never been difficult for me to talk openly about my fears, nor my weaknesses. I am acutely aware of them, as I am of most of my emotions. In openness we risk rejection and criticism, but on Everest, maintaining appearances can have deadly consequences.

With Jamie, Jeff, and Steve, I shared my terrible fear of the cold, my ability to focus (both a strength and a weakness), my personal intensity (again a weakness and a strength depending on the situation), and to some degree, my anger. I can have a short fuse, although over the years I have learned to manage my anger. This anger is rarely directed toward others, but most often toward myself when I do not meet my own expectations. Like Jamie, I have very high standards and thus can be very hard on myself.

My idiosyncrasies include my total disdain for losing things — something that can happen easily because my pace of living is often so brisk. However, my strengths include a fierce tenacity. Once I decide to do something, I will do whatever it takes to get the job done, for as long as it takes. But just as I can be intensely driven, I can also be intensely kind, loving and gentle. I am a bit like a thoroughbred racehorse — fast moving, a bit unpredictable, but never, ever boring.

By the time the evening was over, we had all started to gel as a team. That dinner started to establish the kind of candid communication style that was critically important to our ultimate success. We met on two later occasions before the expedition to climb, plan, brainstorm on coping strategies for crisis intervention, and to socialize and have fun. Those meetings were an important part of our team-building process.

While Jamie and I were in the process of checking out the candidates that Steve recommended, Steve was in the process of coming up with a short list of Nepalese Sherpas who would be the Eastern addition to our team once we got to Everest. He worked through his counterpart in Kathmandu, a man called Sonam Gyalpo, who ran a trekking/expedition agency called Great Escapes Kathmandu and who had worked with our 1994 expedition. Steve contacted Sonam and gave him a description of the kind of Sherpas we were seeking. They had to be experienced, strong and most of all, compatible. We recommended Steve consider Ang "Kami" Tshering, who had been on our 1994 trip, and Lhakpa Tshering Sherpa and Ang Temba Sherpa, members of our 1991 expedition. All had previously summited Everest. Lhakpa, in fact, had been on 17 expeditions to the mountain. At 43, he was moving in on the world's record for the greatest number of trips to Everest.

Our Sherpa team would prove to be absolutely essential to our effort in 1997, just as they had been in 1991 and 1994. Steve assembled an elite group of not only one of the strongest Sherpa teams in the history of the mountain, but certainly one of the most affable. Because many of the Sherpas climb together on expeditions from all over the world, they, like Westerners, learn quickly with whom they most enjoy climbing. Our team selection strategy for them was exactly the same as it was for the North Americans — compatibility first and experience second. In the end, this strategy worked. Our two teams became one.

Very few Everest expeditions would succeed without the Sherpas. Indeed, the mountain might never have been climbed in the first place without them. Not all Everest expeditions choose to use them, but most understand that a team without Sherpas is a weaker team, not only physically, but spiritually. They bring to an expedition a resilience, balance, and cultural diversity that can do nothing but strengthen a team. They have no mountain-sized egos and do not need to prove anything to anyone. They know they are the best high-altitude climbers in the world, and they have absolutely no equals anywhere for sheer strength of numbers. There are about 3,000 Sherpas.

Yet the Sherpas are far from perfect. They have quite a liberal sexual ethic, for example, and regard the occasional lapse of fidelity in marriage as just that, a lapse. As alcohol is part of almost every religious and spiritual ritual they have, some have become terrible alcoholics, known to go on weeklong binges at a time, especially after long expeditions. Given the stress levels of some expeditions and the degree of risk and responsibility some of them must assume tending to Westerners during a trip, that might not be surprising. I make that statement, not to condone such behavior, but to attempt to add some degree of realism to the harsh realities these men and women face almost daily. Very few of us face the real potential of death every day we go to the office.

To our Sherpa team, we added a full-time cook in base camp and Advanced Base Camp, two base camp cook boys, a mail runner, and an expedition liaison officer from the Nepalese Department of Tourism. We also added Dave Rodney, a Calgary climber and educator who would be responsible for collecting and writing all our expedition's daily website updates as well as shooting some of our documentary video footage below Camp One. He was joined by Bruce Kirkby, a technical and photographic wizard from Toronto who would ensure our satellite telecommunications system in base camp ran smoothly. Jamie and I had handled both these communications responsibilities in 1991, but we'd learned from our experiences.

Our team selection strategy for the Sherpas was exactly the same as it was for the North Americans — compatibility first and experience second.

This time, we had found others to handle the expedition's communications needs so we could concentrate on climbing the mountain.

That summer we also met another potential candidate Steve recommended — Dr. Doug Rovira, of the University of Colorado School of Medicine in Denver. He was a cancer researcher/physician and chairman of the safety committee of the Colorado Outward Bound School. He had a long list of outdoor accomplishments to his credit, including a trying expedition to Alaska's Mount McKinley, the highest peak in North America, during which bad weather had forced him off the peak. He was fresh back from that trip.

My first impression of Doug was that he was highly intelligent and articulate. I liked his analytical nature. It was something like mine, and I quickly felt at ease with him. He reminded me a lot of some of my father's scientific research colleagues.

"Climbing," Doug said, "beats the hell out of drugs and rock 'n' roll. I've known every nook and cranny about Everest since I was a kid. I've always known I would go to Everest. It was just a question of when.

"In the American connotation, Everest is the only mountain in the world — or at least the only one they care about. But I have other passions besides climbing. I have two children. Everest is secular, my children are sacred."

Doug went on to explain his personal medical style. He said he wasn't an advocate of a lot of drugs and prescriptions on a mountain, but preferred to let nature run its course. That seemed fine by us at the time. What did concern us more was that he said one of his biggest fears about Everest was boredom. He said he liked to lead, but disliked the mundane load-carrying that is as much a part of Everest as driving to work is for many North Americans. Some of us don't like it, but we do it because it is part of getting to where we choose to go.

Doug said his biggest fear was being absent from his two daughters, Madeline, then 9, and Elizabeth, then 6, for the two months or so the expedition would take.

> "Everest is secular, my children are sacred."
>
> – Dr. Doug Rovira

FROM EVEREST TO ENLIGHTENMENT

"My kids need me a lot more than my life insurance policy," he said. "Everest is not worth the ultimate sacrifice and I'm not sure it's worth the sacrifice of fingers and toes either."

He explained that his mother had developed leukemia in 1993, and he had postponed making an attempt on Mount McKinley's Cassin Ridge then so he could be with her. She died a year later. Clearly, Doug was a family man, a man of honest values and good intentions, like millions of other fathers and husbands worldwide. We liked that about him. We felt that if he could commit to our expedition with that type of passion, he could be a powerful force on Everest.

I pressed him on the issue of commitment during our first meeting at Steve's office in Boulder.

"I feel the need to take the gloves off here," I said looking him straight in the eye. "What we're talking about here [an Everest expedition] many people can't even imagine, let alone comprehend. We need to know that if we're at 26,000 feet, the tent is parting from its anchors and the wind is blowing at 80 miles an hour, that you'll be 100 percent there to solve the problem with us, not two percent back with your wife and family. We'll need *all* of you, not just to make it to the top of this peak and back down safely, but just to survive."

There was a long pause. Doug looked singularly distant. He waited for about 10 seconds, then calmly, replied:

"If I make a commitment to you, it will be total. You have my word on that."

A week later, after carefully checking his references, which came back with stellar reports, we offered Doug the position of team physician. He accepted.

All told, our team consisted of 13 climbers and eight support team members for a total of 21: Jamie and myself as the two Canadian climbers; Jeff, Steve, and Doug as the three American climbers; the eight Nepalese climbing Sherpas; two cooks; two cook boys; a mail runner; a liaison officer; and fellow Canadians Bruce and Dave on communications in base camp. It was quite a diverse crew of personalities, skills, and styles, but we were confident it would gel into an effective team. Ultimately, it did.

"My kids need me a lot more than my life insurance policy."

– Dr. Doug Rovira

In the process of further interviewing Doug, he articulated what Jamie, Steve, and I had been trying to say about the team since the expedition's inception:

"When this trip is over," he said, "I'd like for the world to look at our expedition and say, 'That's it. That's how you climb Everest. Those guys did it right.'"

From that point forward, that became our mission.

> *If there is a deeper and more lasting message behind our venture than the mere passing sensation of a physical feat, I believe this to be the value of comradeship and the many virtues which combine to create it. Comradeship, regardless of race or creed, is forged among high mountains, through the difficulties and dangers to which they expose those who aspire to climb them, the need to combine the efforts to attain their goal, the thrills of a great adventure shared together.*
>
> — SIR JOHN HUNT,
> Leader, 1953 British Everest Expedition

"When this trip is over, I'd like for the world to look at our expedition and say 'That's it. That's how you climb Everest. Those guys did it right.'"

– DR. DOUG ROVIRA

The Trials of Training

If anything goes wrong, it will be a fight to the end.
If your training is good enough, survival is there;
if not, nature claims its forfeit.

— Dougal Haston,
renowned Scottish high-altitude climber

IN ADDITION TO choosing a team, perhaps one of the hardest parts about preparing for Everest in '97 was that training always had to be worked around our speaking, business, and traveling schedules — every day. This meant that no matter where Jamie and I were, what continent we were on, or what time zone we were in, we had to run, swim, bike, hike, climb on an inclined treadmill, or walk on a rotating set of stairs, even when we were tired.

I remember one particularly lonely training session in Toronto. Jamie and I had flown in from Calgary after a long day of negotiations with Colliers. It was 12:30 a.m. on a cold winter's night. As I still hadn't trained that day, I strapped on my running shoes and headed out for a run around the terminals at Toronto's Pearson International Airport.

There's something special about midnight runs. Even at an airport as busy as Toronto, the place was virtually deserted. Because there were no sidewalks between terminals (who in their right mind would want to walk the distance with luggage after all?), I ran along the road. I remember being passed by a couple of officers in a Royal Canadian Mounted Police patrol car and wondering if they would pull over and ask me what the heck I was doing running there at that hour.

Fortunately, the patrol car cruised past without so much as even slowing down. I guess they had lunatic Everest climbers training there on a regular basis.

Wherever we went, training took priority. In Portugal, Jamie and I didn't spend a minute lounging on the beach by the sea. We rented motor bikes, drove to the nearest "mountain" — 3,000 feet tall — and ran up the thing one morning. To do this, we had to rise at 4:30 a.m. so we could be finished before the heat of the day made training counterproductive.

We discovered that the road to Everest was dangerous — especially the Portuguese roads. If you let your eyes off the rear view mirror even for a second, a car could roar past at breakneck speed. You were actually a hazard *not* driving over the speed limit. This pleased Jamie to no end, because he loves speed, but scared the heck out of me. I don't care for it. Together, we played cat and mouse as Jamie roared ahead, only to slow down and let me catch up, then tear by me again, head bent over the handlebars with face glowing as that childish grin of his spread from ear to ear. As usual, Jamie squeezed every bit of enjoyment out of the journey. Mostly, I was apprehensive. We often have different perspectives of the same journey, but I did get a laugh out of his shenanigans.

Speaking in Barbados was much the same story. Again, we had to adapt to the locale. I chose to swim lengths of the beach in the surf. That was a big mistake. In 45 minutes, I was stung twice by Portuguese man-of-war jellyfish. Being a land-locked Canadian, I didn't even know what a jellyfish was until one stung me. Wow! Do they ever hurt! It was like someone was dragging red-hot steel cable over your back. In an instant, I was wincing in pain. I wore a T-shirt next time, and swimming goggles to protect my eyes, but I didn't stop swimming. I knew that if I couldn't handle a jellyfish, there was no way I'd cope with Everest.

The next day, I went running instead. By 6 a.m., I was out doing battle with the local dogs and hopping over cow pies. In 75 minutes, the heat and humidity, even at that hour, left me weak and disoriented. It was a beautiful place to be, but because we had chosen to climb Everest, there was little time to savor our surroundings. That, I hoped, would come after the expedition. That was also a mistake, but you learn.

Perhaps the most challenging part of mixing international travel with training was keeping to a schedule. Often, upon landing, Jamie and I would head straight out for a run. Usually, that was the last thing we wanted to do, but again, it came with our choice. In the months and years leading up to Everest, we traveled from Calgary to Atlanta, Miami, London, Salzburg, Denver, Cleveland, Vancouver, San Francisco, San Diego, New York, Montreal, Chicago, Toronto, Dallas, Phoenix, Washington, Orlando, Los Angeles and many, many more points all over the world, sometimes back to back. During this time, I invested over 1,000 hours of training and countless more hours preparing to train.

At times, it was difficult to understand how an hour or two run around Central Park could possibly translate into anything on Everest, but in the end, it did. The more time and effort we invested, the more we wanted to realize a return on our investment. That investment helped keep us motivated and consistent in our training, in all weathers, all time zones and all places, day and night, worldwide.

Nine months before expedition departure, Jamie and I began to seriously ramp up on our training, a process we had already been involved in for years. In recent months, I had been working with Cal Zaryski and Grant Molyneux. We developed a custom-made, seven-step training program aimed specifically at my Everest needs. The steps were: aerobic base, specific strength, endurance capacity, anaerobic capacity, mental preparation, rest and recovery, and acclimatization.

The first stage, to establish my aerobic or cardiovascular base, involved running, swimming and cycling indoors and outdoors for up to two hours at a time six days a week. This stage took about six to eight months to initiate and continued through all phases of my three years of training. I never stopped working on this component, and I continue with it today.

Next came specific strength. To develop the exact muscles used in climbing, I spent as much time as possible hiking up mountains in the Canadian Rockies to achieve as much vertical gain as possible, usually 3,000 to 5,500 vertical feet on those days when strength was my focus. I often did this with up to a 50 pound pack so as to make the important transition from "aerobic fitness" to "pack fitness" — a whole order of strength and endurance different from that required for long-distance running and cycling. In winter, I would often go out on snowshoes and deliberately chose hiking trials I knew no one would be on. That way, I could be assured of heavy slogging uphill through the deep snow with a heavy pack. Thus, I was training my body not only to push down against gravity, but also up against the resistance of the snow, sometimes several feet deep. This was ideal training for Everest, especially in extreme cold and wind. And, I could do it without a partner, day or night, no matter where I was in the mountains. For added safety, I usually traveled with a cellular phone, although it often didn't work in the more remote areas into which I would disappear. Thus, I was 100 percent responsible for my own safety. Above 26,000 feet, I knew, there would be precious little hope of anyone being able to save me if I got into trouble. I had to be self-sufficient, calm, and in control.

Because of my heavy speaking schedule worldwide, I could not always get out to the mountains to train, so the bulk of my day-to-day physical training usually took place in the fitness centers of hotels. Usually, this involved loading up a back pack with 50 pounds of weight (usually water, which once used, could be poured down the drain), strapping five pounds of weight on each ankle, cranking the incline on the treadmill up to its maximum of 15 to 25 degrees and walking on it in a specific target heart rate training zone for two hours at a time. For me, Cal determined that this zone should be between 140 and 150 beats a minute — enough to gain sufficient cardiovascular benefit, but not too intense to cause injury or difficulty in staying motivated.

FROM EVEREST TO ENLIGHTENMENT

During these treadmill-training sessions, I typically "ascended" some 4,000 to 6,000 vertical feet. At other times, I would train with the 50-pound pack and ankle weights on a mechanically rotating set of stairs called a stepmill (not to be confused with a Stairmaster, or Stepper, which are significantly easier).

As you can well imagine, this was not the most stimulating training one could do. Frankly, it was *boring*! But it was necessary to prepare myself not only physically, but mentally, for the mundane slogging I would be required to do on Everest for weeks.

I did not climb Everest in a single step on a single day at a single moment. I climbed it during those endless hours on treadmills scattered in hotels and health clubs from Los Angeles to New York and from London to Paris. And while most people associate those places with glamour and excitement, there was nothing glamorous or exciting about what I did there. I suited up and I showed up. I invested in my dream, my future, and in my very survival.

I did not climb Everest in a single step on a single day at a single moment.

> *As I had done for many years past, before big expeditions, I got up early in the morning, filled a knapsack with stones, and took long walks up and down the hills around town.*
>
> — TENZING NORGAY,
> *Man of Everest*

In life, I believe that sometimes we are all on treadmills. When was the last time you felt that despite all your efforts, you were going absolutely nowhere? Our everyday Everests are not climbed in a single day or even in a single step either. They are climbed by taking an apparently endless series of small steps that, over years and decades, may amount to something. Even if we never get to where we're going, there is always the struggle uphill against gravity, and sometimes against ourselves, against our fears, our isolation and even our boredom.

The interesting thing about treadmills, and about life, is that it often seems like nothing's changing. Yet there is a great deal of change, most of it invisible. On a treadmill, we are changing physiologically — getting stronger, fitter and increasing our endurance. We are also getting stronger mentally. The solitude offers us an opportunity to get in greater touch with our bodies and our inner selves — provided we do not allow ourselves to become distracted by televisions, headphones, and music.

In the West, we are conditioned to detach from the boredom of our "workouts" by listening to music or by watching the soaps or CNN. In reality, the simple act of listening to our breathing can be tremendously restful and physiologically more beneficial. The Sherpas have mastered this art. They combine it with chants to simultaneously relax their bodies for maximum performance and ask the gods for safe passage through areas of great danger. Unlike us, the Sherpas train almost from birth, beginning as youngsters by carrying loads of 10 or 20 pounds to and from the fields each day. As they get older, the weight of these loads increases to the point where they can comfortably carry 100 pounds at 13,000 feet — an effort that would kill many North Americans.

Our everyday Everests are not climbed in a single day ... they are climbed by taking an apparently endless series of small steps that over years and decades may amount to something.

With the Sherpas in mind, whenever possible, I tried to train with earplugs so I could get in greater touch with my breathing. This was important to my ultimate success on the mountain because I used it to prevent overexertion. On the treadmill, I learned how to use my energy efficiently and not only move and think like a Sherpa, but breathe like one as well.

In life, we can choose to get off our treadmills or continue climbing. We can either allow ourselves to become disillusioned, disappointed and give up, or we can choose to persevere. In persistence there is power. In tenacity there can be triumph.

It is not always the best policy to persevere, however. In 1994, John McIsaac decided to turn back just 162 meters from the summit. To do so was the wisest decision he could have made. It took more courage than to continue. He is alive today because of it.

The treadmill and stepmill training sessions were grueling. But they were not without their finer moments. One training session will remain with me forever. As I had my head down sweating on the treadmill at Bankers Hall Club in Calgary, a man happened by.

"Do you accept donations?" he asked.

Pulling myself out of the narrow world I perceived, I stuttered....

"Well, well, well yes, of course."

He disappeared. I went back to my training.

"CAN, WILL, CAN, WILL," I said to myself with every step. I CAN climb Everest. I WILL climb Everest. It became my training mantra — one word for each step.

A few minutes later, the man reappeared. To my amazement, he handed me $100 cash.

"Why thank you," I said. "Thank you so much."

He turned to walk away.

"Just a minute," I said. "What's your name?"

"Hal," he said. "The name's Hal."

Hal Kuntze had apparently seen one of our public-speaking presentations a few months earlier and had been observing me at a distance during my indoor training sessions. He said he had been taken by our story, was inspired by my efforts, and wanted in some way to support our Everest dream.

With the $100, he attached a note:

"Please accept this small donation from a fellow adventurer. I know it's not much, but I hope it helps in realizing a life-long dream. (It just happens to be one of mine too!) Best wishes and good luck — only 162 more meters! — Hal Kuntze"

"A great friendship started that day," Hal remembers. "I appreciated the opportunity to talk to a guy that had unwittingly been inspiring me for months. Alan's generosity in answering a few questions is what really stands out to me.... He promised to be careful enough to always 'live to climb another day.' It comforted me to hear that kind of sensibility from someone so driven — those words live with me today."

"CAN, WILL, CAN, WILL," I said to myself with every step. I CAN climb Everest. I WILL climb Everest.

I flew through the rest of the training session. It's amazing what kindness and care from others can do.

To make my hours on the treadmill, stationary bike, and stepmill more bearable, I taped small photographs of the view from the summit of Everest to the machines. These I combined with a small card on which the words "CAN/WILL," were typewritten. With all of them taped to the machine on which I was training, I would disappear within myself and spend hour after hour visualizing every step I would take to the summit and down again. Over time, this visualization, which psychologists call "imagineering" created a powerful mental and emotional imprint of what I hoped the summit experience would be like. I visualized a perfect summit day — blue sky, no wind, no threat of storms and a breathtaking 360-degree panoramic view hundreds of miles to the horizon and beyond.

While training, I practiced a breathing technique developed in India — inhaling and exhaling only through my nose. This was difficult at first and sometimes a little frightening. In the beginning, I felt like I was suffocating. Over time, however, as my fitness level improved and my breathing technique became better, things got easier.

> *It's amazing what kindness and care from others can do.*

The purpose of the technique was twofold. First, it would force my body to use the full depth and capacity of my lungs and thus use air more efficiently (as I would have to do on Everest). When you breathe only through your nose — how our bodies are designed to work — at high respiration levels, the air entering the nose actually spins downwards into the lungs in a vortex. This downward spinning motion drives the air deep into the bottom of the lungs and results in a far more efficient use of oxygen. If you practice this, you will soon feel the sensation of the spinning air in your nasal passages. It's surprising how hard you can train without having to open your mouth once you've mastered the technique and your cardiovascular system is in top form.

The second goal of nasal breathing was to relax me so I could perform better under physical stress. The earplugs also helped do this, even though, of course, I would never dream of wearing them on a mountain for fear of not hearing avalanches, ice block collapses above me, or my fellow climbers.

According to my readings, one of which was a fantastic book called *Body, Mind and Sport*, by Dr. John Douillard, of Boulder, a training session should never be a "workout" in which the goal is to reduce the boredom and discomfort by reading magazines, watching news broadcasts or listening to music. According to him, any person can achieve peak performance with less effort, create a semi-meditative mental state and a heightened sense of physical and emotional well being if they master the ancient art of nasal breathing during exercise.

Nasal breathing apparently allows the body to achieve a deeper level of internal relaxation and a higher level of physical and spiritual benefit even when a person is exercising strenuously. Thus, the goal of my indoor training sessions was not only to become fitter, but just as importantly, to become acutely aware of my body's internal voice. Once I learned how to hear that voice, I knew how to respond to it.

These two mental training techniques, imagineering and nasal breathing, were coupled with another I learned from a friend, Vince Poscente. Vince was a speed skier — an athlete whose goal it was to point himself straight downhill and go as fast as he possibly could — without turning! After only five years of training, Vince had gone from a recreational skier to becoming Canada's fastest man on skis. He competed in the 1992 Olympic Winter Games in Albertville, France.

To prepare mentally for the Games, one of the techniques he used was to stick yellow dots up all over his home in Calgary, the kind of dots you buy at office supply stores to color code items. Whenever he looked at a dot, he said to himself, "I am the fastest speed skier in the world and the Olympic champion." Although he narrowly missed winning the gold, in the process he set numerous national speed-skiing records, including a top speed of over 135 miles an hour — faster than free fall. Today, he makes his living as a professional speaker based in Dallas, Texas, teaching these and other leading-edge high-performance techniques to audiences worldwide.

"A training session should never be a 'workout'."

– Dr. John Douillard, author, *Body, Mind and Sport*

Vince is a visionary. Another of his many novel training techniques was his now well-known "Yahoo Theory." It was simple, but powerful: "If that yahoo can do it, so can I!" In preparation for Everest, I too began to stick yellow dots up all over my apartment — on the microwave, the television set, even on the door to my bathroom. Every time I saw a dot, I said to myself, "I am the first Canadian to climb Everest without the use of bottled oxygen."

As insignificant as these affirmations and techniques sound, combined with other steps I took, they had powerful results. I believe, in fact, my mental training techniques were one of the major factors in my success on Everest. In the end, the Everest challenge was to be about 60 to 70 percent mental. The rest was physical. Before I got to the mountain in '97, I had believed the opposite. Now, I know that once the body is trained to perform for long periods under load, provided it is well hydrated, fueled with food and rested, it is the mind, and not the body, that drives it onwards. The mind is driven by the passion in the soul — the burning and boiling desire to achieve an objective that over time becomes so deeply ingrained and important that it effectively becomes part of the soul. You meld these two together — body and soul — through the power of thought, emotion, and imagination. Thus, the triumvirate — body, mind, spirit.

To build up our endurance for long hours of climbing, Jamie and I began a series of what became known as "Everest Summit Cycles" in the Canadian Rockies. These were designed to simulate in Canada what we might expect on Everest, without the altitude. (There was no way to simulate altitude except to train inside a specially designed low pressure, or hypobaric, chamber. These facilities were difficult to access and prohibitively expensive to use.)

To mirror what our bodies would be expected to do in the days leading up to and down from the summit of Everest, Cal contacted Steve Matous and learned the exact climbing time and elevation changes between our camps on Everest. If, for example, on Day One we were to climb from base camp to

Another of his [Vince Poscente] many novel training techniques was his now well-known "Yahoo Theory." "If that yahoo can do it, so can I!"

Camp 2, a vertical gain of 4,500 feet in a time of roughly six hours, that is what we would do in the Rockies on our first day of training. If on the second day on Everest, we would be required to climb from Camp 2 to Camp 3, a vertical gain of 3,000 vertical feet in four hours, again, that is what we would do in the Rockies.

On June 21, 1996, the summer solstice and the longest day of daylight in the year, Jamie and I set out at 3 a.m. on our first 20-hour training day. We departed on foot from just south of Lake Louise, about 100 miles west of Calgary, and hiked to the summit of Mount Temple, 11,620 feet high. We then descended to a valley and hiked up Mount Eiffel, an elevation of 10,115 feet. The challenge called for approximately 17 miles of cross-country slogging and involved a total vertical gain of about 8,200 feet — over half the 12,000-foot gain from Everest's base to its summit. We finished, as we had started, in the dark, at 11 p.m., tired, sleep-deprived, but proud of our accomplishment. It would be the first of many longer and more difficult mountain training sessions.

Over a series of months, Jamie and I completed three, five-day-long summit simulation cycles before leaving for Everest. The fourth day always included 20 hours of continuous movement, day and night, in winter.

To further prepare myself personally, I also performed one 24-hour solo climb up and down the trail of Sulphur Mountain in Banff, 75 miles west of Calgary, during which I ascended and descended the peak six times — a total vertical gain of 14,000 feet. My biggest challenge that day/night was staying awake. At one point, at about 3 a.m., I bent over on the trail to rest my hands on my knees and take the load of my backpack off my back. I woke up seconds later just before my face hit the snow. It was so difficult to stay awake that several times I actually found myself falling asleep in mid-stride. It was then I learned that one of the causes of falls at high altitude was not misplaced steps, but *falling asleep*.

These long days and nights were challenging affairs. Yet, they were absolutely essential to allow Jamie and me to get

The mind is driven by the passion in the soul.

used to working as a team in extreme cold. One thing was certain — in spite of its rigors, it was a lot more enjoyable than slogging for hours on a treadmill indoors, something Jamie totally disdained and completely avoided. As a former cross-country ski racer, he preferred to train outdoors whenever he could, whereas my years of training in chalk-clouded gymnastics gyms as a youth had made me more accustomed to the boredom of training indoors.

Most of my training was done by myself. Through the long hours of tedium, I maintained my motivation by reminding myself that my life might depend on keeping moving. It's easier to stay motivated when your life depends on it. As it turned out, it did.

Training partners were difficult to find. Not surprisingly, not many people want to go out for 20 hours, especially in the dead of the Canadian winter, and "have fun." In addition to Jamie, I was particularly fortunate and grateful to have Cal join me on some portions of my summit cycles, as did my friend Milan Hudec, a Calgary climber and mountain enthusiast. Even at almost 50, Milan was an ideal long-haul day/night training partner. Like Jamie and Cal, he never complained and most importantly, he never gave up.

Extreme goals call for extreme measures.

Training day and night in extreme cold may seem like lunacy to many people and, of course, it is. But extreme goals call for extreme measures. Considering achieving the summit of Everest wasn't the personal goal of either Cal or Milan, it was touching to have such fine friends support me in my dream. I will never forget the long, cold, and dark hours we shared together. It went far beyond male bonding. It forged true friendships, friendships that will last a lifetime. Of all the rewards Everest has brought me, these are without question the greatest gifts I have received.

Sudden Setbacks

It is not the critic who counts, not the man who
points out how the strong man stumbled or where
the doer of deeds could have done them better.
The credit belongs to the man who is actually in
the arena; whose face is marred by dust and sweat
and blood; who strives valiantly; who errs and
comes short again and again; who knows the great
enthusiasms, the great devotions, and spends himself
in a worthy cause; who, at the best, knows the triumph
of high achievement; and who, at the worst, if he fails,
at least fails while daring greatly, so that his place will
never be with those cold and timid souls who know
neither victory or defeat.

— President Theodore Roosevelt,
who climbed the Matterhorn in 1881

IN THE SUMMER OF 1996, I came to know Diane much better. Every chance I could, I would drop in on her for a visit. Every new meeting made me more convinced she was what I had been searching for in the 10 years since my divorce. She was bright, attractive, athletic and very, very energetic. She listened well, and she was kind and loving. I marveled at her ability to manage three active teenagers on her own, run a household, train for marathons, and hold down a full-time job, all at the same time. I felt close to her quickly and the intensity of my affection for her ignited my most powerful personal drive — my passion.

On September 15, Diane was to run a marathon in the Canadian Rockies, west of Calgary. For years, I had dreamed of proposing to a woman on the high mountain saddle of one of the nearby peaks, just east of Banff. I had become the first person to fly off the peak in a hang glider years earlier, and it had always had a special place in my heart. Although we had only known each other for four months, I knew Diane would not be back in the Rockies before the snow flew and thus, it would be too cold and inhospitable on the mountaintop until the spring. By then, I would be on Everest, and I knew there was always a possibility I might not come back from the mountain. If the worst came to pass, I wanted her to always know how much she meant to me. So, I took a risk and seized my chance to make the moment extra special.

I wrote a proposal for marriage in the form of a poem. In it, I told her how I felt about her, how much I respected and admired her, and how much I loved her. Then, I had my words put to paper by a professional calligrapher who designed them into a small book wrapped in gold ribbon. I ordered a dozen of the finest long-stemmed red roses money could buy, booked a helicopter for the day before Diane's run and looked forward with great anticipation for our day to arrive.

I will remember that day for the rest of my life. The weather was unsettled. The first signs of winter were in the air. It was overcast and cold, with an unpredictable wind. I was thankful I had not waited any longer because I knew what it was like on the top of a mountain in the Rockies in winter.

When we got to the heliport, the pilot took me aside quietly and told me that because of the weather, we would only have about 30 minutes on top. He said a cold front approaching from the west might strand us up there if we lingered longer.

"Will that give you enough time?" he whispered in my ear as Diane unsuspectingly looked on. I nodded yes. In the end, his words were foretelling.

The chopper took off shortly after 4 p.m. I had loaded Diane's poem and roses into a tall cardboard box and secretly stowed them in the biggest backpack I owned. As the chopper lifted from the ground, Diane looked suspiciously over at me as if to say, "What's going on?" She looked apprehensive. I hoped it was just the uncertainty of her first helicopter ride.

"You're on another adventure with Alan," I replied, smiled, and swallowed hard.

Ten minutes after we took off, the whirlybird alighted on the windblown patch of moss and grass I had dreamed of for a decade. At last, I had found the woman I wanted to marry. At last, my moment had arrived. Finally, I would turn my back on all those frustrating years as a single man and join with Diane in wonderful union.

As the wind began to whip a light rain into our faces, I pulled out an umbrella to shield us from the rain drops. Slowly, while reading the poem, I got down on one knee and when the final line of my poem came, so too came my words:

"… will you marry me?"

There was a long silence. I searched Diane's face for some clue to her reply. It should have been instantaneous. It's supposed to be, isn't it?

When she hugged me, my heart fell. I knew. My arms went limp around her. She did not speak for the longest time.

"I need more time," she finally said. "I love you, but I need more time."

In the life of a man, there is no moment of greater vulnerability, none more emotionally exposing, than when he proposes. The second those four words came from my mouth, I lay bare my soul and gave to Diane all I had to give at that moment — my heart, my dreams, and myself. There is only one answer that can solidify your soul at that moment, and if you do not hear it instantly and convincingly, it is as if something inside you shatters like a piece of porcelain dropped on a cold stone floor.

That's how I felt — shattered. I was unable to move, breathe, or speak. The mountain wind blew up my back.

I turned and looked down into the valley. Tears began to stream down my face. I have never felt more alone in my life. It was as if the mountain had become the moon and I alone walked its desolate surface, like a ghost.

In the life of a man, there is no moment of greater vulnerability, none more emotionally exposing, than when he proposes.

After what seemed like an eternity, I got up and walked away. Diane stayed behind.

"Wow," I thought to myself. "Did I ever mess up. I totally misread her."

The chopper was due to return five minutes later. Unfortunately, the winds continued to increase and the clouds grew around us. It looked for the longest time that we would be totally enveloped and then, we would have to hike all the way down together, but apart. I knew that could take up to two hours. Under the circumstances, I knew they would be two very, very long ones.

If I had to live my life over again, there is very little I would change, but I would change that day. I would never have booked that chopper or written that poem. I would have checked in with her verbally and asked her where she was at in terms of our relationship. She would have told me, and then I could have changed my choices. That might have changed everything.

But a little loneliness can be a dangerous thing. We're all a little lonely. Some of us are a lot lonely and lonely a lot. We fill up that loneliness temporarily with others.

"I can't think of a more romantic or perfect proposal than the way Alan proposed to me that day," Diane recalls. "He had taken care of all the little details and had not spared any expense. I remember telling him the poem he had written for me was the most meaningful and most special gift I had ever received. It will always be that, and I will treasure it for the rest of my life. He will never really know just how much that poem touched me and continues to mean so much to me."

During our time on top, Diane held me close and tried to comfort me, but I might just as well have been a million miles away. That day, and those painful moments, set off a chain of frustration in both of us that would carry us many months forward into the future, through Everest and beyond, and lead to one of the most difficult personal disappointments of our lives. I needed to know then if her answer really was that she needed more time, or that it actually was "no." In the hours of discussion that followed, she tried to assure me it was just as she had said — that she just needed more time. That helped to reassure me, but it did not make me feel secure.

From that point forward, I always felt like I was standing on the edge of a mountain with Diane — that no matter how hard I tried to woo her, she had the power to push me off the cliff.

After what seemed like an eternity of silent waiting, the chopper finally arrived about 20 minutes later. Once at the heliport, we drove to Banff.

Neither of us slept much that night. I had booked a room at one of the finest hotels, complete with chocolate-covered strawberries, candles and soft music. Instead, we talked and talked and talked. I cried. So did she.

"By the time the starting gun went off for the beginning of my marathon the next day, we'd already been through an emotional marathon of our own," says Diane. "Both of us were wrung out, red-eyed and exhausted. I think Alan had hoped I would start my race flying — joyous in the knowledge that we would spend the rest of our lives together. Unfortunately, that's not how it worked out. The timing just wasn't right for me."

To my amazement, Diane somehow still finished the run — all 26 miles, 385 yards of it. She was understandably disappointed and frustrated with her time, but relieved at having finished. In a marathon, if you cross the finish line, you win. Too bad relationships aren't that easy to define.

In a marathon, if you cross the finish line, you win. Too bad relationships aren't that easy to define.

Within minutes of congratulating Diane, I had to jump in my truck and dash to the Calgary airport to fly to Cleveland for a speaking presentation for Colliers. As I drove the 70 or so miles, I determined to be patient and to gradually win her over. That became my new goal. Unfortunately, that thinking was as flawed as the one behind my marriage proposal, the same way that trying harder is a mistake in golf. At that point in my life, I believed that "if at first you don't succeed ... try harder." It doesn't work in golf any more than it does in relationships. Both are living, breathing things. They take on an energy of their own. Diane had made an admirable and impressive decision, albeit a painful one for me.

"As the mother of three children, I wasn't sure if Alan knew what he was getting himself into as a potential stepfather. Nor was I completely sure yet how I felt about him. I still had reservations — about who he was, his traveling lifestyle and his independence. I had only been out of my 15-year marriage for three years and so I was still pretty apprehensive. His less-than-reserved approach was not what I needed at that moment. I needed him to go slow and easy, to be casual and laid back and just let the relationship, and me, evolve. Mostly, I just wanted to have fun."

My story had a happy ending, at least temporarily. Six weeks later, after a lot more talking, Diane finally accepted. I was over the moon — but there was a catch. Because of her three children, Diane asked that I not share my news with anyone until she had time to tell them herself. She told only her mother. That should have been a warning sign for me that she was still unsure because months later, she still had not told her children.

At that point in my life, I believed that "if at first you don't succeed ... try harder." It doesn't work in golf any more than it does in relationships.

Out of respect for her position and to honor her request, I told only my parents and Jamie and asked that they keep my news confidential. I was bubbling inside and wanted desperately to share the joy of my news with others, but because of my commitment, I could not. I told myself that the fact that I couldn't tell others wasn't really that important, that what mattered was that she had accepted. The reality, I would learn, was that she hadn't and, in fact, ultimately never would. Even with a "yes," I was still dangling on the edge. I felt simultaneous joy and fear. It was an uncomfortable state in which to be.

I did not know it then, but my relationship with Diane was a critically important part of my emotional training for Everest. It was preparing me for an emotional Everest I could hardly have imagined. The Sherpas, regrettably, could not help me in this climb. I would have to carry the burden myself.

When all of my mental and physical training was almost over, Cal began to put the top on the pyramid of my body's preparation — nine sessions of anaerobic bursts. For sheer discomfort, these took the cake. After a 15-minute warm-up on a stationary bike, I'd power away for 17 minutes at 90 percent of my maximum heart rate, usually between 160 and 170 beats a minute. Then, at the 17-minute mark, I'd pull out all the stops, pedaling full-out for three minutes. Cal called this "red lining," the point on an automobile's tachometer when the needle goes into the red and the engine can suffer damage if its revolutions per minute remain too high for too long. I felt like I was coming apart and the rivets were popping. It was very uncomfortable.

While Jamie was on a speaking tour of several Colliers offices worldwide, he continued to train and help Steve organize the expedition. Unfortunately, the toll became too much for Steve. Faced with the prospect of having to spend up to three months away from his wife, Connie, and Cooper-Tashi, with just three months to go before expedition departure, Steve tearfully let us know he would not be able to join us on the mountain.

"As the months of organizational work progressed," Steve remembers, "I was deep in the operational end, but more confused on a personal end. I was starting to be torn in half. I wanted to be with Cooper and I really, really wanted to go to Everest. I had originally thought that Connie and Cooper could just come to Everest with me. But the previous spring we have gone there [to Nepal] and I had realized that wasn't going to happen.

"… As long as I can remember, I've been a climber. As long as I can remember, I've wanted to go to Everest. It's always been a major part of my life. Here I was realizing that that might need to change. It felt like a life struggle — like I was losing a limb. Even after I'd made it, I second-guessed it a lot. I really wanted to be there."

My first reaction to Steve's decision was one of shock and disbelief. Understandably, I was disappointed, and I'll admit, a little angry. How could he desert Jamie and me now with such little time left? Where would we find another leader half as capable, experienced, and affable? The number of people who were qualified to lead an Everest expedition, we knew, was very small. Of those, the number who might be available to leave the country for three months on short notice and be compatible with both our goal and our team was even smaller. I feared that number was zero.

Jamie helped ease my frustration. He explained what a gut-wrenching decision it had been for Steve, that Steve fully understood the implications of his decision, and that he felt absolutely dreadful about having to make it. The reality was, Steve believed he would feel even more dreadful if he went to Everest and left his young family behind. The decision he made took courage.

"This expedition is everything I've worked for my whole life," he explained. "Finally, someone is willing to pay me to organize and lead an expedition. No more fundraising, no more endless beating of the bushes for money. I get paid to do exactly what I love to do — logistics, planning, strategizing and leading."

Steve's decision, understandably, left us in a difficult spot far beyond the simple leadership void it created. After the disasters on Everest in 1996, the last thing we wanted was for our sponsors to get cold feet again. We couldn't afford to have anything else shake their confidence.

Jamie and I decided to keep silent about the loss of our expedition leader with 90 days to go. In his organizational role, Jamie moved swiftly to develop a short list of possible candidates. The list was exactly that — short. There were only two — Lloyd Gallagher, the former deputy leader of the 1982 Canadian Everest Expedition, and Jason Edwards, an American climber we had met on Everest in 1994.

Gallagher had impressive credentials. Besides his Everest involvement, he had gone on to become the coordinator of emergency services for a major Canadian park. This meant he was responsible for overseeing all emergency search and rescue operations, supervising the training and deployment of emergency personnel, and overseeing the establishment of standards and procedures for everything from locating lost children to plucking off mountains critically injured climbers stranded high on isolated rock faces by helicopter. Essentially, this meant that if you got yourself into trouble anywhere in "his" mountains, he got you out of it — day or night, 365 days a year, no matter what the weather. It was a tremendous responsibility, one for which he had earned high respect amongst his peers, not only for his professionalism, but for his consistently affable personality. Everyone I knew thought the world of him, including the Sherpas who had worked with him. I felt the same way.

If Lloyd had been 20 years younger, there is no question we would have chosen him. I held him up on the same level with Bill March and Laurie Skreslet. In my mind, we would never have been on Everest without him. Together with his colleagues, he had paved our way to Everest. Unfortunately, we felt we needed younger, fresher legs high on Everest. So, after much soul-searching and evaluation, we decided to go with Jason. He was in his late 30s, very fit, and brought to the climb extensive high-altitude experience, particularly on Everest. He had also had lots of experience with the Sherpas. It was still a very difficult decision.

"I was excited and I was into it," recalls Jason of the opportunity. "It didn't intimidate me a bit."

The loss of Steve as the expedition's climbing leader on the mountain worked out for the best. Shortly before our team left North America, he developed a herniated disk in his back, probably from the stress of mounting a $1 million corporately sponsored expedition. In spite of it, he agreed to accompany the team as far as Kathmandu to ensure everything there was in order before he returned to his family in Boulder. Fortunately, because of Steve's Herculean efforts to that point, he was quickly able to bring Jason up to speed and pass him the leadership reigns so that once in Kathmandu, Jason could completely take over. Without question, we absolutely could not have made it to the top without both of them. Thanks to Steve's superb organizational effort all the way to Kathmandu, and Jason's considerable physical and logistical strength from there to and from the mountain, the loss of Steve led to an overall gain for the entire team. Steve got what he wanted — time with his family, and we got what we needed - climbing and leadership strength high on Everest.

"We didn't have any agendas manipulating anything," Jason recalls. "This was the Alan and Jamie program. We knew that from the beginning."

So there we were — after three years of fundraising, training, and organizational work, two previous Everest expeditions and for me seven other high-altitude climbs, everything was finally ready. After Cal had overseen my last anaerobic "red line" training session, I was ready for the final and most important phase of my training — rest and recovery. During this time, I tapered down on the length and intensity of my few remaining training sessions, concentrated on eating properly and getting lots of sleep. Then, I disappeared to a personal sanctuary with friends where I took refuge from the world of phones, faxes, and meetings. I was careful to take only a few social calls and removed myself as much as I could from the stresses of last minute details It was hardly the isolation the Sherpas enjoy high in their mountain paradise, but it was wonderful nonetheless. In those final days before departure, I prepared psychologically for the biggest physical, mental, emotional, and spiritual effort of my life.

During that special time, my mother visited me in Calgary and gave me the following note:

My send-off —
For the laughter and joy you brought us as a boy, I thank you.
For the perseverance and toil as a college student, I thank you.
For your aching heart and its insights into healing and
*   moving forward, I thank you.*
For your Everest efforts one step at a time toward
*   the supreme effort, I marvel.*
My wonder at the wisdom earned, humbles me. I thank you.
Through all this, I repeat, what you do is enough.
May our love surround you,
Mum.

There could not have been a better way for my mother to say good-bye to me, nor a finer way for me to say hello once again to her love. It is one thing to love your children. It is quite another to support them in an endeavor from which they might never return. Perhaps this is one of the reasons why my parents, particularly my mother, have been so expressive of their love for me. With all the physical risks I have taken in my life through hang gliding, parachuting, climbing, white water kayaking, white water rafting, and so on, she has never been able to take my presence for granted. She knew I could die any day — any of us can.

Whatever the reason for their commitment to me, such is the love my parents and my brothers have for me. It is constant and unshakable. Those closest to me have always supported me, no matter how they might have personally felt about the potential outcome of my actions. I have been free to fail, even to die, going after my dreams, but most of all, I have felt safe to succeed. In being permitted to explore who I am, I have been able to fully discover who "I" actually am.

Sometimes I think I am one of the luckiest guys on the planet.

Quite probably, I am.

It is one thing to love your children. It is quite another to support them in an endeavor from which they might never return.

The Dream Takes Flight

So if you cannot understand that there is something
in man which responds to the challenge of this
mountain and goes out to meet it, that the struggle
is the struggle of life itself upward and forever
upward, then you won't see why we go.

— GEORGE LEIGH MALLORY,
British mountaineer and Everest climber

THE DREAM BEGAN at 3:50 a.m. on March 19, 1997, with Diane at my side. I had been up into the wee small hours the two previous nights with Cal, his girlfriend, Christine, and Milan, taking care of last-minute packing that seemed endless. There are always so many last-minute things to attend to before leaving for a major expedition, and this trip, like my two previous ones to Everest, was no exception.

Diane had flown in to Calgary to trek into base camp with me and then return to her commitments as a teacher and mother three weeks later.

"I had also been through something of a marathon to be with Alan. After several tries over many months, I had finally convinced my school board to give me the time off. I had prepared daily lesson plans for my substitute teacher, looked after my financial commitments, arranged for my children to be cared for while I was away, and made numerous personal presentations to potential sponsors in search of the over $5,000 I would need to get to and from the mountain."

In the end, only one thing was lacking — financing. As if providentially, at the last minute I came into some unexpected money and was, therefore, delighted to help.

Were I to live my life over again, I would not have brought Diane, or any intimate, on the trek into base camp. The harried nature of our departure from North America, the sudden physical and psychological adjustment to the developing world, the considerable stresses of adapting to high altitude while trekking through Nepal, and the pressures of climbing the world's tallest peak were too much to expect a new relationship to bear. I was feeling the full anticipation of the biggest effort of my life and was naturally on edge. In hindsight, I have learned that such efforts are probably best made alone, except in cases in which one's intimate partner is a full participant in the endeavor. On the other hand, perhaps the trek into "the ultimate challenge," as Everest has been called, is also the ultimate test of a relationship. Ours was not to pass the test.

But that was yet to come. That dark winter morning in Calgary, I was excited. At last, the day had come. At last, all the fundraising, organizational work, book writing, packing, training, training, and more training was over. Now, it was time to live the dream.

Hurriedly, we loaded a rented van driven by Bruce Kirkby, our satellite telecommunications coordinator. Bruce is a tall, strapping, and powerful man. Although he has a degree in engineering/physics, he had spent most of his recent life working as a river guide in the wilderness of the Canadian Yukon. A friend of mine, Rob Aikens, of Ottawa, had referred Jamie and me to him. Rob had also expressed an interest in being the telecommunications coordinator, but in a touching display of personal integrity, had recommended Bruce over himself.

"Bruce comes with my highest personal, professional, moral and ethical recommendation," Rob had said. "He's the best man for the task."

Rob was to prove right. In addition to his considerable intellect and outdoor experience, Bruce had an affable personality and easy-going nature that made him ideally suited to the rigors of an Everest expedition. In fact, he had been so keen to join our team that he had originally applied to be base camp cook. That's how enthusiastic he was — he was willing to do almost anything to get to Everest.

Although Bruce's telecommunications position would be a volunteer one, the chance to go to Everest seemed enough to satiate his considerable passion for adventure. He is not motivated by money. He is driven, amongst other things, by his desire to explore. His job on the mountain would be to operate and maintain our link to the outside world, our telecommunications system.

Along with Bruce's roommate, Colin, we were joined that morning by David Rodney, the climber and educator who was to work closely with Bruce. While Bruce's job was to ensure our communications link with the world remained open, David's job was to provide the information our sponsors and, indeed, the world would receive through that link. Thanks to Jamie, our expedition would have two websites — one maintained by Lotus and the other by VR Didatech Inc., of Vancouver, Canada's largest distributor of educational software. Through VR, David would help develop a unique interactive educational curriculum on Everest and exchange e-mail with 300,000 students around the world. His job was to keep these students updated daily on our progress on the mountain and answer their thousands of questions on life at high altitude. These questions, it turned out, would cover everything from tactics to toilets.

Like Bruce, Dave was to prove to be an invaluable asset to our team and especially to me. I did not know it then, but in the ever-widening gap in my relationship with Jamie, Dave was to fill an emotional void and make a vital contribution to my life.

At the Calgary airport, our quartet of Diane, Dave, Bruce and myself began the long and involved process of checking in 13 excess bags, and paying well over $1,000 in excess baggage charges. To their credit, the check-in agents with Canadian Airlines International handled the whole affair smoothly and professionally without the slightest sign of being flustered. Perhaps they understood the magnitude of what we were proposing to do. We were all greatly relieved.

Together, we moved smoothly through U.S. customs at the Calgary airport and boarded our 7 a.m. flight to Los Angeles. From there, we were to bridge the Pacific to Seoul, South Korea on Thai Airlines, fly on to Bangkok, Thailand, overnight there, and travel to Kathmandu the next day.

The trip went smoothly. In Los Angeles, we boarded our flight to Seoul and Bangkok with none other than Pete Athans of Colorado, who held the American record for the greatest number of Everest ascents — four.

"I was thrilled to meet him," Diane recalls. "Unlike some of the sports world elite, he was gentle, humble and articulate. He radiated a quiet confidence. He was the kind of sports hero I wished all sports heroes could be — sensitive, perceptive and intelligent."

Athans had been to Everest a dozen times and in the process had distinguished himself, along with another of his American colleagues, Ed Viesturs, as a consummate climbing professional and true gentleman. He had an aura about him — solid, self-assured and grounded. He was like Everest.

"I will always remember that flight to Seoul with Alan," Diane says. "We were very much in love."

I wrote in my diary that day:

"There is a tremendous feeling of peace — that I've done everything I could possibly do to prepare for this goal, trained as hard as I could possibly train, worked as hard as I could possibly work. Like the movie, The Right Stuff, I feel like it's finally time to 'light this candle' and get on with it.

"It's wonderful to have Diane along. As usual, she is a constant source of good humor and energy. She is vital. I am so fortunate."

After what seemed like days of travel later, we finally arrived in Thailand. Four hours of fitful sleep later, we awoke in Bangkok to the first day of spring amid balmy temperatures, lush flora and bright sunshine. By mid-morning, after a hearty breakfast that included guava and pineapple juice, fresh bananas, and other tropical delicacies, we were on our way to Kathmandu. By early afternoon, our plane touched down there.

It was quite a moment. My very first thought was, "Wow! This is awesome. We've actually done it. We're actually here."

The first thing I noticed was how dry Kathmandu looked. When we had landed there in the spring of 1994, the city had been much greener. Now, it was brown. This bodes well for the future, I thought. Perhaps it meant less moisture down low and hence, less snow high up. That could mean easier going on the trek in and less snow to wade through once on Everest. I was filled with optimism.

The first familiar face we met in Kathmandu was that of Jason Edwards, our climbing leader. He looked flustered and tired, and small wonder. He had just spent the last week or so preparing for our arrival and along with Steve Matous, Jeff Rhoads and others, had been working full out in the heat of Kathmandu. Not surprisingly, he reported that Steve, Jeff, and the others were already sick with diarrhea and dysentery and that he had only just begun to recover from it himself.

Often the most difficult part of climbing many of the world's tallest peaks is maintaining your health while traveling through the developing world in which many of them are located. Most of the world's population does not enjoy clean drinking water, adequate plumbing, sewage treatment, waste disposal systems, or even food that is "safe" to eat.

It is almost impossible to avoid getting sick at least once while you're traveling in these areas. While diarrhea and vomiting can be serious even for a casual visitor, for a high-altitude climber, they can quickly escalate into something life-threatening. Dysentery can lead to such rapid dehydration that the victim may succumb to high-altitude sickness.

Most of the world's population, including many who live in Nepal and Tibet, exists on the very edge of survival and cannot even begin to dream of climbing Everest. Their everyday Everest is keeping their children from dying of diarrhea, tuberculosis, chronic infection, or any of a multitude of other infectious diseases.

This fact came pounding home to me again the moment Diane and I stepped out of the airport in Kathmandu. There,

> *Most of the world's population does not enjoy clean drinking water, adequate plumbing, sewage treatment, waste disposal systems, or even food that is "safe" to eat.*

we were besieged by a small crowd of boys clamoring for the right to carry our luggage in the hope of bringing home a tip for their families.

"I felt a combination of guilt and privilege when a van sent by Great Escapes Trekking appeared to whisk us away to the comfort of our hotel," Diane recalls. "As the van pulled up at the entrance of the Everest Hotel and the bell man hustled to collect our bags, I marveled at the neatly manicured lawn and garden, and especially at the circular swimming pool and reclining sun chairs. I could see that within sight of where we were standing, just outside the hotel grounds, barefooted workers pushed carts of heavy iron rebar painstakingly uphill and crippled beggars panhandled for pennies. I tried to remind myself that the expedition was bringing hundreds of thousands of U.S. dollars into the country, but it did little to quell our uneasiness."

Our brief stay in Kathmandu was to be a pivotal one in my relationship with Diane. I was jet-lagged from two days confined to an aircraft and out of sync with North American time by some 12 hours. As a result, I did not sleep well while I was there. Diane, on the other hand, adapted smoothly and easily. On the second night, probably as a result of the combined stresses on me, our state of excited bliss evaporated into a lover's quarrel. Sensing that both of us needed space, Diane left the room and went for a walk. Diane and I bounced back, as we always had, but I felt I had almost made my last withdrawal from her goodwill bank account.

Fortunately, our time in Kathmandu was just a few days. Steve knew from experience that the longer we stayed there, the greater the chance there was that we would get sick. So, he arranged for all of our eight Sherpas to come down from the Khumbu Valley and assist with last-minute packing and organizational efforts in Kathmandu. The result was that I was relieved of the burden of any such stresses. Already, the Sherpas were carrying loads for us, although we were still hundreds of miles and many days journey from Everest.

On March 23, we all assembled at the Kathmandu airport for the 45-minute helicopter flight to the Sherpa village of Lukla, in the high foothills of the Himalayas. There, we would begin the 30 or so mile trek on foot to base camp. Steve would have to stay behind to ensure our oxygen cleared Nepali customs, then he would return directly to Colorado.

It was a painful parting with Steve.

"There were tears," Steve remembers. "I was still missing Cooper — 50 percent of him is me. Part of me was on its way to a helicopter and part was in Colorado. It was a major emotional moment for me. Talk about a conflict."

"Be safe and have fun," Steve said as his wiped the disappointment from his cheeks.

"We will," I said proudly. "Thanks to you Steve, we will."

I hugged him.

"My gut, my belly was totally on fire when they got into that helicopter," Steve remembers.

It is impossible for me to convey how much Steve put into our expedition, the thousands of hours he spent on the telephone, the months of preparatory planning, and the sleepless nights that in the end maximized our chances of success once in base camp. Steve was like the blacksmith who day after day pounded out the shoes that went on the horses that pulled our team to the top and back down again safely. With his hands, his head, and his heart, he forged our dream from a hot idea into a cold reality.

As we stepped into the Russian Kazan helicopter packed to the rafters with gear and passengers, Steve waved good-bye. I knew he must have felt like a mother giving away her offspring. The belly of the helicopter, after all, now carried his brainchild — and his children. It was now our job to go to Everest with all the tools he had given us and execute the mission.

"In retrospect, it was the right decision for me to stay behind in North America with my family," Steve reflected months later. "There's something about children that you'll never be able to reclaim. I can always go back to Everest. It will always be there."

> *"There's something about children that you'll never be able to reclaim."*
>
> — STEVE MATOUS

There, inside that helicopter, I felt excitement and guilt. Was it right that Steve should be staying behind? Had we really made the right call in consenting to go with another leader? That leader was a fine one with a proven track record, but — it was silly to second-guess anything now. We were on our way. We were off to Everest.

"There was no pre-flight briefing, no safety demonstration," Diane remembers. "The leather bomber jacket-clad "flight attendant," a gruff Russian, passed around a Tupperware container filled with cotton balls for our ears and months-old candies that had welded themselves to their wrappers in the heat."

Over the huge load of packs and poles, haul bags and boxes of telecommunications equipment covered with fish netting to hold them in place, I peered over at Bruce and a few of the Sherpas and gave them a thumbs up. They all flashed me a broad smile.

As the machine shimmied and shuddered while the rotor got up to speed, I craned my neck to catch one last glimpse of Steve. Alas, my window was too tiny to see him from where I was. I took comfort in the fact that I knew he was there. He always had been.

His presence never left us.

As the chopper's wheels finally lifted from the ground, I felt my heartbeat jump just a little.

The dream had taken flight.

The Trek Begins

It's good to have an end to journey toward;
but it is the journey that matters in the end.

— Ursula K. LeGuin

"Forty minutes of breathtaking flight later, we peered out the windows of the chopper to see the tiny airstrip at Lukla thousands of feet below," Diane remembers. "From the air, it looked so small, like a postage stamp stuck to the side of a mountain. It seemed impossible anything could land there."

Perched precariously at 9,200 feet, it was easy to understand how the airstrip at Lukla had claimed the life of Sir Edmund Hillary's wife and 15-year-old daughter during a plane crash there in 1975. As we approached the suspended runway, it occurred to me that this might very well prove to be one of the most dangerous parts of our Everest adventure.

"The runway, which sloped gradually uphill, was only a few hundred yards long," recalls Diane. "It was only wide enough for a single light plane. Only a few feet before its beginning, the ground fell off steeply into thin air. If you undershot the approach, you plowed instantly into the side of the mountain. If you overshot, the outcome was the same."

If I was grateful for one thing, it was that I was not in the specially fitted Twin Otter fixed-wing planes that landed there many times daily. They came in at full throttle, hammered down into the runway, and immediately threw up full flaps and reversed their propellers in what at first appeared from both the air and the ground to be a certain suicide mission. As their engines roared, they sent up a wildly spinning cloud of dust, then miraculously came to a stop just seconds before what seemed like inevitable disaster. In all my travels, I have yet to see an airstrip like Lukla's anywhere in the world and hopefully, nothing will "better" it in my lifetime. The aerial view of the approach reminded me of a description a jet fighter pilot had once given to me about what it was like to land a fighter on the deck of a steeply swaying aircraft carrier in high seas.

I swallowed hard and tried to remind myself that, fortunately, the runway wasn't actually swaying — although it looked like it was as we rattled around in the belly of the chopper, buffeted by the wind. Our Russian pilots were very experienced and, in fact, had been specially selected for their skill in flying this make of helicopter into this location. Small consolation, I thought. It wasn't hard to imagine our less than streamlined ship as a tangled, twisted mess of smoking wreckage in the valley bottom thousands of feet below.

Moments later, it was all over. With all the cool of morticians, the Russian pilot and his colleague gently maneuvered the chopper onto terra firma. It seemed effortless, the way anything difficult done well so often does. Moments after that, when the massive rotors had finally stopped spinning, our sardine can in the sky popped open and along with the two dozen or so other relieved passengers, Jason, Jeff, Bruce, Diane, myself, and some of our Sherpas clambered out and peered into the awesome beauty of a Himalayan day.

Lukla was spectacular. What it didn't have in state-of-the-art airport facilities, it more than made up for in ambience. This was a real live Sherpa village in the high Himalayas. The Sherpas have existed here for centuries, having originally arrived by trekking hundreds of miles on foot over the high mountain passes carrying sugar, salt, wood, and other staples to and from ancient Tibet. Today, they make their living as farmers, tea house operators, trekking guides, and high-altitude climbing Sherpas for expeditions from all over the world.

There is still a great deal of foot traffic between the increasingly well-known villages of Namche Bazaar, Thyangboche, Pheriche, and Gorak Shep en route to the desolation of Everest base camp at 17,000 feet. The hardy yet humble Sherpas exist as the tillers of the thin soil and the human tractor-trailers of this part of the world. There are no roads or telephones here, no flush toilets, and no running water — except the millions of gallons of freezing melt that tumbles in the spinning silver ribbons of waterfalls from the massive glaciers above. The area is a fitting ceiling to planet Earth, a paradise in the hills suspended above and beyond the ordinary.

Behind the loosely constructed barbed wire perimeter of the "airport," dozens of locals waited patiently in the hope of securing portering opportunities that would take them further up the valley for a few dollars in daily wages. The sweet smell of burning juniper wafted peacefully over the tiny tin-roofed homes, shops, and tea houses of the several hundred or so residents.

"The day was glorious," Diane remembers, "Bright sunshine, a few high scattered clouds against a brilliant blue sky and about 70 degrees. I breathed in the fresh mountain air like it was life itself — which, of course, it was. After the pollution-choked air of Kathmandu, Lukla was like heaven. At least we weren't very far from there."

That day in late March, I felt like I always did the first time I set foot in rural Nepal — like I'd stepped back in time. There were no cars, traffic lights, cell phones, or sidewalks. Our load of visitors and the dozens of others that arrived on other chopper flights and by Twin Otter constantly throughout the day created something of a continuous rush hour in the tiny village. The influx and exit of hundreds of Westerners mixed seamlessly with the locals, creating a stimulating bustle of trade, tourism, and everyday life.

Kathmandu was at least a week's journey on foot from here and because most of the Nepalese could not afford the luxury of a swift aircraft flight to the country's capital, Lukla had become the gateway to the spectacular Khumbu Valley, massive

Everest and the rich Sherpa culture. The village was teeming with commerce, trekkers, climbers, and locals in a fascinating blend of East and West, old and new.

I marveled at the apparently blasé attitude of the Sherpas to what was obviously just another day in the life of Lukla on a clear day. Provided the weather was good enough to allow safe landings and take-offs, this was the way it usually was here. When the weather was poor, however, visitors could neither arrive nor depart, and there was a steady build-up of stranded visitors that made for stiff competition for the seats of the local tea shops and for the beds of Lukla's many spartan but cozy guest lodges. When the clouds eventually parted, the accumulated backlog of Westerners waiting to depart to and from Kathmandu suddenly scrambled to catch flights at both ends. Thus life in Lukla could be a little frenetic at times. It was an exciting place.

After being ushered abruptly off the airstrip by Nepali policemen fervently blowing whistles, the first obstacle I had to overcome was a large sleeping cow just outside the runway fence. It occurred to me how easily it would have been for him to awake and aimlessly wander out into the path of a plane or helicopter, but the policemen, I came to understand, were responsible for herding them as well as the tourists. One way or another, we were all being herded. Cows, the providers of life-giving milk, meat, and cheese, are sacred in this part of the world, not to mention a source of financial wealth and social status. I knew that as a visitor, I was also something of a cash cow, and that I looked more out of place. But on this journey, although I would be "milked" for money, I would also be given something priceless in return.

Diane, myself and the others were quickly directed to the office of Richen "R.K." Karma Sherpa, one of Steve's business partners and the unofficial king of Lukla. R.K. spoke fluent English. He was neatly dressed in Western clothing and it was obvious by the manner with which he conducted himself that he was also a veteran at dealing with impatient, demanding Westerners. Although calm and composed, he spoke and moved at a pace more in keeping with Los Angeles than Lukla. He immediately set about the task of working with some of our Sherpas and other locals. Together, they created individual porter and yak loads from our thousands of pounds of gear.

As all this went on, the white-faced "sahibs" (clients) were treated to a feast of boiled eggs, potatoes, fried rice, and rehydrated Japanese noodles at one of the local tea houses. We washed the whole works down with bottled water and canned soft drinks and soaked in the soothing warmth of the sun. It was so good to be out of Kathmandu. Not only was the air cleaner here, but even with the steady drone of arriving and departing aircraft, it was still a lot quieter.

Shortly before 1 p.m., Diane, myself and the others sported light backpacks and began to head down the path to our day's destination, the nearby Sherpa village of Phakding, just a few hours walk away.

"It was an incredible stroll, certainly one of the most memorable of my life," she recalls. "The trail gradually wound its way downwards a few thousand feet along the steep eastern side of the Dudh Kosi River, which has as its source the Khumbu Glacier at the foot of Everest. Above this frigid and swift-flowing river, the views of the surrounding countryside were stunning. Everywhere I looked, there was a breathtaking panorama of jagged mountains, plush green trees, and hanging waterfalls. It was like paradise on earth."

There is no question whatsoever that Nepal is one of the most beautiful countries in the world. If it were 10,000 miles closer to North America, it would be the West's number one tourist destination. It is a land of tremendous range and contrast, yet while it is one of the most naturally beautiful places on the planet, it is also one of the poorest economically. However, while most of the 20 million people who live there are poor in comparison to our considerable financial wealth in the West, they are far richer spiritually and light years ahead of us in their attainment and understanding of the importance of inner balance and personal peace.

> *While most of the 20 million people who live in Nepal are poor ... they are far richer spiritually and light years ahead of us in their attainment and understanding of the importance of inner balance and personal peace.*

Daily living for most Nepalese, although sometimes a struggle against disease and hunger, appears from the outside to be punctuated by an overriding gentleness and calm. They are an unhurried people, quiet and even amidst considerable adversity, surprisingly at ease with themselves, each other, and with their environment. While you may stroll smoothly among them wearing more on your back than some of them may own in a lifetime, there is no feeling of resentment or animosity toward you. It is a remarkable feeling.

This attitude toward life is also held equally by the Sherpas.

"The Sherpas have a joy of life amid adversity," Laurie Skreslet says. "They prove that you can still have fun in the midst of hardship. At the end of a long day, when everyone else is exhausted, they can still dance. You get out of life what you choose to get out of it."

Crime as we know it is virtually non-existent in Nepal. Even late at night, I have never had any fear of being jumped, mugged, or robbed, even when alone in a completely unlit street and carrying the Nepalese equivalent of a huge amount of cash. You are free to go about your business, just as the Nepalese are free to go about theirs. You feel safe there, at peace. This is perhaps one of the most magical things about Nepal. Although every visitor must cope with the constant challenge of maintaining his or her health, you needn't worry about your emotional or spiritual wellness while you are there. Here, Hindus and Buddhists have existed harmoniously side by side for centuries. What's a few hundred thousand visiting Catholics, Protestants, Anglicans, Baptists, or Lutherans? Religious tolerance or, more accurately, respect for others, is not just touted here. It is practiced — daily.

Three hours of spectacular hiking later brought us down to the bank of the Dudh Kosi River and the tiny Sherpa village of Phakding. With its stone fences, scattered tea houses, and potato plots, it was an idyllic place to pitch a tent. We delighted in crossing the gently swaying, albeit dilapidated, footbridge over the roaring river. There was the odd foot-board

> *"You get out of life what you choose to get out of it."*
>
> – LAURIE SKRESLET, FIRST CANADIAN TO CLIMB MT. EVEREST

missing, but it was obvious from the stiffly drawn and staunchly anchored steel cable that you weren't about to be dumped into the drink.

"My first thought was that I had just walked into a post card," says Diane. "A small group of children in wrap-around, gray robes and sneakers raced about excitedly, welcoming us and squealing with joy and laughter. Some pointed curiously at us and asked after our hats, for candies, and of all things, pens."

After a delicious dinner of rice, lentils, and fried banana fritters prepared by one of our skilled expedition cooks, we retired to our tents and crawled into our sleeping bags for the night.

As Diane and I lay there together listening to the roar of the river, a calm came over me that I had not felt in weeks. Finally, we were on the trail. I could feel the solid soil beneath my body and inhale the cool, pure air into my lungs. We were amongst the Sherpas. We were on our way.

My Emotional Everest

The greater the obstacle,
the more glory in overcoming it. — MOLIÈRE

THE NEXT 11 DAYS of the trek passed largely as planned. Every day, we walked a few more miles, increased in altitude two thousand feet or so, and rested whenever necessary to allow our bodies to "catch up" to the increasingly thin air. A highlight of this time was that we got to visit many of the homes of the Sherpas with whom we would be climbing. They welcomed us warmly into their one-room stone and timber enclaves, fed us sweet Sherpa tea (regular tea with lots of milk and sugar) and cookies, and plied us whenever possible with chang, the locally brewed beer. We returned the favor by presenting them with small photographs of the Dalai Lama, the spiritual leader of Tibetan Buddhism. These were cherished more than money, especially by the Sherpa children. They shrieked with joy the moment they set their eyes on them, danced about like they'd just been given candy, and ran to their friends to show off their precious new gift. With the billions spent on complex Christmas and birthday presents, elaborate computer games, virtual reality, remote-controlled cars and battery-powered dinosaurs each year back home, I longed for a return to this, a simpler, albeit harder life.

"... the practice of love and compassion is not mainly a religious matter," the Dalai Lama once said. "But compassion and love — without these we cannot survive."

There was compassion and love here too, even amid the hardship. You sensed it, as you sensed the struggle for survival. It showed in the faces of the children, and in the eyes of their mothers and fathers.

Each home was of similar design. There were two stories. The bottom floor was reserved for livestock. In the winter, the body heat from the animals rose up through the wooden floor into the sub-divided kitchen and one-room living and sleeping area on the second floor. This room, which served as the focal point for all family activities, consisted of a central stove on which tea was kept warm. Wide benches ran almost the entire perimeter of the inside of the living and sleeping area of the room. These doubled as beds and were covered with thick wool and yak-hair blankets. The walls were decorated with pictures of the Sherpas on the summit of Everest, certificates of achievement from the government of Nepal and large shelving units housing most of the family's possessions, including old back packs and dusty climbing gear. Scattered amongst these were large, hand-made brass and copper pots which I gathered were about the only outward display of wealth that seemed to be permitted in the culture. At one end of the room, there was always a brightly decorated Buddhist shrine, complete with pictures of the Dalai Lama. There was no central heating, only the odd bare light bulb powered by hydroelectricity, no carpeting, no furniture aside from a few worn and weathered wooden coffee tables and no books. However, although permeated with the smell of years of burning yak dung and juniper bows for heating and cooking, everything was neatly arranged and cleanly swept. The bathroom was an outhouse.

Generally, each home was damp, cold, and dark inside. But what brought light and warmth to it was the degree to which we were welcomed. Although I speak only a few Sherpa words, it was impossible to miss that our Sherpa hosts were thrilled

"... the practice of love and compassion is not mainly a religious matter," the Dalai Lama once said. "But compassion and love — without these we cannot survive."

FROM EVEREST TO ENLIGHTENMENT

we were there. And they would do anything in their power to ensure we felt completely at home. This included repeated and persistent offers for more chang or tea, which came in the form of the phrase "shey, shey," meaning "more, more." No sooner had we taken a single sip of their fine tea than our cups were topped up again. It was thus almost impossible to finish a visit in anything under an hour and a half, and preferably it lasted the entire day. Welcome to Himalayan hospitality — Sherpa style. Here, the emphasis was on friendship, not money, on what's happening now, not what still had to happen that day. Although everyone was busy tending to animals, tilling the soil, and preparing the year's seeding, there was always time to visit. There was a focus on the immediate, perhaps because in an environment as harsh as this one, at altitudes from 9,000 to 17,000 feet, tomorrow really might never come. You could be killed climbing, your child could die of any number of diseases, or your spouse could freeze to death if she failed to keep the home fires burning.

I was reminded of an incident that had occurred in 1994, during my second expedition to Everest from the Tibetan side of the mountain. Then, I had been told by one of our Sherpas to pay close attention to my clothing while setting up my tent in base camp.

"The Tibetans will remove anything you leave unattended," he explained.

"Why?" I inquired. "That's theft."

"You do not understand, Alan," he replied. "To the Tibetans, you do not need your down parka."

"What do you mean? Without it, I could freeze to death on the mountain."

There was another one of those long pauses, the kind I had learned meant something that I should have known was coming.

"The Tibetans believe you do not need to climb the mountain. You chose to climb it. They do not choose to live here. This is where they were born, and it is the only life they know. They are now prisoners in their own land. Your parka would be needed to survive the cold nights and winter."

How relative life is, I thought, and how my views were based so much on my own reality. As it has been said: "We do not see the world as it is. We see it as we are." The Sherpa reality became starkly clearer.

I was fascinated by the Sherpa culture, descended as it was from life in Tibet. It was the apparent de-emphasis on time that captured me most. I was to discover quickly, as many Westerners have before me, that although you may return to the time-dependent West, a part of you never leaves the timelessness of the Khumbu. It stays forever cozied up with that bottomless cup of tea or chang, wrapped comfortably in yak-hair blankets and chatting easily for hours at a time around the stove about life adventures, or saying nothing at all. English is not the only language spoken here. Silence is acceptable too. Here, you may visit only with yourself, or with the deity of your choice. There is a pervasiveness of acceptance.

"The Sherpa people are incredibly warm and gracious," Dr. Doug wrote home. "It has been wonderful wandering through village after village on the way to the mountain. I met with the lamas at the monasteries in the Sherpa villages of Thyanboche and Pangboche. I would give them a khada silk scarf with a small donation for their monastery wrapped inside. They hung the khada around my neck, said a prayer (om mani padme om — the jewel is in the lotus) and gave me red silk strings to tie around my neck. We throw blessed rice at that which we fear and walk around carved prayer stones called mani on the left [because the circle of life runs clockwise]. I don't know what any of it really means. What I do know is that I am in the company of a people who are at peace with their harsh environment, with each other, with me and with their God. It is a very spiritually uplifting experience."

Steve Matous agrees. "What's always impressed me is how much they [the Sherpas] welcome you," he says. "I remember going to visit one of the Sherpas in Nepal. He had to be away from his village that day and couldn't see me. His family had never met me, but they asked me to sit next to the fire. That is the most special seat in the house. 'Have some tea,' they

> "We do not see the world as it is. We see it as we are."

said. 'What would you like to eat?' That would not happen in North America."

In this soothing sanctuary, two events were to occur that would stand out for me in sharp contrast. One was reasonably minor, the other, major. Within days of beginning the trek, I came down with a very bad head cold, something that at more hospitable altitudes would have been nothing, but here, as we gradually hiked up to 17,000 feet, became increasingly uncomfortable. As my body struggled to adapt to the altitude, it also had to work to try to cope with my coughing, hacking, and substantial nasal and sinus congestion. During the uncomfortable acclimatization process, it is often difficult to sleep at the best of times and a head cold only compounds the discomfort. Add to this my anxious emotional state and the trek turned into a far greater challenge than I had anticipated.

The problem with sickness at altitude, even if it's minor, is that the body does not have the ability to recover the way it conventionally does at lower elevations. The partial pressure of oxygen in the air, the pressure that drives air into our lungs after exhalation, gradually becomes less and less the higher you climb. The body requires oxygen for almost all its important processes, including its ability to combat disease. If you get sick at any point in an expedition to high altitude, you can expect to carry some of that sickness with you for most, if not all, of your trip. Although there are exceptions, for me, this is usually the case.

In the larger scheme of the challenges I had to overcome, a head cold was to prove minor, but it marked the beginning of what would be a series of health challenges that would dog me throughout the expedition. Essentially, I was sick most of the trip and for many weeks afterwards as well — par for the course for just about any Himalayan expedition.

What was far more serious and, indeed, perhaps potentially life threatening, was what happened between Diane and me. During the trek in, I gradually noticed she was becoming more and more distant emotionally and physically. My intuition started talking to me and I began to feel emotionally insecure.

By the time we reached the Sherpa village of Pheriche at 14,000 feet, only days out of base camp, both my health and the health of my relationship with Diane were in need of attention. Although we were walking through some of the most beautiful scenery in the world, my heart was heavy. I tried to put these concerns aside, attributing them to my head cold, lack of sleep and the usual discomforts of acclimatizing. But it was more than that.

"What is it sweetheart?" I finally asked. "Is there something wrong?"

"No," Diane replied. "Everything's fine."

I sensed otherwise.

"Everything may be all right my love, but your body and your actions are speaking loudly to me. What is it?"

"I never came out and stated that I did not want to marry Alan that night," Diane insists. "He put those words into my mouth."

Whatever the case, in the wee small hours of Easter Sunday, just days from beginning the biggest physical push of my life, the painful truth came out. Our engagement was off.

"I would never consciously do anything to hurt Alan — or anyone for that matter," Diane explains. "I would never have chosen that time to suggest I had some doubts about us. The timing was his, not mine."

In my view, it really didn't matter whose timing it was or who had brought it out. What mattered was what reality was. My reality hit hard.

At first, I felt numb — like I had been hit by a heavy blow — no matter who you chose to believe dealt it. Obviously, something was wrong. Diane held me and told me that she loved me, but as I had on the top of that peak when I had proposed to her, I did not hear her words. Silence hung like the darkness in the tent.

Then, the strangest thing happened. In my mind, I carved out some peace. I resigned myself to the fact that I had done everything I could to woo her. I had courted her, proposed to her, pursued her over hundreds of miles and now traveled to the ends of the Earth — the third pole, with her.

You cannot make someone love you. They must decide to love you. Love is a conscious decision, as well as an emotion.

If Diane was to marry me, I resolved, she would. If she wasn't, she wasn't. This was a very uncharacteristic reaction for me. I am usually very focused on my goals and as one of my goals was to marry Diane, I would usually have simply persevered more at that point.

I didn't, if only for a few hours. I was deeply disappointed and very, very hurt, but I could not change how she felt. It was her decision. I was a big part of it, to be sure, but I was not the one who had made the call. She had, and whether she had consciously chosen to tell me at that moment or not, I had got the message.

Somehow, I instantly understood that if I let Diane's decision get to my core, it could kill me on Everest, or potentially contribute to the deaths of other members of our expedition if I let it distract me on the mountain. I knew Everest was unforgiving, totally. The situation certainly wasn't the way I would have wanted it, but I knew that if I hadn't raised the issue with her, I would have had to live under a cloud of doubt for the rest of the expedition. I didn't want that. At least this way, I knew.

The words of Laurie Skreslet came back to me at that moment: "Make sure your emotional house is in order." I knew now there was no way my house could be, and it would be that way throughout the expedition.

John Lennon once said: "Life is what happens to us while we're making other plans." Obviously, fate had other plans for me. I hoped with all my heart that I could somehow survive Everest and at the same time climb my emotional mountain.

No man can deliver the goods if his heart
is heavier than his load. — FRANK IRVING FLETCHER

"I asked him if he wanted me to go home," Diane recalls. "He said no, not this close to base camp. He said he knew what it was like to come back to North America after not having

You cannot make someone love you. They must decide to love you.

made it to the goal and my goal had been to reach base camp. He said he didn't want me to have to endure the pain of having to explain why I hadn't made it to everyone back home. I appreciated that and marveled at his ability to see past where we were as a couple. He told me he loved me and wanted me to stay. I told him I loved him too. We talked about living together instead of getting married and that seemed like a better idea. Alan is a tremendously focused person. He is a wonderful partner, but he can be very intense. It is one of his greatest strengths. It's part of how he takes on big challenges. He focuses that intensity on one thing. When he does, amazing things can happen. But if one of those 'things' is you, it can be a little overwhelming."

Hours later, after more discussion, we both turned over and went to sleep. The bad news was our engagement was off. The good news was, I thought there might still be some hope of saving our relationship. As I am an optimist, that was enough for me. There was a lot of uncertainty, but there was a lot of uncertainty in climbing Everest too. This was no different, as none of our Everests are.

I did not know it then, but I had already reached base camp in a way. I had reached the base of a mountain I had been trying to climb with Diane for almost a year and for many years before that since my divorce. It was obvious that for the moment, I would have to climb solo, at least until I came back from this physical mountain. That's the way we'd planned it anyway, except that I hadn't planned on doing it under these circumstances.

"The next few days were difficult for both of us," Diane remembers. "Because of Alan's health, we decided to stay an extra day in Pheriche."

As if in concert with my emotional and physical state, within hours of my decision to stay behind, the sky quickly clouded over, the temperature dropped, and snow began to fall. The next day, Diane and I hiked up to the village of Loboche at 16,000 feet.

There, things went from bad to worse for me physically. The first night, the altitude drove my head cold deeper into my chest and I coughed almost all night. Finally, at 3 a.m., exhausted from blowing an endless stream of colorful discharge from my nose, I started on antibiotics, decongestant spray, and Tylenol. Three hours of fitful sleep later, I dragged myself out of the tent and tried to walk around camp. By afternoon, I was so tired, I had a cry just to release some of the tension. The tears flowed freely. They were tears of grief as much as anything. That night, I took my first sleeping pill of the trip, something very unusual for me, but sometimes necessary to preserve your sanity and health at altitude. You cannot recover if you cannot sleep.

The next day, April 1, was the day Bruce, Jason, Jeff, Diane, and I were to trek in to base camp. Most of the Sherpas had already gone ahead to assist in the construction of base camp. I had looked forward to arriving in base camp with the rest of the team for a long time, but it was obvious it would not be wise for me to ascend higher until my health improved. Diane stayed behind to see me through another night, but after another miserable time in the tent hacking up phlegm and keeping both of us awake, I decided it would be best if she continued to base camp without me. I would descend to Pheriche in hopes that the lower altitude would help my immune system.

Shortly before 10 a.m. on April 2, I said good-bye to Diane in Loboche.

"It was a sad parting," Diane remembers. "We knew there was a possibility we might never experience base camp together, as had been our dream, but Alan seemed resigned to the reality of his health. To climb higher, we knew, would only make things worse."

I kissed Diane good-bye, told her I loved her, and sent her on her way with a porter. Slowly, she disappeared from sight around a rocky moraine. In moments, she was gone. I turned immediately downhill and started to hike back to Pheriche. It was a long and lonely walk.

By noon, I had returned to the village at 14,000 feet. There, I found a room in one of the Sherpa tea houses and went to sleep for the rest of the day and night. It was heavenly. I was amazed with the difference a few thousand feet in altitude made. By morning, I felt substantially better, having awakened for only two hours during the night to hack and cough before finally getting back to sleep. The tea house was dark, damp and cold, but at least it seemed to be well run.

Bleary-eyed, I staggered out of my little enclave and almost straight into one of our Sherpa trekking leaders. He directed me to the tent of Jamie and our team physician, Dr. Doug Rovira, only a few hundred feet away. They had been a day or two behind us on the trek in, but now that I had been delayed, they had caught up.

It was great to see them. I dove into Jamie and Doug's arms, hugged them both and basked in the warmth of the familiar. Then I treated myself to a two-minute-long hot shower courtesy of my tea house, washed my now very dirty handkerchief and celebrated reunion and rejuvenation.

But my respite, like most on the trip, was brief. That evening, my mind became preoccupied with Diane's decision. Within hours, my head was spinning with unanswered questions. I prayed she would descend from base camp and come to see me. I desperately needed reassurance.

"Descending didn't even occur to me as an option," she recalls. "For starters, I'd have to be accompanied by a Sherpa. All of them were naturally hard at work establishing base camp. Secondly, I'd have to explain my reasons to Jason. As expedition leader, of course he had other more important things on his mind besides me."

I wrote in my diary that day:

"This is a terrible, dark and lonely time. God I hope I can get some answers."

The next day, fueled by my desire for those answers, I hiked all the way from Pheriche to base camp — an altitude gain of more than 3,000 feet. I was like a man possessed, possessed by a need for personal peace. Dave Rodney and a porter accompanied me. Because the porter had not yet been to the altitude of Loboche as I had recently, we left him there. He was to join us the next day in base camp if he was feeling up to it. To our total surprise, however, he appeared behind us a short distance below base camp showing the first signs of altitude sickness. At first, we offered him water and food, but he refused it. Even if they are thirsty, hungry and tired, the Nepalese sometimes refuse assistance from Westerners. It could be an issue of pride or cultural differences, but they see their role as one of service.

A few minutes later, it became obvious the porter was in difficulty. So, Dave and I began force feeding him water and food. This helped a little, but within hours, he was having trouble walking.

Under such circumstances, it is always safest to descend. The problem was, we were already much closer to base camp and the medical attention Dr. Doug Rovira could offer than we were to barren Loboche, which had no medical facilities. Lightly falling snow and low cloud made the trail difficult to follow. As it was already getting late in the day, Dave and I decided it was safer under these conditions to continue the few hundred feet higher than all of us trying to descend to Loboche in the dark. Even a descent was a gamble. If the porter's condition improved in the tiny village, that would be great, but there was no guarantee it would. We thought it best to continue to medical help. We knew there was a portable high-pressure chamber in base camp, should the porter's condition become life-threatening.

Thankfully, a long line of chortens, stone markers, dotted the route. Were it not for them, we might not have found our way to base camp. The "trail" consisted of crumbled rock that, once covered with snow, became virtually indistinguishable from the rest of the stony landscape. Since none of us had been to base camp before, it was a bit like the lame leading the blind.

In an impressive display of commitment and charity, Dave shouldered the porter's load, which was one of my haul bags, as well as Dave's own personal backpack. For the last 90 minutes of the trek, Dave carried about 80 pounds at 17,000 feet. I carried my own backpack. He would not allow me to carry my haul bag. This later earned him the nickname among some expedition members as "Sherpa Dave."

> *Well, it had been a great effort.*
> *And I had made a great friend.* — TENZING NORGAY,
> *Man of Everest*,
> referring to Swiss climber, Raymond Lambert,
> after coming within 750 feet of the summit with him
> during the 1952 Swiss Everest Expedition

We finally pulled into base camp at dusk. The moment I got there, I sought out Diane's tent and threw myself inside.

"It was so great just to hold him again, to feel his touch and to know he was back," she recalls. "Unfortunately, our reunion was short."

Moments after my arrival, Jason burst into the tent and proceeded to chastise Dave and me for gaining elevation too fast and for jeopardizing the life of our porter in the process. Since I had already slept at Loboche, just 1,500 feet lower than base camp, and our porter had come against our instruction, I felt Jason was being excessively severe. We had made what we felt was the safest decision. His scolding markedly reduced the excitement of our arrival, but we could completely understand and appreciate his position. His job as climbing leader, after all, was to ensure the safety of all team members. He was simply fulfilling that role.

The first night at a new and higher altitude is always difficult and that night was no exception. Dave, the porter and I experienced the usual array of acclimatization discomforts — headaches, insomnia, and an overall sense that something wasn't quite right. Jason ensured someone tended to the porter all night, giving him liquids and keeping him warm with hot water bottles. He suffered no serious ill effects and recovered quickly from his hypothermia and mountain sickness.

The next morning, it was time for Diane to leave base camp and begin her long journey back to Canada. So, having come up from Pheriche the day before, Dave, myself and our porter, together with Diane and her porter, left for Pheriche at mid-morning. By dusk, we were back there and shortly after that, Diane and I were wrapped up comfortably together in a sleeping bag in one of the Sherpa tea houses.

"The room adjoining ours was occupied by a Buddhist monk," Diane recalls. "The monk chanted to late in the evening and started again with his rituals early the next morning. It was quite a way to spend our last night together — serenaded, if you will, by a Nepali lama. He burned incense, threw rice and read aloud from ancient texts. Only a drape of cloth separating our two rooms."

That night will remain with me for a long time, not only because of our adjoining inn-mate, but because of the conversation that took place between Diane and myself. We sat up until late in the night talking about where we were as a couple, where she was as a person, and where we both needed to go, if anywhere, from here. She said she just wanted to comfort me, nurture me and hold me — to make everything all right. Of course, that was impossible. So, we finally agreed that we would wait and see what happened, but that the overall plan would be for me to come and live with her and her children after the expedition.

The next morning, it was time for Diane to go. It was as hard to see her leave as it was for her to have to watch me stay.

"I didn't want to go," she says. "I was worried about Alan and I just wanted everything to go well."

I kissed Diane many times, held her one last time, and then finally, let her go. I watched her walk slowly off down the trail with her porter into the postcard of the Himalayas. Within minutes, she was just a dot on the massive mountain backdrop. Seconds later, she blended completely into the canvas and disappeared.

I turned and walked away. Dave put his arm around me. He didn't say a thing. He didn't need to. I knew he knew what I was feeling.

Dave and I stayed behind in Pheriche that night. It was hard to be there without Diane. It was, after all, the same place in which I had first learned of her decision. I was plagued with painful flashbacks of that night.

Two days later, very early on April 9, Dave and I headed back to base camp. All the way hiking up there, I thought about Diane, how much I would miss her and what a doubly big mountain I now had to climb — one inside, as well as one outside. The inner one somehow seemed bigger.

The outside one crystallized clearly into view at 8 a.m. that day. Dave and I pulled into base camp just as the special puja ceremony got under way. Its goal was to ask the mountain to bless our expedition and permit our safe passage to and from the summit. As one of the local monks chanted mantras, read aloud from ancient texts, threw rice and burned juniper, I looked up at the infamous Khumbu Icefall and remembered the words of Laurie Skreslet months earlier. The Icefall was huge and savage looking, far bigger than I had imagined. It struck fear into my heart.

In that instant, I knew where I had to put my total focus now. I knew that if I did not put Diane out of my mind immediately, I could lose my life on Everest. If there was ever a moment of clarity in my life, that was it. The Mother Goddess now demanded my complete attention. She was no longer some cold and distant image I could fantasize about while gazing at photographs taped to a treadmill. I was now staring straight into the maw of her frozen face. Her crystalline tongue lay bare and prostrate before me.

> *For weeks, for months, that is all we have done.*
> *Look up. And there it is — the top of Everest.*
> *It is no longer just a dream, a high dream in*
> *the sky, but a real and solid thing, a thing of*
> *rock and snow, that men can climb.*

> — Tenzing Norgay,
> *Man of Everest*

I could not see the summit from base camp. It was too high above us — elusive, ethereal, the way it had always been to me in books and photographs. All I could see was her west shoulder, which I knew from maps was many thousands of feet below the top and a long way from the base of her neck along the wind-whipped west ridge.

I knew then that for the next two months, there could only be one woman in my life. If I failed in my relationship with Chomolungma, I knew she would not simply walk out of my life. She would kill me — instantly, remorselessly, indifferently — the way she had so many climbers before me. Whether that was my dharma or not, I could not know.

That's how I got past the pain of losing Diane. I buried it in the recesses of the Icefall and went stone cold inside. I shifted my focus onto that towering black mass looming up in front of me. It stood defiant against the sky — tall, dark, and ominous.

Together with the monk, our Sherpas, and my other climbing friends, I prayed for our safe passage and focused ever-tighter on what it was I'd come here to do.

… on a mountain I can put away all other thoughts —
of the world, the problems of living, even of home
and family — and think of nothing, care for nothing,
except what lies ahead. There in base camp and in the
days to come only one thing, of all things, mattered
to me. And that was Everest. To climb Everest.

— TENZING NORGAY,
Man of Everest

The Climb Begins

*For it is the ultimate wisdom of the mountains
that man is never so much a man as when he is
striving for what is beyond his grasp and that
there is no battle worth winning save that
against his own ignorance and fear.*

— James Ramsey Ullman,
author of *Man of Everest*

THE PUJA WAS SPECTACULAR. The entire team was decked
out in our bright yellow, red and black sun ice one-piece
climbing suits. They stood out sharply against the white snow
backdrop and brilliant blue sky of base camp. Under a slight
breeze, birds swooped and darted here and there over the
hand-built stone altar the Sherpas had constructed over the
previous days. As wave after wave of sweet-smelling smoke
from the burning of juniper boughs twisted and turned its
way skyward from the altar, the local monk's chants created a
scene of stirring spiritualism.

It is forbidden for any climbing team to set foot on Everest
without a puja ceremony. The Sherpas believe that you must
ask permission to tread upon Chomolungma's skin, and that
to ascend to the summit without such license is tantamount
to violating the Mother Goddess in the most intimate way.
Whether you believe in such things or not is immaterial.
What is material is that you respect the culture and spirituality
of the Sherpas.

I decided I'd do anything the Sherpas asked me to do. This
was, after all, *their* mountain and I was just *their* guest. It would
be rude for me to do otherwise.

Now we were getting down to it! Now we were actually going to begin the long process of trying to get up this mountain. And what a mountain it was. What size! What majesty! What presence! It was Everest. It was awe-inspiring.

An atmosphere of reverence, respect, and faith descended over the whole camp then, and over the dozen or so other expeditions from all over the world assembled there. I do not consider myself a religious man, but I am a spiritual one, and I sensed the presence of a Higher Power. It was impossible not to. We were, after all, higher than almost any other inhabited place on Earth, and certainly any other permanently inhabited place. (The highest inhabited place on Earth is the Rongbuk Monastery on the Tibetan side of Everest. It is 16,500 feet above sea level and is the year-round home of several dozen very hardy Buddhist monks. As the crow flies, it was only a few miles from where we were at about 17,300 feet.)

Most of the other teams in base camp were commercial trips consisting of guides and clients, some of whom had paid up to $50,000 to be guided up the peak. Our expedition, a corporately sponsored affair, was one of less than a handful of similar trips — tangible evidence, I believe, of the relative difficulty of raising corporate cash versus contributions from private individuals aspiring to climb to the peak.

The three-hour puja ceremony was spectacular. Clearly, the monk was trying to communicate directly with Chomolungma herself. We were to be quiet and restrained. I felt strangely detached from the scene, understanding its significance, but in true Western fashion, being too preoccupied with the magnitude of what might lie ahead. As I had only just returned to base camp a few hours earlier, I was really still renewing my acquaintance with Everest. I found myself staring again and again into the Icefall, trying to imagine myself there. It was just so big, so vicious looking. I found myself drifting off in the juniper smoke, not in a deep communion with the mountain, but in an encounter with my own fear. It was a silent struggle, but a real one.

"On cue, the Sherpas erected a pole and strung great streamers of prayer flags across the glacier," Doug recalls. "Our Sirdar (Ang Temba Sherpa) reminded us that several of the teams which had suffered fatalities in the '96 disaster the spring before had begun climbing before their puja ceremony."

After hours of chanting and offerings, the reading of ancient text, the burning of juniper, the pounding of a hand-held drum, and the clanging of cymbals that echoed out over Everest, the monk retired to the seclusion of a private tent where he continued to ask for our safety on the mountain. I too sought solace in my tent, where I read Diane's final good-bye card, shed a tear and placed it in a pocket at the back of my tent. I never looked at it again. I couldn't afford the luxury, or the pain.

Base camp was a global village. There were a total of 14 teams from Russia, Malaysia, the United States, Britain, Japan, Canada, Italy, and Indonesia spread out over the constantly shifting moraine of boulders, rubble, and ice pushed out at the bottom of the Icefall. It fanned out for several hundred yards like the shattered cement blocks of a demolished high rise.

So much is made of politics, of nationality.
Not on a mountain itself: there life is too real
and death too close for such things, and a man
is a man, a human being, and that is all.

— Tenzing Norgay,
Man of Everest

Each team had its own cook and mess shelters, its own altar, and at least three or four long lines of multicolored prayer flags that radiated like the points of a merry-go-round from a central bamboo pole 10 to 20 feet tall. On each flag was written, naturally, a prayer, and the idea was that as the wind blew, each prayer was sent up to the Mother Goddess to ask for her guidance to and from the heavens above.

The cook and mess shelters were especially impressive. Most consisted of stone walls at least six feet high on top of which were placed wooden cross-members that formed the trusses for a makeshift ceiling made of a waterproof plastic tarpaulin draped over top of the skeleton. This tarp was held in place by rope lashed back and forth over the top of it. The whole building took days to construct, stone by hand-placed stone.

The Sherpas acted as architects, engineers, and construction workers in the building of these amazing shelters. They had both the experience, and most importantly, the physical strength and adaptation to the altitude to lift the large stone blocks, some of which weighed well over 50 pounds. Gently, they would place these stones into their exact position in a fashion not unlike the way the Inuit of the Canadian Arctic build igloos out of snow blocks. I marveled at the precision of these craftsmen and, ultimately, at the rigidity of the finished structure. It redefined "solid as a rock."

> *You do not climb a mountain like Everest by trying to race ahead on your own, or by competing with your comrades. You do it slowly and carefully, by unselfish teamwork.* — TENZING NORGAY, *Man of Everest*

"Base camp is on a glacier covered by rocks and boulders," Doug remembers. "A glacier is really a living thing that creaks and groans as it moves down valley so it's sort of like living on the back of a sleeping dinosaur. Add the intermittent crashing of seracs [ice blocks that fall off glaciers] pounding down the surrounding peaks and it is rarely quiet for long."

On Everest, I learned quickly to park my pride and ego and conserve my energy. For me, that meant ensuring I stayed focused on my task — to summit the peak. I would be dishonest if I did not say that that compromise bothered me. I frequently felt guilty watching others doing physical work like building mess shelters and carrying loads, and although I'd paid my dues and then some to finance and assist in the orchestration of the trip, that rationalization did not fully placate me. I felt inadequate when I watched the Sherpas, Jeff, Jason, and some of the others perform tasks I knew I was incapable of performing — a bit like a child who needed to be taken care of. That is a painful admission for any person, especially for a climber, but it must be tempered with realism. Especially during the initial phases of an expedition to high-altitude, it is unrealistic to hope everyone will be at the top of their game. I recognized the huge efforts others were making on my behalf and I deeply appreciated them. My role would come later — the mountain, the weather, and my health permitting. It was all part of the strategy and plan, but it was still hard for me to watch. I wanted to feel strong.

Is this the way you climb Everest? By letting others carry your gear to the high camp from which you'll do your thing? The world's leading mountaineers will answer instantly, and unequivocally, no.

I am not one of the world's leading mountaineers. I have never made, nor will I ever make, that claim. That titles goes to the likes of Peter Habeler, Reinhold Messner, Barry Blanchard, Sharon Wood, Laurie Skreslet et al. What I may be reasonably good at doing, if that can be said, is determining what I do well and what I don't do so well. I let others do what they do best, and I try to stick to what I do best. I think I'm good at putting one foot in front of another in adverse conditions. I seem to be able to raise money. I can also train hard, day after day, consistently, rain or shine, tired or rested.

Some of the teams in base camp were not climbing Everest. They had as their objective Mt. Lhotse, Everest's sister peak, at 27,891 the world's fourth highest. Most expeditions, including ours, had received permission to climb the South Col route, the line first pioneered by the 1953 British Everest Expedition led by Sir John Hunt.

The biggest and most lavish base camp in "the village," as some of us called it, belonged to a Japanese cosmetics billionaire who was in the process of launching a new perfume. Apparently, he saw no better place to do it than at the base of the world's tallest woman. His expedition, which we guessed cost at least $5 million, featured a staggering 25 high-altitude climbing Sherpas and daily helicopter sightseeing flights to base camp from Kathmandu. During these expensive forays,

Japanese visitors must have paid exorbitant amounts of money to have their photograph taken in base camp holding the banner of the product's logo. These visitors were only on the ground for five or 10 minutes at most and the danger to participants, not to mention the climbers in base camp, was such that all the sightseers used bottled oxygen, and the helicopter never even stopped its engines. It was commercialism out of control.

The Sherpas who worked for the Japanese team spent innumerable hours painstakingly constructing a helicopter landing pad out of stones. To land safely, the chopper had to fly low over camp, rattling tents and threatening to uproot hundreds of prayer flags with the wash from its rotors. Then, ever so delicately, the pilot had to gingerly maneuver his bird into position and land. This was a risky game at best, and I never got used to watching it. It's one thing to be safely inside a cement building when a helicopter passes overhead. It's quite another when the only thing separating you from instant decapitation is a one-sixteenth of an inch thick piece of nylon tent fabric. Later in the expedition, a helicopter did, in fact, overshoot the landing pad and crash within 100 meters of our tents, but fortunately, no one was injured and the pilot and one passenger (not a sightseer) walked away without a scratch. The helicopter was severely damaged.

The sightseeing flights created a circus atmosphere in base camp and I, for one, felt that while the odd helicopter arrival or departure might be acceptable, multiple flights daily were ridiculous and dangerous. Base camp wasn't supposed to be an airport.

To make the whole comical affair seem even more ludicrous, the Japanese billionaire, the self-declared autocratic leader of his trip, ensured he had a 10-foot diameter satellite dish in base camp so he wouldn't miss daily TV news reports. Unfortunately, or fortunately, depending on your perspective, Everest had other plans for him. Everest would not look upon his naiveté, surplus of capital, but deficit of experience at high altitude, with favor.

Over the years, Everest has seen people try to ski down her, snowboard, hang glide, balloon, climb blind and on and on. It has become one of the world's highest stunt grounds. In the ever-increasing competition for the mountain of money needed to finance an expedition, human beings have chosen to become more inventive about ways to create "firsts" in attempting to climb the peak. By and large, the mountain, in her majesty and might, has successfully spurned the majority of these attempts and made it clear that she does not take kindly to such irreverence. Most expeditions have discovered that at 26,000 feet and above, there is barely enough energy to survive, let alone hang glide, balloon, ski, or snowboard. My personal feeling is that these kinds of activities have no place in a sacred space. Arguably, neither does climbing.

The very next day, April 10, 1997, at 4 a.m., our expedition began in earnest when Jeff Rhoads, Jason Edwards, and our eight climbing Sherpas left base camp with the first loads of equipment needed to establish Camp 1 above the Icefall. All men came back with thrilling stories about the challenges of the Khumbu; its massively deep crevasses, huge ice blocks, and dozens of ladders perched precariously over gaping holes hundreds of feet deep.

*So once again came the hard, drudging work of
all big mountain climbs — the searching-out of
a way, the cutting of steps, the fixing of ropes, the
carrying-up of the heavy loads.* — TENZING NORGAY,
Man of Everest

In the interest of safety, each of the teams in base camp paid the Sherpas of one of the British teams to maintain the route through the Icefall. It was felt this would reduce the amount of time everyone was exposed to the danger — everyone, of course, except the Sherpas who had to maintain the route. Within hours of a collapse, they had reestablished the route, or found a new one, much the same way ants reestablish their hills after a rain. As if by magic, 8-foot-long aluminum ladders, the same kind you use to paint the side of your house, would appear with mile upon mile of rope and stacks of other safety equipment needed to make the route "secure."

In the Icefall, you felt the same way you always felt on Everest — dwarfed. Entering it, especially in the dark, was a bit like being a beetle making its way through the staging of a production at the Metropolitan Opera House in New York, in mid-performance. The whole twisted and broken melee was in constant motion, creaking and wailing like a tortured beast. You felt infinitesimally small and horribly unimportant, which is exactly what you were.

Everest gives us an instant awareness of our complete insignificance. Its sheer size boggles the mind. When you are looking down into the dark, deep chasms of the Icefall, it is obvious how inconsequential you are. I like that about Everest. There is very little gray area, only black rock, yawning, dark crevasses and blinding, white snow. She lets you know exactly where you stand — cowering at her feet.

I did not participate in the first of several carries through the Icefall. I was not well enough. I did not know it then, but this was to be the way it would be for me throughout most of the expedition. I started sick and I spent most of my time that way, with only brief respites. For my first few days in base camp, I was weak, nauseous, congested and fluish. Part of it was the naturally unpleasant process of acclimatizing to 17,000 feet. The other part was my head cold.

"The whole time, I really couldn't see Alan climbing the mountain without bottled oxygen," Jeff remembers, "especially as he was sick. He was just like the rest of us — plugging along doing the best he could. Talk's cheap in the locker room, so I just thought, 'When it really comes down to it, we'll see.'"

There are dozens of stories of climbers enduring horrendous hardship on Everest, so a head cold and the flu are nothing there. Some of the climbing world may scoff at the mere mention of such trivialities, but I will never forget how unpleasant it was. Call me a wimp, but in spite of temperatures well above freezing during the day, I found myself curled up in the fetal position in my sleeping bag, shivering uncontrollably and close to vomiting. Within hours, I had soaked my bag with sweat.

I still work with companies that spend inordinate amounts of time and money focusing on what the competition is doing. As a result they are usually looking up the mountain at the competition rather than down on them from above.

I tried to drink as much as I could and take a couple of short walks around base camp, but it was very difficult. Finally, sick of feeling sick, I took an anti-nausea pill. It was of little help. It completely knocked the stuffing out of me to the point where I had a hard time getting to and from the stone outhouse, about 100 feet from my tent. It was a less-than-stellar start to the expedition, but I took comfort in the fact that there was still a lot of time ahead.

The next day, activity in the Icefall was delayed by a collapse about 1,000 feet above base camp. Fortunately, no one was hurt, and the Sherpa crew from the British team immediately went to work to make repairs. I decided to go for a short walk to the foot of the Icefall, but coughed so hard from the altitude that I vomited my breakfast. I spent the rest of the day lying low in my tent, trying to beat the bug.

My body does not adapt particularly quickly to altitude. It usually takes me a full six weeks to adjust, and during that time I must constantly remind myself to be patient and have faith. This is difficult to do when it seems everyone around you is acclimatizing faster, or climbing stronger, or seeming happier.

Knowing something and putting it into practice can be two different things.

I remember as a gymnast the first time I learned not to pay attention to my fellow competitors. One day, I realized there was only one gymnast on the apparatus at a time. While this may seem like obvious common sense to anyone with any intelligence, it wasn't immediately obvious to me as a youngster and, amazingly, it is still lost on some adults today. I still work with companies that spend inordinate amounts of time and money focusing on what the competition is doing. As a result, they are usually looking up the mountain at the competition rather than down on them from above.

On Everest, I knew this, but knowing something and putting it into practice can be two different things. I remember how frustrated I felt that I couldn't join the team on those first carries through the Icefall. I knew I wasn't pulling my own weight. I felt weak and undeserving of being there.

I slept only 90 minutes that night. Dawn didn't come early. It seemed like it might never arrive. For breakfast, I managed to force down a cup of tea and two hard-boiled eggs — a caloric intake that would have lasted me about 15 minutes at lower altitudes, but it was all I could put down. At 6 a.m., as agreed, Jeff Rhoads and I headed into the Icefall for the first time.

I was feeling too rough to be afraid. It was all I could do just to keep moving. I know there have been lots of times in my life away from mountaineering when it was important to focus only on the immediate and not let the possibilities of the future overwhelm me. This was one of those moments. I would never have dreamed it would come this early in the expedition, but there it was, in my face, the way Everest was. I felt inadequate.

Amid a biting wind and spindrift snow, I moved painstakingly slowly. Jeff was as patient as a priest. I imagined what he was probably thinking: "Whoa. If this guy is going this badly now, there's no way he'll ever get up this thing. What kind of a trip have I got myself into?"

In true Jeff fashion, he didn't say a thing. He just let me be who I was at that moment. When you're under the weather, the last thing you want is for someone to point out that you're weak. He kept quiet.

"I knew we weren't going to go very far that morning," Jeff recalls. "Alan was moving really slow. His strength just wasn't there."

Together, we climbed about 700 vertical feet above base camp before I vomited again.

"Nice work," Jeff piped up sarcastically. "At least you didn't let it go on the trail. You're not the first guy to puke in the Icefall. You hit the wall, no big deal. You've still got plenty of time to acclimatize."

I forced out a smile, wiped my mouth and pushed out some more steps. We got only as far as the second ladder across a narrow crevasse before it became obvious I could climb no higher that day. I apologized to Jeff and together we descended. No sooner had we arrived back at base camp than I immediately had a sudden bout of diarrhea.

As I hung my butt over the plastic barrel in the drafty stone privy, I shivered. I spent the rest of the day in my tent, then

When you're under the weather, the last thing you want is for someone to point out that you're weak.

dragged myself to the mess tent for dinner only to vomit once again on my way to the outhouse. That night, I put on an adult diaper and was up four or five times to stagger my way again over the rocks, snow, and ice to the loo.

> *I vomited so much I thought all my insides*
> *were coming out....*
> — TENZING NORGAY,
> *Man of Everest,*
> on his expedition to Mt. Nanda Devi, 1936

Although I felt like I was the only one hurting, the reality was that everyone, in one form or another, was.

"I don't think Alan was much sicker than anyone else," Doug recalls. "Jamie was pretty sick. Jason was the healthiest. It's just a very tough environment in which to stay healthy. When you're trying to climb the biggest mountain in the world, symptoms really magnify. Medicine just doesn't seem to help."

Jason agrees:

"Sicknesses on longer trips like Everest don't concern me," he says. "I expect everyone to get sick one to four times. It's just a matter of getting through it."

If you lose your focus mentally, the game is over.

The problem, of course, is that you never really do "get through it." You never really recover, you just chug along at much less than full strength. It's a bit like having a seven-week-long case of the flu while you're living outside in a tent in winter. Over time, that begins to wear on you, not just physically, but mentally. If you lose your focus mentally, though, the game is over. The key on Everest is to stay in the game, to somehow maintain your body so that it can keep going and discipline your mind so that it can continue to drive your body just long enough to get you safely to the summit and down to base camp before you collapse, or go crazy.

Base camp does little to rekindle your steadily waning motivation. It is a bleak and desolate place. There are no trees, no animals, no life of any kind, save people and the odd scavenging bird. From the south side of the mountain in Nepal, you cannot even see the summit. While the view down the Khumbu Valley toward the Sherpa village of Gorak Shep only a few miles away can be a spectacular one, it is often obscured in cloud. If you look toward the mountain, you can usually see Mt. Pumori on your left, the Lho La pass between Everest and the Main Rongbuk Glacier beyond, Mt. Nuptse on your right and, of course, the Icefall straight ahead. To say that it is not still a spectacular threshold for the tallest point on the planet would be an understatement, but neither is it necessarily inspiring. You feel confined and isolated in base camp, surrounded as you are by massive mountain ramparts.

What adds considerable drama to base camp is the regular avalanches from the Lho La and Nuptse. They periodically roar down their respective faces, snapping the gazes of all the climbers in base camp skyward to see if anything is coming down into the Icefall. Once in a while it is, particularly if there has been a slide from the west shoulder of Everest.

This is precisely what happened one morning in the wee small hours of 1982 when three Sherpas on the first Canadian expedition to the mountain lost their lives in a huge avalanche that cut loose thousands of feet above. They had little hope of saving themselves. Death came out of the darkness swiftly and decisively.

That incident left a permanent impression on my psyche. I was back in Canada working as a newspaper reporter when I read the accounts over the news wire. I was horrified.

"Poor bastards," I thought. "They didn't stand a chance."

Obviously, base camp is not a Club Med. If it were, more people would go there and that, of course, would make it less difficult to reach. Nevertheless, it does operate like a small city. The morning rush hour is between 4 and 7 a.m. as dozens of climbers head up into the Icefall with their day's loads of equipment and supplies. The "afternoon" rush hour is between 10 a.m. and 1 p.m. when they, and other climbers already higher on the mountain, come down. For much of the rest of the day, it's just a bunch of tired climbers hanging around coughing, sipping tea, cat-napping and socializing in tents, cooks preparing thousands of meals, Sherpas enjoying rousing games of cards, yaks and porters coming and going with loads of supplies from the valley below, and trekkers from all over the world staggering in and out eager for conversation.

In the silence of your tent, you find yourself asking the perennial question — why?

What's the sense in risking your life for something as apparently insignificant as a patch of snow in the rarefied air? Getting there, after all, won't save any lives. Taking that summit shot won't make the planet a better place, and it won't help feed the homeless.

The answer to the age-old question "why?" is *not* "because it's there." Those words were said by British mountaineer and Everest climber, George Leigh Mallory, to a very persistent journalist, in the early 1900s. After many unsuccessful attempts to explain his motivations to the reporter, Mallory stormed off in frustration. As he did, he said those now famous words. They have stuck because we seem to like simple answers to complex questions, but a mountaineer's — indeed any adventurer's — personal motivations go far deeper than such superficialities. They are different for every adventurer.

> *The answer to the age-old question "why?" is not "because it's there."*

I climb and adventure because I'm curious. I'm curious to find out what it might be like to climb Everest. How would it feel? What would it take? It has nothing to do with any attraction to danger, thrill seeking, or adrenaline rushes. That's not fun. That's frightening. High-altitude climbing isn't "sexy," or "exotic." It's mundane, risky business.

I adventure to explore and discover who I am, and in doing so, come to a better understanding of others. My goal, ultimately, is to go and see something with my own eyes, and thus more fully *see* myself. I want to learn. I want to know. I want to actually experience, not only through books or films, but in person.

Climbing Everest doesn't make any sense. But exactly how much of our lives actually does? Putting a basketball through a hoop, or hitting a golf ball, doesn't make a lot of sense either. Neither does battling rush hour traffic just so we can get to work. What about 50 years of marriage?

I believe that we do these things because at some deep level, they help bring happiness, peace, or meaning to our lives. They help ground us. I have never seen a family that is anything but semi-organized chaos, but even amid its constant change, there is the constant of home and, if we're lucky, love and sanctuary. As Dave King, Canada's former national hockey coach once said, "Win or lose, when you come home, your dog treats you the same way."

We do apparently senseless things because they help us meet a need, or a perceived one. That was a large part of the attraction of Everest for me. I needed, or I perceived I needed, a victory. However, I discovered that the allure can be deceptive. Everything comes at a cost, and sometimes that cost isn't apparent until the event is over.

John F. Kennedy, in proclaiming man was going to stand on the moon, made no sense either. The cost was astronomical. Yet perhaps better than anyone, he came closest to explaining the method in the madness of this thing called "the adventure of life" when he spoke these words during a public address on September 12, 1962:

> *"But why," some say, "the moon?" Why choose this as our goal? And they may well ask, "Why climb the highest mountain?" Why, 35 years ago, fly the Atlantic? Why does Rice [University] play Texas?*
>
> *We choose to go to the moon!*
>
> *We choose to go to the moon!*
>
> *We choose to go to the moon in this decade and do the other things, not because they are easy, but because they are hard, because that goal will serve to organize and measure the best of our energies and skills, because that challenge is one that we're willing to accept, one we are unwilling to postpone and one we intend to win.*

"We choose to go to the moon in this decade and do the other things, not because they are easy, but because they are hard ..."

– JOHN F. KENNEDY

15

Into the Icefall

And up on the mountain we began our ant-like labors. What is a man on an ice-world up in the sky? At that altitude he is no more than a will straining in a spent machine. — Gaston Rébuffat

A FEW DAYS AFTER my sickness began, my health improved and I was back in the game. On April 15, Jason, five of our climbing Sherpas and I headed into the darkness of the Icefall at 4 a.m. It was a mind-boggling labyrinth of crevasses, ice block seracs, ladders, and anxiety, especially by headlamp. In just 50 minutes, I'd reached my previous high point, a climb that had taken me an hour and 45 minutes only a few days before. The body is an amazing organism — highly adaptive and incredibly resilient, but also amazingly fragile. It usually comes around if we are patient.

I will never forget that morning. Because the Sherpas respect the Icefall as much as anyone, and because many of their friends have died in there over the years, they constantly mumble their mantras when they climb through it in the dark. This, they hope, will appease the Mother Goddess and allow them safe passage. The deep, melodious sound of their voices added a whole new dimension to the twisted mass of frightening shadows, popping and creaking ice, and the snorts, coughs, spitting, hacking, and vomiting of their fellow climbers.

The Icefall is a moving graveyard for about 20 climbers, many of whom are Sherpas. That morning, I felt the presence of Something. It was not only the spirits of the dead that visited me in the haunting darkness. For the first time, I began to touch the metaphysical mountain, the aura of Everest herself. There was something uncanny and unmistakable there. And, there was something special going on. I was taking my first steps into the infamous Khumbu Icefall, surrounded by real live, mantra-chanting Sherpas, by huge ice blocks, sinister shadows and by a strange spiritualism older than Everest itself. You could not help but feel the connection to some higher power. It was all around me, in the air and in the ice, and most importantly, inside me. I felt it, deeply. We were not alone.

The first time I crossed one of the ladders spanning a crevasse, I was petrified. With only a single strand of limp, quarter-inch-thick climbing rope on which to hold with each hand, I had to carefully ensure my crampon-shod boots were placed exactly on the 10-inch-spaced rungs of the ladder, step by tentative step. As I am not very fond of heights, I was somewhat relieved to realize that in the dark, I couldn't see the bottom of the crevasse.

Every person is afraid of heights — every person.

Every person is afraid of heights — every person. It is a natural human fear the same as the fear of fire. Over the years, the way I have learned to manage my fear is by concentrating on what I must do to keep from falling, rather than focusing on falling itself. Thus, I look only at my feet and hands — and not into the empty space beyond, except to check on the weather.

There are three steps to learning how to manage our fears. The first is to acknowledge that we are afraid. The second is to focus on the known, and the third is to take action.

Most of us get stuck on step two. We focus on the unknown, not the known. In the case of heights, we peer over the edge and look down into the abyss. We imagine ourselves plummeting earthward like a rock … faster, faster, faster. Suddenly, even though we haven't moved an inch from the edge, our heads start spinning too, we feel dizzy, light-headed and nauseous. This is called vertigo.

Our mind is a powerful thing. It can be used to create the most wonderfully pleasant images or the most horrific disasters. Our minds choose what we see. On the basis of our choice, we also choose our outcome. Thus, if we want to start to overcome our fear of heights, we have to start changing our picture. In other words, we have to imagine something different.

Laurie Skreslet said: "When we run away from fear, it gets bigger, but when we advance toward it, it shrinks."

As I gingerly made my way across that ladder, under the weight of my body, the ladder began to bow, swaying up and down and creaking with a terrifying sound. Periodically, gusts of wind would buffet me from side to side. To prevent myself from pitching sideways into the crevasse, I squeezed the safety lines like they were life itself.

The steel points of my crampons dug sharply into the soft aluminum rungs, sometimes holding my feet momentarily as I tried to bring them carefully forward. Up and down, side to side, forward and back I swayed. The whole experience was unnerving. I seriously contemplated crawling. But I was an Everest climber. They didn't crawl! Crawling was for babies. I may have felt like one, but I could overcome this.

"You CAN Alan," I told myself. "You WILL."

Some of the ladder bridges were four and five sections across — a horizontal distance of 50 or 60 feet. They were lashed together with rope. It was pitch black, freezing cold, my heart was racing, my chest was heaving and my legs felt like rubber. My whole body began to quiver. It was all I could do to keep from shaking myself right into the blackness below.

Everest is most alive in the Icefall. There, she speaks to you in wails, groans, and sudden cracks. Her molars of sharp-edged chunks of ice yawn at you from all sides. With every new crevasse you cross, you penetrate deeper and deeper into her body. She is hungry.

She speaks to you. She says you shouldn't be there, that you shouldn't have come. Every fiber of your being wants to turn tail and head back to base camp. But you know that if you want the summit, you must continue, slowly trudging upwards, hour after stressful hour, knowing full well that your next step could be your last, that that huge black mass above you is

> **"When we run away from fear, it gets bigger, but when we advance towards it, it shrinks. "**
>
> – LAURIE SKRESLET

actually an ice block the size of a city block, waiting to topple over on you.

No one stops in the Icefall — at least not for long. The only time I ever stopped was to vomit, drop my drawers with sudden diarrhea, or to take a pee.

The route through the Icefall winds its way back and forth and up and down with no apparent rationale. Everyone on the mountain follows the same line. I tried to imagine how the first Sherpas that season might have felt choosing the route. There was certainly no clear way to the top, in fact, you couldn't even come close to seeing the top, especially in the dark.

When the first gray rays of the day fell into the Icefall, I gradually began to realize what was actually around me. It was a bit like waking up to a nightmare, instead of coming out of one. Once, I looked up to see an ice block easily the size of a house teetering over me at a 45-degree angle — toward me! I never looked up again. You learned quickly to keep your focus on your feet. That's how I managed my fear.

"You CAN Alan," I told myself. "You WILL."

As horrible as the whole experience sounds, there was an awesome, if not deadly, beauty to it too. The green, blue, and turquoise colors of the ice, its unending variety of shapes and sizes, angles, and edges created a living beauty that overwhelmed me at times. I felt like I was in an elaborate entryway, a gateway to some celestial shrine. Despite the danger, I found myself incapable of resisting the impulse to peer out of the corner of my eye to sneak a peak at the crystalline world around me. It both frightened and inspired me.

I learned a powerful lesson crossing those ladders in the Icefall, one that I continue to use today. To cross the ladders, you *had* to look down. You had to see where you were placing your feet. In looking down, you had a choice of where you looked — as far as the rungs of the ladder, or way the hell and gone down into that terrifyingly deep hole beyond.

So often in life, we focus on the hole — on all those terrible things that could happen to us, on all those things outside our control when the only things we should be focusing on are those things within our control — the tiny steps we need to take this minute to get us to where we want to go.

This was both the power and the pariah of the Icefall. You could either learn how to deal with the danger and rise to the challenge, or you could allow yourself to be completely overwhelmed by it. Some climbers chose the latter. You saw them repeatedly crawling across the ladders. After a while, you never saw them in there again. They never got over their fear. They never really crossed the crevasse.

It took me three hours to reach the top of the Icefall that morning.

"The top of the Icefall is guarded by a huge, overhanging block of ice that is surmounted by a five-ladder section (about 40 feet high)," Doug remembers. "It is sort of like climbing a four-story building on a rickety ladder."

At the top, at the section Doug describes, the movement of the ice had contorted the top five-ladder section into a twisted, bowed out malignance. From below, it looked like a piece of twisted roller coaster track that forced you to climb almost backwards up an overhang as you made your swaying ascent. The twist was just enough to make you tilt to one side as you climbed, but not enough to completely turn you all the way over onto your back. So, you clung tenaciously to every rung of the ladder, fighting gravity. One or two more degrees of bend and you'd have been bucked off into the depths below.

By all conventional measures, this is insanity. But you are forced to face your fear. If you win, you gain far more than a "triumph" over Everest. You learn to better manage yourself.

Half an hour after cresting the top of the Icefall, we had reached our Camp 1 at 19,000 feet in the Western Cwm (Cwm, pronounced "Coom," is the Welsh word for valley). As I arrived there, coughing hard and feeling all the strength of a limp noodle, I gazed up toward Everest. Surrounding me on three sides were massive ramparts thousands of feet tall. The expansive faces of rock, snow, and ice dwarfed everything around them, including the pitifully tiny forms of climbers like me at their feet. I again felt minuscule, diminished and completely insignificant. Ice blocks the size of tractor-trailers had tumbled from high above. They lay shattered in the middle

> *So often in life, we focus on the hole — on all those terrible things that could happen to us, when we should be focusing on the tiny steps we need to take this minute to get us to where we want to go.*

FROM EVEREST TO ENLIGHTENMENT

of small impact craters only a few hundred feet away. All it would take, I knew, was a bit of bad luck and I'd be squashed like a bug.

"The Western Cwm is the throne room of the mountain gods," Doug wrote, "... our route and camps are well situated and safe from the massive destructive force of avalanches. The sound, though, is a roar so loud it can't help but strike terror. This place must certainly be the throne room of the Almighty Herself. I cannot imagine another place like it on Earth."

I spent only 15 minutes resting and rehydrating in Camp 1. Then, I "hurried" down through the Icefall, or as fast as you can hurry when you're sucking wind. By 10:30 a.m., I was back in base camp, accompanied on my descent by our Camp 2 cook, Shyam Prasad Pun, a patient and glowing man of considerable spiritual and physical strength.

During the course of our expedition, I would get to know our Sherpas, cooks, and support staff well. To a man, they were an impressive bunch. The team consisted of Ang Temba and Lhakpa Tshering Sherpa, who had been with us in 1991, Kami Tshering Sherpa, who had joined us in 1994, and newcomers Tashi Tsering, Pema Temba, Gyalbu, Nurbu and Mingma Dorjee Sherpa. All were veterans of innumerable Everest expeditions, all but one had been to the summit at least once and Gyalbu and Nurbu had been to the top three times. Without question, ours was one of the most powerful Sherpa teams ever assembled for an Everest expedition. Credit for such an accomplishment can only go to Steve Matous and his Kathmandu business partners, Ang Jangbu Sherpa, himself an Everest summiteer, and Sonam Gyalpo Lama, a veteran of decades of experience assisting Everest expeditions in Nepal.

We can either learn how to deal with danger and rise to the challenge, or we can allow ourselves to be completely overwhelmed by it.

Throughout the expedition, our Sherpa team worked feverishly for brutally long hours without a word of complaint. By Western standards, the roughly $5,000 each of the climbing Sherpas was paid for two and a half months' work was a pittance considering the level of risk they assumed, and they completely redefined service to us, their customers. We all knew it would have been impossible to find such strong, committed, and easy-going men in the West. I shudder at the thought of a "union" wage for such perilous work.

"The modern expedition to a 26,000-foot peak would grind to a complete halt but for the efforts of its Sherpa employees," Doug wrote. "They prepare the base camp clearing tons of scree and talus [rocks and boulders], fetch water, prepare meals, establish camps, stock the camps with tents, sleeping bags, food, fuel, and oxygen, fix ropes and ladders over difficult sections, and break trail on the summit day. On our trip, they've even carried personal gear for two of our climbers. All this is done with no apparent expectation of thanks or recognition. I've never heard a Sherpa speak of himself and when asked about their accomplishments, they are quick to change the subject."

I celebrated my first successful trip up and down through the Icefall with a wonderful sense of relief. I'd survived. There, I learned others had had different experiences.

The leader of the Japanese team, the cosmetics billionaire, had entered the Icefall with half a dozen of his team members. He was already using bottled oxygen — a luxury usually reserved for about 24,000 feet and above. Within hours, he had returned to base camp. A few days later, he choppered out to Kathmandu, called back to base camp through his satellite telecommunications system and canceled the entire expedition. Twenty-five climbing Sherpas, innumerable support staff and eight of the most experienced high-altitude climbers in Japan were sent needlessly packing. Some of the Sherpas went to work for other expeditions. Others simply walked back home down the valley and called it a season.

The remaining 13 teams on the mountain scrambled to acquire Japanese equipment that had already been moved above the Icefall. Most teams, including ours, were unable to secure any. The leader of the Japanese team had apparently issued strict orders to leave nothing behind. While we all understood the wisdom of that from an environmental point of view, from a safety perspective we could not. If any of us could save ourselves the danger of even one trip through the Icefall, it was worth it. We would still carry all the gear down ourselves when we were done.

Wave after wave of confused Sherpas was sent up again through the Icefall to carry all the expedition's equipment down to base camp. It was subsequently returned to Kathmandu.

The withdrawal of the Japanese team tarnished the early period of the climbing season on Everest that spring. On the bright side, our telecommunications system, which to that point had mysteriously been almost non-functional, suddenly began to work the minute the Japanese leader's television-receiving dish was dismantled. To that point, a beleaguered but ever-determined Bruce Kirkby had been working day and night trying to make what should have been a relatively straightforward e-mail connection with Lotus's website in Cambridge. With the combined corporate weight of Colliers, Lotus, and all our other sponsors and suppliers bearing down on him with each passing day, he had tried everything from reprogramming our computers to relocating our entire satellite telecommunications system and tent to a different place in base camp. As this was his first time to Everest and the first time he had ever manned a telecommunications system of this kind in the mountains, he was under considerable pressure.

In classic Bruce form, he rose to the challenge beautifully without a word of complaint and even amid the considerable stress, maintained his equanimity. A huge cloud lifted from above his head the moment he reestablished contact with Massachusetts.

It was ironic that our transmission challenges likely had more to do with interference from a team 100 yards away than a computer half a world away.

With that technological crevasse cleared and my physical fear faced, the most difficult step in our journey was now behind us. We had survived Everest's chilling handshake.

Humbled

Men always talk of the conquest of the mountains.
And here he comes across the glacier, looks up
only once, very slowly. He glances at me, comes on
with sunken head, is no longer consciously there.
Going up to him I say, "Reinhold, how are you?"
A few sobs are the answer.

— NENA HOLGUIN, greeting her boyfriend,
Reinhold Messner, the world's greatest living mountaineer,
after his historic first ascent of Everest solo,
without the use of bottled oxygen, in 1980

AFTER SUCCESSFULLY navigating through the Icefall for the first time, over the next 10 days or so, my health gradually improved and I was able to climb higher on Everest. Meanwhile, our team made rapid progress ferrying loads of equipment and supplies higher as well.

In just a few weeks, our powerful climbing Sherpas carried gear to Camp 2 (Advanced Base Camp) at 21,000 feet, and Camp 3 at 24,000 feet half-way up the face of Mt. Lhotse. Jeff, Jason, and Jamie followed soon after, with Jamie spending a very uncomfortable first night in Camp 3. The next morning, pale and sick, he descended to Advanced Base Camp. En route there, he vomited three times. We passed as I was on my way up from Camp 2 to Camp 3 that morning.

Jamie recommended I climb up to Camp 3 that day, stay there for a few hours, then descend to Camp 2 and sleep there again that night. The next day, if I was feeling good, I could climb up again to Camp 3 and spend the night there. I should not, he said, go directly from Camp 2 to Camp 3 in one day and try to overnight there the first night as he had. I could get sick.

I heeded Jamie's warning. The last thing I wanted to do was get sick again, especially the way he had been. His was likely altitude sickness produced by ascending too fast. The general rule in high-altitude climbing is not to ascend more than 2,000 vertical feet a day, especially not without having previously visited the higher altitude for a short period.

Life in Advanced Base Camp, much like life in base camp, was taken up mostly with the mechanics of living — eating, sleeping, maintaining gear, and drinking as much water as possible to assist the acclimatization process. Perhaps the greatest adventure on Everest takes place in your mind because the greatest part of your day is usually spent alone. In our busy world in the West, we often take almost no time to be alone. We spend the majority of our waking hours going as swiftly as possible from one task to the next, tending to the needs of children, significant others, co-workers, colleagues, clients, and friends. But on an expedition to a high mountain, you have many, many uninterrupted hours of solitude waiting for weather and waiting for your body to catch up to the altitude. This is perhaps the greatest gift of any Everest expedition — time with yourself, time to reflect on who you are, where your life is going, and what's really important to you. In essence, you are altitude's prisoner and you must learn the art of patience, retreat and reflection.

In our busy world in the West, we often take almost no time to be alone.

Of one such period, Doug wrote:

"I think about the blessing of family and friends — life's greatest gift. I think about the comforts of home. Having not had a real shower in five weeks, my usual one seems such an extravagance. I think about my children and how their day-to-day experience and growth is so fascinating and precious. I think about my career and what a blessing it has been to stumble upon something I love doing so much I can do every day.... I've been given health and fitness, and I am ever so grateful. Finally, I've thought about you [his friends] during one of those sleepless, stormy nights. Those thoughts have been filled with great memories and hopes for your health and happiness."

Just as I struggled to adapt to 21,000 feet and above on Everest, so too did the other members of our expedition. All of us fought the usual headaches, nausea, and general lassitude, which is as much a part of life on Everest as sunburn is at the beach. Most of all, we struggled with our own humanness.

"I'm greatly disappointed that this [Advanced Base Camp] seems to be some sort of altitude ceiling for me," Doug wrote home. "In two attempts to climb to Camp 3 (half way up the Lhotse Face at about 23,700 feet) I've been unable to take more than a dozen plodding steps before having to stop and gasp for breath and wait for my pounding heart to slow to a rumble. I have always expected to be a real tiger at altitude; I'm eating a big chunk of humble pie by barely being able to move up here.

"... I had hoped to acclimatize well enough to climb to Camp 3.... Alas, I never made it to 3. I just felt too short of breath. Even at my plodding pace of one step to each breath, after 10 steps, I would have to stop and breath and let my pulse drop below 150 [normal is about 70 for most people at sea level]. Back at camp I had a small pulse oximeter [a device that measures the percentage of oxygen the blood is carrying]. My oxygen saturation never bettered 65%. [At sea level, it should be at least 98%. At 65%, you are usually hospitalized and close to death at sea level.]"

Just as we all had to face the raw realities of who we were, to use Jamie's words, Doug still managed to find solace in the situation. He sought refuge, as many of us did during the expedition's trying times, in the quiet company of the Sherpas.

"Sitting with nine of them in our round tent at Advanced Base Camp, the contrasts could not have been more marked," Doug recalled, " — one white-faced, the others dark; one wealthy, the others of much more humble means; one who thinks little of flying to several cities in a day for business, the others who live in villages without roads; one the employer, the others employees.... I speak ten words of their language, they speak one hundred of mine. Yet I have rarely felt as content. In my oxygen-deprived state, I wonder why the

---

Most of all, we struggled with our own humanness.

rest of the world doesn't feel as safe and comfortable, even happy, with its diversity."

So it was that each of us began to find our own way to where we were going. As a result of our differing health, rates of acclimatization and respective decisions to climb with and without bottled oxygen, Jamie and I unconsciously began to climb separately as two teams within a team — he with Jason, our expedition leader, and myself with Jeff, our deputy leader. As in 1994 (see *The Power of Passion*), we didn't realize the potential long-term ramifications of our different decisions until it was too late.

I learned after the expedition that my initial plan to attempt Everest without the use of bottled oxygen brought considerable pressure on Jamie from Jason, Jeff, and some of the other team members. They demanded he try to sway me, saying not only that mine was an unsafe plan, but that I was an unsafe climber.

"I was very worried about Alan going without gas," Doug recalls. "Something wasn't firing right for him. He wasn't as strong as he needed to be, but I had no tools with which to check him to see if I could determine what was wrong. At first, I tried to reserve judgment about his decision. I didn't know if he'd get stronger when he went higher. Some climbers do. But when he didn't [get stronger], I was surprised he didn't see that. Jason was very concerned, as were others on the mountain.

"Finally, I said, 'This is a really bad idea.' Jamie hauled me aside and just lit into me. I've never seen him so angry."

Because of his loyalty to me, Jamie backed me in my plan to try to climb without oxygen. He may have disagreed with it, but he knew how important it was for me to try. I am no daredevil. Unfortunately, the other members of the team didn't know that. They hadn't known me as long as Jamie had.

Jason was also concerned:

"I was concerned about it [my position to try to climb without bottled oxygen] from the beginning," he recalls, "but willing to give Alan the option as long as it was a viable one.... I planned it out that the option of using oxygen was always clear. It would be easy to switch."

> *"I wonder why the rest of the world doesn't feel as safe and comfortable, even happy, with its diversity."*
>
> – DR. DOUG ROVIRA

On April 26, after a day of rest in Advanced Base Camp after climbing up to Camp 3 and, at Jamie's suggestion, descending back down to sleep in ABC, I once again hauled myself up to Camp 3. It was a spectacular climb on alternating steep, hard ice and steeply inclined snow. All the while, you were clipped safely into anchored rope. Nevertheless, in places the terrain approached an incline of almost 60 degrees, and if you somehow got unclipped from the safety rope and lost your balance, there was nothing to stop you from plummeting 3,000 feet straight down the Lhotse Face to your death.

I gained a whole new respect for Hillary and Tenzing that day. This was not a "yak route" as some had maintained. It certainly wasn't the most technically difficult climbing terrain I'd ever been on, but it was certainly some of the highest and most exposed. I tried not to look down. A few weeks later, a Sherpa from another team apparently neglected to clip his harness into the anchored rope here while descending from Camp 3. He lost his balance, and went for "the big ride" all the way into the Western Cwm. His limp and lifeless body was pulled from a crevasse at the bottom a short while later.

Camp 3 was equally unforgiving. Although the view was astounding from its 24,000-foot perch, the terrain was so steep there that literally 10 inches outside the front door of your tent, the world dropped away abruptly. Again, if you fell, you were dead. The year before, a climber had perished here when he'd left his tent in the dark to answer the call one night and failed to clip into the safety rope surrounding the tents. With his feet shod only in the inner insulating liners of his climbing boots, he slipped and tumbled all the way down the Lhotse Face.

Predictably, my first night in Camp 3 was an unpleasant one. Life there consisted entirely of melting snow for water, answering the call, staying warm at night and during the early morning, and trying to stay as comfortable as possible during the late morning and scorching ultraviolet heat of the afternoon. It was such a physically confined spot that movement outside your tent for any significant distance was impossible, and thus once inside, you were basically stuck there. The altitude hit you hard at 24,000 feet and you found yourself bumping your head against the floor of the next great elevation adjustment level, 26,000 feet. It was the start of the "Death Zone," where the partial pressure of oxygen can only support life for very short periods of time.

"I took my heart rate in Camp 3," Jamie remembers. "In North America, it would have been about 45 beats a minute. Here, as I lay motionless in my sleeping bag, it was 122 — the equivalent of a light jog in Calgary. That's how hard my heart and lungs were having to work to deliver oxygen to my starving muscles."

At about 24,000 feet, your rate of physiological and psychological deterioration begins to increase exponentially. Once you climb to Camp 4 at 26,000 feet, it doesn't even make sense to overnight there. The already serious game of high-altitude climbing becomes a whole order more serious. Not just hours, but minutes count. The best way to summit safely is to climb as "fast" as you can, tag the top and return as quickly as possible to the relative safety of Advanced Base Camp.

The problem is, you can't exactly hustle anywhere at these altitudes. Making a meal can take as long as two or three hours because of the time needed to melt snow. Going to the bathroom outside your tent can take 10 to 15 minutes. Everything is slowed down — especially your thinking.

After surviving the night alone in Camp 3 with only a mild headache that soon went away, I decided to reconnoiter the route to Camp 4 above by climbing up to a feature called the "Yellow Band" of rock at about 25,000 feet. This is a prominent band of light-colored stone that circles the entire summit pyramid of Everest.

My plan ran into its first snag when I couldn't eat breakfast because I was nauseous from the altitude. All I could manage to hold down was half a quart of sugar-free apple cider. I have no idea why we purchased sugar-free mixes for our trip. As one of the biggest single struggles we have on Everest is keeping our weight loss to an absolute minimum, it was ludicrous to have diet drinks along. I laughed when I read the package.

For another high-altitude climber, climbing on no breakfast might not have been so bad, but my metabolism must have food, especially when I am working hard. If there's no fuel for my fire, I very quickly burn out.

This is what happened to me the first time I tried to ascend to the Yellow Band. Just one hour above Camp 3, I was reduced to a snail's pace as I struggled to will out every step. I felt like I was an actor in some kind of bad slow-motion movie. It took so much effort just to take a single step. I reminded myself that it would probably be even tougher higher up, so I tried to view this experience as a learning opportunity — a chance to further harden myself for the hardships that were to come. Again, the primary challenge of Everest is fought within yourself, where all of our battles are won or lost in life.

On Everest, it is so easy to allow yourself to become demoralized. All you want to do sometimes is just say "to heck with it" and go home. Over and over again on Everest this is the challenge — to maintain your motivation. There is no magic formula to this. I do it by remembering all the years of effort I have invested in the dream and how much I want to realize a return on my investment.

Sometimes, there is an almost overpowering urge to quit just because it hurts. When we're tired, hungry or sick, we may be sure we've made the right decision, but remorse can be delayed.

In my "breakfastless" state, it took me over two hours to reach the Yellow Band from Camp 3, an elevation change of just 750 feet. Without even looking at the view, I staggered my way back down to camp and collapsed into the tent.

That night in Camp 3 was terrible. The soup I managed to hold down for dinner gave me terrible gas during the night, I peed constantly and had to get out of the warmth of my sleeping bag to empty my pee bottle in the dark. This was no easy feat considering the drop outside my front door so, although I was tired and bleary-eyed, I focused all of my available energy on grasping the safety rope and watching my footing.

> *It is so easy to allow yourself to become demoralized. I maintain my motivation by remembering all the years of effort I have invested in a dream and how much I want to realize a return on my investment.*

1. The Colliers Lotus Notes Everest Expedition Team, 1997: (back row, from left) Jason Edwards, Expedition Leader; Jamie Clarke, Co-Business Manager; Jeff Rhoads, Deputy Leader; Dr. Doug Rovira, Team Physician; Bruce Kirkby, Telecommunications Coordinator; Dave Rodney, Communications Coordinator; (front row, from left) Steve Matous, Expedition Organizer (Great Escapes USA); Alan Hobson, Co-Business Manager. (Photo: ABL Photo, Calgary)

2. Our high points in 1991 and 1994 on the north side.

3. We could be brothers. Me and my mentor, Laurie Skreslet (right), of Calgary, the first Canadian to climb Everest. Courageous, noble and charismatic. The quintessential mountaineer. (Photo: Alan Hobson)

4. The dream-maker. John McLernon, chairman and CEO of Colliers International. Warm, approachable, and astute. (Photo: Colliers International)

5. Sweat equity. Grueling treadmill training at maximum incline. 50 lbs. on my back and 5 lbs. on each ankle. It focused my mind and strengthened my body. (Photo: Cal Zaryski)

6. The best friends a man could dream of having. My parents, Isabel and Peter Hobson. (Photo: Isabel & Peter Hobson)

7. Preparing for the peak. Winter training in the Canadian Rockies. One of the coldest winters on record created ideal conditions. (Photo: Bruce Kirkby)

8. Not your average airport. The airstrip at Lukla at 9,200 feet. You don't want to overshoot the runway.
(Photo: Ron Crotzer and Steve Matous)

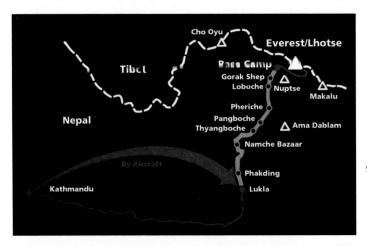

9. The trek route from Lukla to base camp. Ten days to two weeks of gradual ascent. (Graphic: Steve Matous)

10. Powerhouses on legs. Yaks en route to base camp. (Photo: Bruce Kirkby)

11. Frozen fear. The infamous Khumbu Icefall as seen through the door of a tent in base camp. As menacing as it looks. (Photo: Dave Rodney)

12. Jamie (left) and me in base camp. (Photo: Bruce Kirkby)

13. A call to the Mother Goddess. In base camp, two of our climbing Sherpas burn juniper at the stone altar during the sacred puja ceremony. (Photo: Bruce Kirkby)

Summit
Mt. Everest
29,028 ft

Climbing Route

Camp IV
South Col
26,000 ft

Lhotse

Nuptse

Camp III
23,500 ft

Advance
Base Camp
21,350 ft

Camp I
19,700 ft

Base Camp
17,600 ft

Khumbu
Icefall

14. In the footsteps of giants. The South Col route pioneered by Sir Edmund Hillary and Tenzing Norgay in 1953.
We followed 44 years later. (Photo: Lloyd Gallagher; Graphic: John Amatt, One Step Beyond)

16. Our Tigers of the Snow, our climbing Sherpas: (from left) Tashi Tsering,
Gyalbu, Lhakpa Tshering, Pema Temba, Kami Tshering, Mingma Dorjee,
Nurbu, and Ang Temba (Sirdar). Probably one of the strongest Sherpa teams
in the history of Everest. They carried our dream. (Photo: Dave Rodney)

15. Our anchor in the Western
Cwm. Shyam Prasad Pun, our
cook in Advanced Base Camp.
Amazing commitment.
(Photo: Bruce Kirkby)

17. Tireless loyalty and an unbending work ethic. Our base camp staff:
(from left) Padam Bahadur Limbu, Pemba Jeba Bhote, and Ang Dawa.
They worked up to 20 hours a day for two months. (Photo: Dave Rodney)

18. The force of focus. Jamie crossing a ladder bridge over a crevasse in the Icefall. You had to look down to place your feet, but control your mind. (Photo: Jason Edwards)

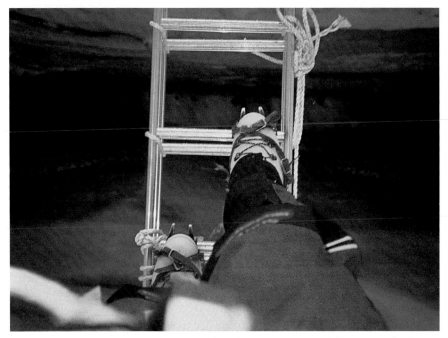

19. It's not "because it's there." There's nothing here but fear. What you see as you cross a ladder over a 150-foot deep crevasse in the Khumbu Icefall. We learned to look only at the rungs. (Photo: Jason Edwards)

20. Camp 2, Advanced Base Camp, at 21,000 feet in the Western Cwm. (Photo: Jamie Clarke)

21. The view from Camp 3, 24,000 feet on the face of Mt. Lhotse, at sunset. No place for sleep-walking. (Photo: Alan Hobson)

23. The reality of high altitude climbing. The author sick and tired — again. Every day is a bad hair day on Everest. (Photo: Jamie Clarke)

22. The launching pad of dreams. Camp 4 on the windswept South Col at 26,000 feet, the bottom of the "Death Zone." A frozen football field. (Photo: Jason Edwards)

Going to the bathroom at 30 below zero on a steep mountain face in the dark ranks up there with the most complex climbing moves I have ever done. How do you go to the bathroom in those temperatures? The answer is … quickly. Believe me, it adds a whole new meaning to the phrase, "Freezing your butt off."

The next morning, I awoke after only about two hours sleep with a bad headache — a sure sign I was dehydrated. At 8 a.m., I was stirred from my hypoxic stupor by a Sherpa I had never seen. He was rummaging around outside the tent collecting oxygen bottles. He said he was from another team, but when I inquired as to its name, I'd never heard of it. As I'd heard stories of other climbers stealing oxygen, instantly, I became concerned. My experience should have told me that Sherpas never steal (although the Tibetans have been known to "borrow" parkas), but I'm afraid when you're exhausted, you don't always think rationally.

In a second, I sprung out of the tent to protect our precious oxygen. Without taking the time to put on gloves or mitts, I moved to count our titanium oxygen tanks. Thankfully, they were all there, but within minutes, my fingers were numb and white from contact with the metal. I was forced to dive back into the tent and heat them on the stove. But I couldn't get my lighter to work!

I began to panic. Quickly, I stuffed the lighter into my crotch — the warmest place on the body. I'm sure my privates must have retracted all the way up into my stomach.

Thirty seconds later, as I watched my fingertips turn progressively whiter and whiter, I pulled out the lighter again and, thank God, finally, it lit! Quickly, I got the stove going and held my hands close to the burner.

Twenty minutes of anxiety followed as I began to realize that my little fit of fear, likely just a byproduct of exhaustion and sleep deprivation, might very well cost me my summit chances, not to mention the ends of a few of my fingers. Thankfully, the feeling in my digits gradually returned, but my hands continued to pulse painfully with blood for quite a while afterwards.

How do you go to the bathroom on Mount Everest? The answer is … quickly.

Unsettled, but still relatively calm (I thought), I radioed to Doug in Camp 2. I learned that the Sherpa had, in fact, been telling the truth. Another team had stored their oxygen tanks next to ours. The tone of my voice must have telegraphed something more serious because Doug immediately ordered me to take a tablet of the steroid dexamethasone and descend to Camp 2 as quickly as possible.

"I remember that radio call very clearly," Doug recalls. "Altitude sickness can be subtle. What was striking to me was that Alan was confused where normally he is absolutely focused. It took him 20 or 30 minutes to light a stove. It was clear to me that something wasn't quite right and I suspected cerebral edema [water on the brain]."

My plan that day had been to climb once again to the Yellow Band, but with Doug's orders it became quickly apparent there was no way that was going to happen. Tired and demoralized, about an hour later, I slowly descended to Camp 2. My fingers were fine.

On the glacier above camp, I came upon Doug, who, like a trooper, had climbed up to meet me. He fired a few packages of a product called "PowerGel" into my hand; a pure carbohydrate gel used by triathletes that looks and tastes a lot like cake icing. Its purpose was to get fuel into my body fast. Once he'd done this, he began plying me with water. Obviously, I was in rough shape. I thought I was just tired, but often, the climber is the last person to know when they have crossed the line.

After my very unpleasant night in Camp 3, it was a huge boost to see Doug. It is impossible to describe the feeling of camaraderie you get when someone comes to your aid when you need it, and I will never forget Doug's kindness that day.

"There was a huge sense of relief when I met him," Doug remembers. "A Sherpa from the Malaysian team had just died falling down the Lhotse Face so I was glad to see Al had navigated that terrain. It's just the kind of terrain people die on. It's not so steep so that you absolutely have to have a rope, but it's steep enough so that if you miss clipping into the anchored rope, you're gone. I was feeling so damn sick myself, but Alan was probably in better shape than I was."

A few minutes later, Doug and I descended the rest of the way to Advanced Base Camp. A few hours after we got there, Jamie and Jason arrived from base camp.

Jamie had been struggling through most of the trip with an irritating sinus infection. By the sound of his cough, I could tell it was not getting any better. Without a clear respiratory system, I knew his summit chances could be seriously jeopardized. Because he had a history of sinus problems, most notably the one that had almost killed him in Tibet in 1994 when he'd had an acute allergic reaction to an antibiotic, I was particularly concerned.

"Jamie just had this unrelenting cough," Doug recalls. "He didn't need antibiotics. He needed something more serious."

Jamie and I met in a tent in ABC to discuss our options. He floored me by suggesting we hire a helicopter to take us to Kathmandu for a few days. There, he hoped his sinuses would have a chance to react to other antibiotics, and I would have a chance to kick the cold that had continued to plague me throughout the trip.

"Can we afford that?" I asked incredulously.

"I don't think we can afford not to," Jamie replied.

At this stage, with the month of May only days away and the summit window soon to open, if at all, we couldn't afford any strategic mistakes. Our health had to improve or we didn't stand a chance of summiting.

While some of the other teams might scoff at our extravagance (even some members of our own team), I felt in my heart that the best thing to do at this point was to get the heck off the mountain for a few days, rest, and recover as much as possible. A quick chopper flight, although very expensive, could have us in Kathmandu in a matter of hours. Once there, we still ran the risk of getting sick from food poisoning or being unable to fly back to the mountain because of bad weather. Thus, there were no guarantees that our plan would work. In fact, if we were delayed more than a few days in Kathmandu, we'd lose all our upper-mountain acclimatization and we'd be forced to re-acclimatize all over again. At this late stage, that would be impossible.

We either had to go for it or go home.

It seemed like we were stuck between a rock and a hard place. If we stayed, we'd probably be too sick to summit safely. If we went, we might get sick there too, or worse still, get stranded.

Jamie and I discussed all our options for about an hour. None of them seemed certain.

Finally, we decided to gamble and go with the chopper idea. We knew this would bring us into disfavor with many climbers, some of whom came from the old school of mountaineering that discouraged any form of technological assistance. But we'd already come this far. We either had to go for it or go home. I didn't want to live for the rest of my life with a sense of "I should have."

As it would turn out, just getting down the mountain to the chopper would prove riskier than we could have imagined. The Icefall had something sinister in store for us.

Hanging by a Thread

I believe that no man can be completely able to summon all his strength, all his will, all his energy, for the last desperate move, till he is convinced the last bridge is down behind him and that there is nowhere to go but on.

— HEINRICH HARRER,
author of *Seven Years in Tibet*

THE NEXT MORNING, in the darkness of our tents in Camp 2, Jamie and I rose at 4 a.m. We knew that if we were to get safely through the Icefall before the heat of the day made it unstable and unsafe, we had to start early, when temperatures were at their lowest and there was the least chance of a collapse.

I have never gotten used to the early rises so frequent in climbing. We call them "alpine starts," but for me, and especially for Jamie, they don't start fast.

When you wake up in your own bed at home, all you have to do is roll out of it in your pj's, strip to the buff, step into the nice hot shower and voilà, you enter the world warmly.

At high altitude, when you wake up in the morning, you enter the world abruptly. The first thing that hits you is the freezing cold air. It strikes you like a slap in the face, welcoming you suddenly to your new reality. Your first reaction is to dive into your bag and try to come to your senses.

To get out of your sleeping bag without freezing, you have to get dressed in your bag before you actually get out of it. This is akin to putting on all your clothes, including your winter jacket, hat, scarf, and gloves, before you pull back the sheets. The last thing you want to do is get out of your bag buck-naked. That would definitely be a rude awakening, one even ruder than rising at 4 a.m.

You may be one of *those* who can spring out of bed at 3 or 4 a.m. singing "It's a wonderful world," but I'm not. I'm like a lot of people. I dislike getting up before 8 a.m. I do it all the time, but I don't enjoy it. I differ from most people, however, because when I'm in the mountains, I get dressed *before* I get out of bed. Actually, I *start* getting dressed before I even get *into* bed.

There is an art to sleeping in a tent in the cold. I don't have a Teddy bear. I sleep with all my "non-freezables" — the things you've got to keep from freezing. These include my lighter (to light my stove), a butane/propane gas canister of fuel for the stove (if I'm in a camp without a cook), sun block, two-quart plastic bladder of water, and, of course, my two, one-quart pee bottles (for those heavy nights) jammed into a haphazardly shaped and uncomfortable lump at the bottom of my sleeping bag. What can make sleeping in a bag in winter almost enjoyable is if you boil the water you put into your water bottle or bladder just before you take it to bed with you. Result — a hot water bottle from which you can also drink!

The Inuit may have perfected the art of sleeping naked at 40 below zero, but they sleep together. My jammies are several layers of polyester fleece one and two-piece underwear, a fleece neck tube, a wool hat with earflaps, and fleece gloves. In extreme cold, I pull my neck tube up over my face so I can pre-heat the cold air before it comes into my lungs. When I rise in the morning, I usually wake up with a layer of ice against my face as a result of my warm, exhaled breath cooling, condensing and freezing there during the night. There is usually also a thin layer of ice clinging to the inside of the roof of the tent for the same reason.

You can't use an alarm clock to wake you up. They don't work in the cold. You can't use a wristwatch alarm either. You can't hear it when it's buried in your sleeping bag. The technique I use is to put my wristwatch inside my hat on the top of my head. That way, when the alarm goes off, you have some hope of hearing it. If it's windy outside, the walls of the tent are flapping loudly and you have to wear ear plugs to sleep, so you may sleep straight through your alarm, regardless of where you put it. If you do start late, you may find yourself in danger later in the day if you're climbing; the snow starts to melt and avalanches and ice collapses occur around you. Thus, in the mountains, sleeping in can have far more serious consequences than being late for work. If you miss your alarm, sometimes it's best not to leave camp at all and take a rest day. If you have slept through your alarm, you may need the rest anyway.

When you sit up in your tent in the morning, you've got to be careful not to brush the top of the tent or the ice crystals that have formed there during the night immediately fall straight down the back of your neck. You have to make sure you wipe off this layer of frost before you light your stove or leave your tent for the day because, if you don't, when the temperature inside the tent rises above freezing, the ice on the roof of the tent will melt and everything on the floor of your tent will get soaked. If you leave your tent and forget to prevent this mid-morning or afternoon "rain shower," or fail to get back to camp to dry out your gear before the sun sets the next night, your sleeping bag can freeze into an uncomfortable crunchy mess that affords you little or no insulation. Result — a cold night (if you're lucky) and a lesson learned the hard way.

The most difficult part about getting up in a tent in winter is getting out of your sleeping bag. The first thing I do is turn on my headlamp, pull on my down jacket and sit up. Then I fumble around inside my bag and wrestle on my insulated climbing pants. Only then do I finally get out of my bag. You can never stop thinking, or thinking ahead.

"It's always so hard to get going in the early morning," Doug says. "The sleeping bags are so warm and the air is so frigid.… I think it is this moment, perhaps more than any other, that defines the successful mountaineer."

One of the keys to sleeping in the cold is the same as sleeping at home. It's in managing the transitions of getting into your cold bed at night and out into the cold from your warm bed in the morning. The way you do this is to never fully

"It's always so hard to get going in the early morning," Doug says. "… I think it is this moment, perhaps more than any other, that defines the successful mountaineer."

undress. In other words, I never take my underwear off, except to wash it. I do this every few weeks when I'm in base camp. I also get to shower there about once every two or three weeks.

If all of this seems uncivilized to you, you're right. By Western standards, it's primitive, basic living. Most of us haven't had to live like this in the West for decades. In its unpleasantness, however, you garner a whole new appreciation for the luxuries of life we enjoy in much of North America. If we were all like expedition climbers, for example, we'd all smell alike, but we wouldn't have to bathe every day. On a mountain, everyone stinks. You don't get used to it. You accept it. Whenever anyone comes back from the shower, there is a small celebration, and no small amount of envy and cajoling. In the mountains, the small stuff is big stuff.

By 5 a.m., Jamie and I had been through all our morning procedures and had been treated to a hot breakfast of boiled eggs, fried Spam and rehydrated Japanese noodles prepared by Shyam. At first light, we began descending the Western Cwm toward the Icefall. The previous night, before turning in, we had radioed to base camp and asked Bruce to arrange a helicopter for us at 9 a.m.

Although, in theory, we had lots of time, Jamie and I wasted no time getting down to the Icefall. We knew that if there had been a collapse during the night anywhere along our descent route, it might take many hours to get through, if we were able to get through at all. With the chopper costing at least $1,000 an hour at this altitude, we couldn't afford to be late. Our contingency wasn't that big.

The descent down the Western Cwm in the early morning hours is one of the most spectacular in the world. Gradually, you round a corner in the Cwm and there, straight ahead, is the Lho La pass and Mt. Pumori. They stab skyward, bare and pure in the grayness of the newborn day. They seem so close you could reach out and touch them, like snow cones, instead of summits.

That morning, there was a crispness and stillness you could feel, as well as hear. It was as if she were sleeping, awaiting once again our feeble attempts to scale her flanks. The reality was that I knew Everest never slept. We were being watched, whether we were conscious of it or not. Others had experienced the magic of the mountain here too.

"We rounded the west shoulder of Everest," Doug recalls of one descent from Camp 2, "and were stunned to see perfect shadows of Pumori and Mt. Lingtren cast on a distant ridge. A little further down the Cwm, the summit pyramids of those peaks, bathed in the exquisite morning light, came into view. In the frigid shade created by Everest, we stood still, in reverence, as if watching the entire world unfold beneath us. I remembered at that moment why I always return to high places. There was not a sound. I inhaled great draughts of the sweet, frosty air hoping to never forget the moment. We all looked at each other with big grins of school boys who have seen something they know their companions will envy. Playing in my mind were the last lines of one of my mother's favorite poems, "High Flight," by John Gillespie Magee, Jr., a pilot with the Royal Canadian Air Force:

> *Oh, I have slipped the surly bonds of earth*
> *And danced the skies on laughter-silvered wings;*
> *Sunward I have climbed, and joined the tumbling mirth*
> *Of sun split clouds — and done a hundred things*
> *You have not dreamed of — wheeled and soared and swung*
> *High in the sunlit silence. Hov'ring there,*
> *I've chased the shouting wind along, and flung*
> *My eager craft through footless halls of air*
> *Up, up the long, delirious, burning blue*
> *I've topped the windswept heights with easy grace*
> *Where never lark, or even eagle flew.*
> *And, while with silent, lifting mind I've trod*
> *The high untrespassed sanctity of space,*
> *Put out my hand, and touched the face of God.*

"At the beginning of our expedition, just after the puja, Ang Temba gave each of us a small portion of rice, blessed by a lama," Doug remembers. "We were to throw the rice at that which we feared or when we felt we were in danger. I amused myself, alone at night, with the thought of desperately digging the stuff out of my sweater pocket while a chunk of the Icefall was toppling over or the lip of a crevasse was collapsing beneath me. On this perfect morning, I asked Ang Temba if it might be appropriate to cast the rice in thanks. He smiled as I tossed my rice across the glacier."

By 6:45 a.m., Jamie and I were out of the magic of the Cwm and about halfway through the madness. The Icefall, as usual, was frightening. But I sensed there was something wrong beyond the obvious fact we shouldn't have been in there in the first place. By that hour, we should have been met by dozens of Sherpas climbing up from base camp carrying loads. No one had appeared.

Shortly after 7 a.m., we found out why. We rounded a bend in the route and came upon what we feared second only to an avalanche — a major ice collapse. It was about 150 feet wide and 50 feet deep. It looked like someone had dropped an entire city block five stories below street level and let the pieces shatter. From above, the area looked like the aftermath of a small earthquake. Huge blocks of ice had fractured into hundreds of smaller ones. Our intended route had been completely obliterated. In its place was a tangled melee of ropes, twisted and broken ladders, some of them partially buried, others sticking out of the ice at odd angles.

Jamie and I looked at each other.

"I hope nobody was in there when that let go," I said. "There's no chance they would have survived."

Slowly, we surveyed the scene. There was no evidence of human remains. The first thing we noticed was a piece of rope coming out of the ice at our feet. It cut into the snow steeply over the lip of the ice block on which we were standing and headed at about a 60-degree angle straight into the collapsed area about 50 feet below. Under the weight of the ice blocks that had fallen, it was drawn tightly.

"This looks pretty solid," I said, pulling on the rope. "What about sliding or rappelling down this? Seems like the simplest solution."

"Maybe," Jamie said, "but what if we weight it and the damn thing snaps under the stress? Whoever's on the rope will fall straight into the hole."

"You see any sure way around this mess?" I asked. "One way or another, we're taking a risk. I'm willing to give it a try."

"Okay," Jamie replied.

Quickly, I prepared to lower myself down the rope using the braking device (called a figure eight) clipped to my harness. On first test, all seemed secure.

"Just in case I don't make it out of here," I said. "I love you."

"I love you too buddy," he replied.

It's hard to describe what it's like to rappel over the edge of a sheer drop. Just half an inch of rope separates you from a fall. In my case, I knew that if the rope broke or pulled, I'd probably fall and break my back or bust my head open. Then, we'd be in real trouble.

Ever so carefully, I began to lean back over the edge of the abyss.

Suddenly, I felt uneasy.

"Something's wrong," my intuition said. "You'd best stop right now."

No sooner had I lowered myself 10 feet over the lip than the weight of my body on the rope, the angle of its descent, and its already considerable tension caused my braking device to jam. I found myself in the middle of the Icefall, dangling freely over a 50-foot deep hole, unable to move up or down.

In a second, reality set in. The safest alternative, I decided, was to try climbing back up the rope by unweighting the braking device from which I was hanging. So, I reached back onto my harness for my jumar (an ascending device that allows you to climb a rope). Quickly, I clipped it onto the rope above my figure eight. I thought that by pulling down on the jumar and doing a modified chin-up, I could unweight the rappelling device just enough to move it back up the rope towards Jamie.

"Just in case I don't make it out of here,"
I said,
"I love you."

Because of my background as a gymnast, at lower altitudes this maneuver would have been easy. But at 19,000 feet, it took every ounce of energy and power. Under normal circumstances, I would have simply attached a smaller rope to my jumar and stepped into it, but considering the angle of the rope, I was sure that would cause my jumar to twist right off the rope and tumble into the abyss. So there I was, straining with everything I had to unweight my body from the rope, move the figure eight an inch or two toward Jamie, weighting the rope again, resting and trying to repeat the process.

Above me, Jamie crouched and strained over the edge to reach me with an outstretched hand. Our fingers stretched fully toward each other, but the two-foot-wide gap between them seemed like a canyon.

"Come on Al!" Jamie said. "You can do it."

In seconds, my heart rate must have rocketed to over 180 beats a minute — red line. My chest heaved. One second, I was pulling down on the jumar with both hands, the next I was flailing madly to free up one hand so I could move my figure eight an inch or two higher. Frantically, I kicked the crampons on the bottom of my boots viciously into the ice block beside which I was dangling. It took everything I had to move an inch.

I struggled for five minutes. I cannot recall straining harder to do something and gaining such little ground with such a massive output of energy. I could feel the blood pounding in my head and the adrenaline coursing through my veins. I had to get back up the rope. I had to!

"Toss me your other hand!" I blurted to Jamie.

To do that, Jamie would have to lie down. If he did, he could fall into the hole himself.

I thought I was going to come apart physically. I became one giant, heaving lung. Everything I had — everything — I focused on moving myself one inch higher.

For a moment, I thought we weren't going to make it. I could feel the energy beginning to drain out of me, like water flowing down a sink.

Then, like an angel, Jamie threw himself into the snow and tossed both hands over the edge. This time, our fingertips just met, then our first knuckles. In one massive heave, he hauled me back onto the top of the ice block. My face plowed into the snow like a battering ram.

I continued gagging and coughing for 10 minutes. I just rolled around like a limp rag. It was a while before I could speak.

At that altitude the work had been so exhausting that for several minutes he could only lie there in the snow, trying to regain his strength and breath....

— Tenzing Norgay,
Man of Everest,
recalling Swiss climber Jean-Jacques Asper
struggling in the Icefall during the
1952 Swiss Everest Expedition

"Obviously, that isn't a viable alternative," I finally said
Neither one of us laughed, but it broke the tension.

As I continued to recover, Jamie headed back up the route down which we had descended. He went a short distance, dug down into the snow and managed to pull out a section of partially buried rope. He cut off a long section of it with his knife and came back down to me.

"What's say we try that again?" he said. "This time, maybe we can rappel on this."

"Is it long enough?" I asked.

"Probably," he replied.

We tested it. Sure enough, it just reached the bottom of the hole. I went first. Jamie followed.

It took us about 20 more minutes to find our way through the collapsed area and regain the original route below. The biggest challenge was making sure we didn't dislodge any of the newly fallen blocks. Some of them teetered precariously on edge, and if you so much as touched one with your boot, it could set off a chain reaction among the other ones. One misplaced hand or foot could cause us to be pinned under an ice block hundreds of pounds in weight.

When we finally regained the route below, I looked at my watch. It was 8 a.m. I was relieved, but I knew we still had a lot of ground to cover if we hoped to make it to the chopper by 9 a.m. So, Jamie and I turned on the speed. At 8:35 a.m., we staggered, panting, into base camp. Everyone there was surprised to see us. They figured the Icefall was impassable. They looked at us like we were apparitions.

I went straight to my tent and began to pack for three days in Kathmandu.

9 o'clock came — no chopper.

10 o'clock — no chopper.

11 o'clock — no chopper.

I began to feel like all our efforts had been wasted. Perhaps Everest was punishing us for deferring to technology. Perhaps she had decided we were unworthy.

Finally, at 12:30 p.m., I heard the faint sound of rotors coming up the valley. Jamie and I scrambled to our tents, picked up our backpacks and hustled over to the landing pad.

The machine never even shut down. Jamie and I piled in with our packs, someone slammed the door behind us and seconds later, Commander Lama, a former member of the Nepali air force, gently lifted the Bell Jet Ranger off the ground. We waved good-bye.

What a relief! We'd done it.

Ten minutes later, we landed at the tiny Sherpa outpost of Syangboche, a trip that would have taken us days to reach on foot. There, we picked up some supplies, but the clouds rolled in and we could not take off. This, as it turns out, was the reason the chopper had been late. A thunderstorm in the area had made it impossible for the helicopter to get safely from Kathmandu. Without benefit of satellite navigational equipment on board, although he knew the route like the back of his hand, Commander Lama had to be able to at least see the horizon. Apparently, it had taken many hours of patient waiting before he could even do this.

After a cup of tea at the tea house beside the landing area, the clouds lifted slightly about half an hour later. Quickly, we

> I began to feel like all our efforts had been wasted.

all loaded back into the bird and with all the precision of a skilled surgeon, the pilot deftly found his way up through a hole in the clouds. From there, he dove his ship, and us, straight down the valley like a missile.

The trip to Kathmandu was without doubt the most amazing piece of flying I have ever experienced and perhaps ever will. It put even my most rousing hang glider flights over the Canadian Rockies to shame.

En route to Kathmandu, we flew through rain, wind, cloud, distant lightning, and close to zero visibility. At one point, as Jamie sat in the front seat, he turned back to me with a look of horror and disbelief on his face as if to say, "I have no idea whatsoever how this guy is flying this thing. I can't even see where we're going." I motioned to the sky above so much as to say, "It's out of our hands buddy."

I tried not to think about how tragic it would be to come all this way only to end it by plowing into some poor peasant's potato field. We sure wouldn't look very heroic then, although it would certainly scare the hell out of the farmer's goats.

Fortunately, someone was on our side. When the rotors came to a stop at the international airport in Kathmandu an hour and 20 minutes after we'd taken off from Syangboche, we stepped out on the tarmac at 4,500 feet into 85-degree heat. I felt like I'd just landed on another planet. Everywhere you looked, there were people — and trees, cows, goats, bicycles and, my gosh, even cars. The reverse culture shock was phenomenal. I turned to Jamie and said:

"Is this actually happening?"

"Sure is buddy," he said, draping his arm over my shoulder. "Welcome back to civilization."

I felt like my body had been sent into sensory overload. All around me, I was overwhelmed with sights, sounds, smells, tastes, textures, and emotions I had not even realized I'd missed for the more than a month I'd been on the mountain. The realization that in our absence, life in the outside world had gone on completely oblivious to us was a surprisingly major adjustment. At the airport, every time we passed someone, I found myself thinking, "That person has no idea where I've just come from and more importantly, there is no reason whatsoever why they should care." It was a healthy dose of reality.

The air was so "thick!" I could actually sense its increased density in my nasal passages and lungs. Although it was heavy with pollution from the diesel fumes so prominent in the developing world, it was also definitely "heavier" than the stuff I'd been breathing on Everest. For a moment, I just sucked it in, savoring it, even with its impurities. Pollution aside, it was good to be back in the land of the living.

Outside the airport, a representative of Great Escapes Kathmandu, Ang Jangbu Sherpa, met us. He had summited Everest some years before. It was great to see his smiling face and hear his reassuring voice. Both Jamie and I knew that unlike everyone else at the airport, he knew where we'd come from. There was a wonderful comfort in that. He seemed to know just the right things to say. It went beyond the natural gentleness of his upbringing. He understood.

Incredibly, there was a taxi strike in Kathmandu that day so at key intersections, there were picket lines. I doubt taxi drivers are unionized in Kathmandu, but they are definitely unified. To get us back to the Everest Hotel, Ang Jangbu and his colleagues had arranged for a private car and two motorcycles to escort us. I felt a bit like a visiting dignitary, on a very small scale, as our mini-motorcade of three vehicles — a motorcycle in front and behind, and our car in the middle — wound its way through the congested and busy streets of Nepal's steamy capital. To avoid the blocked streets caused by protesting cabbies, we had to take a circuitous route to the hotel. About half an hour later, we arrived.

The first thing I noticed was the pool. It sure looked inviting. Many nights in base camp, I had fantasized about the joy of just floating in water, weightless at last and free to dive and sweep my way effortlessly through the warm water. Virtually all of your time at high altitude is spent battling gravity and after a while, you yearn for some solace from the struggle. Ah, to be weightless, I'd imagine. Here was my chance.

First, however, I definitely had to have a shower. After checking in, and getting to my room, that's the very first thing I did. It was heavenly. One of the greatest gifts about deprivation and isolation is how quickly your perspective on life can change. To this day, I never get into a shower without celebrating. It is a marvelous privilege, as is a clean glass of water, electric heat, and light.

I celebrated in the shower that day. I think I was in there for over an hour. It was just so wonderful to feel the hot water stream smoothly down my back, run down the backs of my legs and swirl between my raw and blistered feet. What a treasure it was to know that the supply was virtually unending, unlike the five-minute plastic bag of hot water that had been our shower in base camp.

By the time I'd showered, shaved, and got changed, it was time for dinner.

That evening, we gathered in the Indian restaurant on the top floor of the hotel. We were joined by Jamie's mother, Denise, his brother, Leigh, and about 10 or so other members of a trekking party. They had hiked up to base camp and back as part of an incentive trip for Colliers and Lotus. They had themselves just returned from Lukla by air that day.

Coincidence?

In the Everest Hotel, the place from which my Canadian colleague and friend, John Amatt, had sent television reports back to Canada on the progress of the first Canadian Everest expedition in 1982, we dined on curried chicken and sweet vegetables, spicy Indian wafers and delicious cucumber and yogurt dip. I thought of John then, as I had so often of his entire team while on the mountain. He had been the business manager and a climber on the expedition. Without him, Laurie Skreslet, Bill March, Lloyd Gallagher, Pat Morrow, James Blench, Jim Elzinga and the other Canadians who had preceded us on Everest could not possibly have made it to the mountain. In a very real way, I was following in their footsteps.

As a small team of waiters hustled around our table, it occurred to me again how wonderful it was just to be alive. For the umpteenth time that day, I found myself looking at the restaurant and around me at all the smiling, friendly faces and thinking, "How did I get here?" That morning, only hours before, I had been struggling for my life in the Khumbu Icefall. Now, I was feasting in the lap of luxury. Life has so many wonderful contrasts.

The trekkers were thrilled to see Jamie and me and anxious to share stories of their adventure. Jamie's mother, at 51, had surprised even herself by plodding her way methodically all the way up to 17,000 feet and back down again — a feat that would be unequalled by some of our other trekkers half her age. Jamie comes by his physical and psychological strength honestly.

All the trekkers were particularly keen to get first-hand news of our team's progress on Everest. For a few hours, Jamie and I enjoyed semi-celebrity status, complete with autograph-signing and picture-taking. I felt like a bit of a hero, even though in my eyes, all I'd done was be sick on a mountain for more than a month and gained a little altitude along the way. Nevertheless, support from others was a big psychological boost for both of us. It was nice to feel special.

By 9:45 p.m., I was in bed, dog tired from the day and exhausted from the strain of the expedition. I marveled at how comfortable the bed was. Everything around me seemed so much more vivid, from the warm feel of the carpeting on the sore soles of my feet to the amazingly white towels in the bathroom. Then there were those glorious, glorious gallons of seemingly endless hot water in the shower again. You didn't have to melt ice to make it. All you did was turn on the tap. What a concept!

Slowly, I ran my hands over the bed sheets, pulled the nice warm blankets over my head and thanked God for small mercies. If I could only just remember how special that moment was, and how fortunate I am to live where I do, it would help me to realize what a life of tremendous abundance we all enjoy in the West.

That is another gift Everest has given me, the gift of gratitude.

In seconds, I was deeply asleep.

Up and Down

Climbing is not a battle with the elements,
nor against the law of gravity.
It's a battle against oneself. — WALTER BONATTI

THE REST I HOPED to realize in Kathmandu did not materialize. Although I slept for most of the first night and day I was there, by day's end, I began to feel out of sorts. A day later, I was very unwell. My biggest concern about going to Kathmandu had been the possibility of getting sick. Although the Everest Hotel was one of the finest in the city, polluted water has a way of reaching everything, almost everywhere. All it takes is someone to rinse your fork in unpurified water, and as soon as you put the utensil in your mouth, you run the risk of coming down with something.

That may have been what happened to me. In the wee hours of my last of three nights in Kathmandu, I found myself hanging over the toilet in my hotel room going at both ends. It was so disappointing and frustrating. There I was, surrounded by all the creature comforts, and yet still just as sick as I had been in base camp. I had a bad case, not only of diarrhea and likely food poisoning, but of déjà vu.

> *But I was worried about my health.... I thought about*
> *it all so much that I could hardly sleep at night....*
>
> — TENZING NORGAY,
> *Man of Everest*

It took everything I had to drag myself to the airport for our return flight to base camp that morning. I'd slept for only a few hours. I was pale and drawn, and I felt awful. Every movement was an effort, from packing my bags to getting down the stairs to the lobby. Somehow, I managed to make it to the airport and out onto the runway where Commander Lama was waiting with our chopper. Minutes before the bird was to lift off, at 7 a.m., I threw up again. Dozens of onlookers on the airport's observation deck must have seen me.

Seconds after I'd been sick, Commander Lama nonchalantly handed me an airsickness bag and ushered me into my seat. Then, he fired up the rotors and moments later, we were airborne.

I never got to swim in that pool at the hotel. As we lifted off, I tried to catch sight of it through the window of the chopper, but I was so disoriented, I could hardly figure out which way was up. That weightless dip would have to wait until another day, I thought. At least my head was swimming.

We were going back to base camp, back to complete the mission.

The flight to base camp was nothing like the one we'd taken to Kathmandu. Beneath a canopy of scattered cloud, the sun shone brightly. Even in my nausea, I was still excited. We were going back to base camp, back to finish the mission. My mission, I realized during the flight, was to overcome my latest illness and get back in the game. Now, I really had to deliver — to the best of my ability, for better or for worse, summit or no summit.

The views of the Himalayas were absolutely spectacular. You could see for a hundred miles in all directions as the ramparts of the world's tallest peaks jutted up towards the clouds. The Himalayas are amongst the youngest mountains in the world, and therefore, some of the most jagged. The winds of time have not had as much time to wear them down. So, they stab skyward like standing blades.

The power of these peaks cannot be denied — mile after mile of rock, snow, and ice, spectacular summits and lush green valleys. You cannot help but be touched by it. The Himalayas really do take your breath away, and it is not only because of their altitude. It is because of their power.

After a brief stop in Syangboche, Jamie and I landed in base camp shortly after 8 a.m. on May 3. It happened that the expedition's third corporate trekking party was there to greet us, but unfortunately, I was hardly up to the challenge. I did my best to greet everyone, but mostly I just walked around trying not to vomit. I have photographs of me posing with the trekking team, but I barely remember being there.

Dr. Doug took my temperature. It was 102. At his order, I retired to my tent for the rest of the day until the climbing team convened for dinner that evening.

I did not receive the welcome I had wished. One member of the expedition again made it clear he did not support my decision to attempt Everest without the use of bottled oxygen. My latest illness, he maintained, was only a further indication I was not up to it.

I was too tired and sick to get angry, so I just hung my head beneath the table and tried to hold down some soup. I thanked everyone for their concern, but reaffirmed my decision to climb without bottled oxygen until such time as it became obvious I was incapable of accomplishing the goal. Some of the other team members, I am sure, felt I had already reached that point and, to be truthful, I was beginning to believe it myself. But in my mind, I still hadn't reached a decision. That made all the difference. My mission, after all, was to come safely away from Everest knowing I had given it everything I had. Unfortunately, none of the other team members except Jamie had known me long enough to assess whether I could be relied upon to make a sound judgment. So, they were understandably concerned. Even Jamie's attempts to assuage them failed. In the eyes of some expedition members, I could become a potential liability. If I insisted on climbing without oxygen and got into trouble, they might have to risk their lives to rescue me.

Dave Rodney was a great support, not so much verbally, as morally. He had climbed with Laurie Skreslet and somehow, he just seemed to sense there was still hope for my dream. At the very least, he said he admired my ability to stick to my guns and stay cool and committed under substantial pressure from some of the other team members.

"If there's one guy who can do it [climb Everest without bottled oxygen], it's you," he said reassuringly. "But even if you don't succeed, I agree, it's at least worth a try. You're not out of it yet, so I say, hang in."

Other team members did not agree. Dissension began to build.

"Alan was so adamant about doing it," Jeff remembers, "that it immediately made everyone else adamant about him not doing it."

They were right. If I had been in their shoes, I would probably have felt exactly the same way. Unfortunately, I misinterpreted their position as a personal attack on my dream. They believed in me. They just didn't believe I could climb the mountain without oxygen at that time.

> *It is a Sherpa saying that in a big house there is bound to be some trouble from time to time, and certainly I have never been on a big expedition where everything went smoothly from beginning to end.*
>
> — Tenzing Norgay,
> *Man of Everest*

At that moment, I realized I could no more rebuild their confidence in me than I could climb myself. I was so weak that it took everything I had just to keep from falling over. Still, I felt I had not yet given it my all. Some time was still on my side. Until that time ran out, I resigned myself to bearing their criticisms, knowing they had my own best interests, and theirs, at heart.

Were it not for Dave, I might not have got through that time. His compassion once again shone through. To his credit, Bruce also praised me for maintaining my composure. Although each of them might have quietly disagreed with my position, neither voiced it to me. At the very least, I was reassured that they did respect my goal, and my proposed method of achieving it.

That night, my health took a brief turn for the better. In the morning, I was able to hold down breakfast. Unfortunately, the victory was short-lived. Within hours, my condition returned to what it had been the day before. I could feel myself starting to lose motivation. Doubts began to creep into my mind. It was the lowest point for me on the expedition to that date. I survived only by thinking of my training mantra — CAN ... WILL, CAN ... WILL and all those lonely hours.

While I was recovering in base camp, Jamie and Jason began their first summit attempt. They climbed to Camp 2 in anticipation of reduced winds above. Unfortunately, a tainted can of ham resulted in Jamie also coming down with food poisoning. He spent a very unpleasant night at 21,000 feet before descending to base camp a day later. When he arrived, we swapped horror stories.

The next day, things slowly began to improve for me. Despite continued weakness, I treated myself to a makeshift shower of boiled water. It was very restorative. Then, I steamed my badly clogged sinuses by hanging my face over a pot of hot water with a towel over my head. Thankfully, they started to drain. By day's end, I began to feel better.

The night of May 6, I slept well for the first time since returning to base camp. After purposely eating a large lunch to try to regain some strength, I started to pack for a summit bid. I taped my feet to prevent further blistering and updated my personal medical kit with all the medications I might need above Camp 2. I knew that once past Advanced Base Camp, I would pretty much be on my own medically. Doug had since reached his personal ceiling of 21,000 feet. He would not be able to join us above Camp 2.

Over the next two weeks, our expedition played a continuous game of cat and mouse with winds of up to 90 miles an hour near the summit. While some members of commercial teams lost their patience, packed up and left for home, our expedition waited resolutely. Every day, we studied the weather forecast, which came to us via satellite from Malaysia. When it arrived, we'd pour over it for hours, endlessly discussing our options.

If the winds do not subside sufficiently, there is no way you can safely climb Everest. As we awaited in base camp the destiny Everest would deal us, we knew we couldn't just lie around idly. After five or so days, our bodies began to lose their hard-earned acclimatization to Everest's upper altitudes. So, we either had to climb up yet again through the Icefall to Camp 2, or hang around in base camp and risk losing all hope of summiting. As exhausted as we already were, every few days we'd have to climb up through the Icefall and spend a few days in Camp 2. This was very difficult physically and psychologically.

On May 7, just as I was recovering from my food poisoning (or whatever it was I'd picked up in Kathmandu), I was subject to another challenge of my plan to climb without bottled oxygen. Again, one team member sparked the debate. This time, because I was in better health, I came close to the breaking point. All I wanted to do was dive across the mess tent and strangle him. Frankly, the only "assault" was probably against my own fragile and frazzled ego, but when you're tired, it's easy to lose perspective. I excused myself from the tent.

"I feel almost totally alone now," I wrote in my diary that day. "I wish Skreslet was here to advise me. I'm sure he could help."

"I don't think the oxygen issue overshadowed the trip," Jason says. "All trips have issues and you work through them. It certainly took some work."

I pulled Jamie aside and vented. I told him I felt at least one member of the team should be sent packing. I felt I had made my goal of climbing Everest without bottled oxygen clear long before leaving North America, and now that we were coming down to the crunch, that position was being called into question. I didn't think that was fair.

He listened carefully and tried to remain calm. I can get pretty fired up at times, and this was one of those times. Over the years, I think Jamie has learned just to let me blow off steam. Eventually, I calm down.

Jamie explained that if this expedition member was removed, Jamie's summit chances could be seriously jeopardized. That caused me to pause for serious thought. I wasn't willing to reach the summit, with or without bottled oxygen, if it cost me my friendship with him. Jamie might disagree with that, but that's exactly why I backed off. I loved Jamie.

"Okay," I said. "I'll defer to your position."

Jamie returned to his tent and I returned to mine. I felt confident that by siding with him and putting our relationship first, everything would eventually work out. Sadly, I was to discover otherwise.

I sure didn't feel like we were living up to our expedition slogan of "working together" at that moment. I'm sure Jamie didn't either. It seemed like the whole trip had turned into an hypocrisy. Yet that is the nature of Everest expeditions. Conflict is unavoidable because everyone is under such stress.

That evening, I deliberately took some time away from the rest of the North American team members and shared a feast of boiled potatoes and butter with the Sherpas. This was a regular event that usually settled me. It didn't that night. I felt more isolated than ever. In an attempt to distract myself, I checked with Bruce to see if I had received any e-mail via satellite. Indeed, there were two wonderful notes from Diane. I read them over and over again, trying to rebuild my self-confidence. It was great to read her words of encouragement. In spite of her physical and emotional distance, I felt closer to her then than I had since she'd left, as if she'd somehow sensed my need and intuitively responded to it. I immediately sent her back a reply thanking her for her kindness and telling her how much I loved her. Perhaps there was still hope for us.

A few minutes later, Jeff Rhoads came by the communications tent. He reassured me that he was still behind me, and that he didn't think I was on a suicide mission.

"I wasn't concerned about my safety, or Alan dying," Jeff says. "I just thought he'd end up stalling out somewhere below the summit, be totally crushed, and have to deal with that. Then, we'd both have to turn around."

It was good to hear Jeff's words and know he still believed in me. In reality, everyone did.

Steve got word of our "Great Oxygen Debate" via e-mail.

"I remember thinking, 'This is a pain, but this is also good because this is driving Alan up the hill. This is real motivation.'"

Thankfully, a few days of agonizingly long waiting followed. It gave everyone a chance to cool down. On May 10, I climbed up through the Icefall to Camp 1 to maintain my upper-mountain acclimatization. It was a turning point. My steps came out slowly and laboriously. My legs felt like lead. I knew I had lost a lot battling the bug I'd picked up in Kathmandu and I was thankful I had not waited any longer in base camp.

The next day, I moved from Camp 1 to Camp 2 in my slowest ascent time between those camps on the expedition. I was approaching the edge.

"I'm dead on my feet in Camp 2," I wrote in my diary that day. "I slept most of the day in the kitchen. Finally, at 4 p.m., I managed to move to my sleeping tent just a few feet away. It is very disheartening. I feel like I have gone backwards."

"It was obvious at one point that Alan's speed through the Icefall was average or slightly below average," Jason remembers. "The overall goal of the trip, however, was to have everyone live. It was sad for him, and he was fairly persistent in holding on."

That night, I struggled to sleep. Outside my tent, I could hear the roar of the wind howling across the summit. I was thankful I was not fighting for my life up there. The power of Everest, and of nature, is immeasurable. When it is elevated or enraged, it is best that we leave it alone. If we do not, it can do more than kill. It can obliterate.

Everything was chance and choice now — or destiny, depending on which way you looked at it.

The next morning, we awoke to the sound of the wind still raging above us. For the next two days, our expedition continued to play a guessing game with the weather, trying to decide whether to climb higher, hold our position, or descend. We were pawns on Everest's board, and clearly, she was winning.

Finally, on May 13, the mountain made the decision for us. A fierce summit wind drove us all out of Advanced Base Camp and down through the Icefall.

When it is elevated or enraged, it is best that we leave nature alone.

On the descent, I hacked up phlegm most of the way. Just before 11 a.m., part way through the Icefall, I ran out of energy, having been unable to eat because of nausea that morning. I found myself moving through the danger at a snail's pace. I still hadn't licked the calorie thing. What a state!

As the Icefall began to melt in the day's heat, with every passing minute, I became more and more concerned. All it would have taken was one ice block to teeter over and I'd be pulverized. When Jeff and I became separated, I began to feel even more uneasy. I wondered if today was the day the bullet would come.

At noon, I literally stumbled into base camp, shattered not only physically, but psychologically, from the stress. There, I had a shower and a shave, and tried to pull myself together.

My body was wasting away. I'd lost over 10 pounds, which on my frame is a lot. Psychologically, I was starting to cave in. It was time to do something.

The next day, Dave Rodney and I decided to walk down to the village of Dingboche at about 13,000 feet. My plan was to rest, rehydrate, and recover there for a few days and hopefully, return to base camp sufficiently rejuvenated to launch a summit attempt if the weather window opened.

The day of our descent, May 14, was an absolutely magical one. Within hours of leaving base camp, the sweet smell of sage and juniper wafted through my dried and parched nostrils. It was spring in the Khumbu Valley. For the first time since arriving in Kathmandu, the whole world seemed alive and vibrant again. Gone was the lifelessness and drudgery of base camp. The air was thick, crisp and pure. Toward sunset, the last rays of the day streamed gently through the clouds as they swirled in ever twisting wisps toward the summits. Everywhere you looked, there was running water — from swiftly flowing waterfalls, to gently meandering streams. And there was that color green too! How magnificent it was to see it in the grass and juniper bushes, even in the scattered evergreens, as forlorn-looking as they appeared.

Just as I had felt when Jamie and I had arrived by chopper in Kathmandu, so too did Dave and I sense suddenly that we had been mysteriously deposited on another planet. We celebrated with every step, laughing and joking like a couple of school boys on spring break. The comparatively lush environment of lower altitude seemed so far removed from the bleak moonscape of base camp that the contrast was profound. The change was not only from white to green, but from death to life.

By sunset, Dave and I were resting comfortably beside a yak-dung fire in a cozy Sherpa tea house in Dingboche. There, our hostess, Mingma Sherpa, cooked us a simple, but satisfying meal of noodles and eggs, boiled potatoes, and ketchup, that gave us a surge of energy. Mingma's husband was away on an expedition. After roaming around in our stocking feet, sipping Sherpa tea, and playing with Mingma's two little boys, Dave and I laid out our sleeping bags and prepared to go to sleep.

To be bedded down within the walls of a warm Sherpa lodge is like returning to the womb. It may be dark, but it is always safe and secure.

Although we had left our other Sherpa friends in base camp, the Sherpas were still with us, I thought. There was a sense of sanctuary in Dingboche, as there always was when we were amongst the Sherpas. I felt safe and at peace. Of the many gifts my adventuring has given me, my time with these people is amongst my most precious. To be bedded down within the walls of a warm Sherpa lodge is like returning to the womb. It may be dark, but it is always safe and secure.

Dave and I reveled in that security, rolled over in our sleeping bags, and within seconds, fell soundly asleep.

The Winds of Change

There is no success without hardship. — SOPHOCLES

MY TIME IN Dingboche was very restorative. The first day, I lay around like a dead man, sleeping on and off, sipping Sherpa tea, and eating as much as I could. Meanwhile, Dave took off and hiked to the top of a nearby 18,800-foot peak. Having been confined to base camp because of his communications responsibilities, the descent to Dingboche was as welcome a change for him as it was for me, except that my purpose was to rest. His was to explore.

> *The schedule was arranged so that different teams took turns at the hardest work, and also that every one should come down regularly from the higher camps — not only to the base, but even farther down the glacier to a place called Lobuje, where there was a stream and some vegetation and the men could regain their strength quickly in the lower altitude. I think that much of the success of the expedition lay in the fact that there was time to do such things, while the Swiss had always been forced to hurry on.*
>
> — TENZING NORGAY,
> *Man of Everest*

During our trip to Dingboche, with the exception of his hike, I spent almost every waking hour in Dave's company. I never tired of it. I came to know him quickly as a great friend.

Like me, Dave had his own emotional Everests to climb during our expedition. His relationship of seven years had come apart just before leaving for the mountain and, like me, he was frustrated, upset, and grieving the loss of someone very important to him. We shared a common bond of loss. We supported and comforted each other, talked about our respective relationship challenges, the mistakes each of us had made, how we planned to learn and grow from them, and what fresh new challenges might lie ahead. More than anything, we consoled each other.

At the end of the day, what's most important is the quality of the company we keep, even if we choose that company to be ourselves, by ourselves.

Making new friends is perhaps the most wonderful part of expeditioning for me. Adventuring with others is all about relationships and trust. In a working world so fraught with mistrust, backstabbing, infighting, and politics, it is refreshing to be in an environment in which relying on the other person is not only important, it is absolutely essential. During an expedition, you see almost every aspect of a person — what they're like under stress, when they haven't eaten or slept in three or four days, or how they perform when the chips are down.

The bonds that tie everyone together on the planet are important. At end of the day, what's most important is the quality of the company we keep, even if we choose that company to be ourselves, by ourselves. Sometimes, our adventures bring us closer together and sometimes, they tear us apart.

To that point on the expedition, only one team had successfully achieved the summit, the Indonesians, with the help of Russian guides. Somehow, they had slipped to the summit before the high winds and miraculously returned safely. It was no surprise that a Sherpa had been pivotal to the ascent.

"After 16 hours of breaking trail in windblown snow above 26,000 feet," Doug recalls, "in temperatures of −40°F, Apa Sherpa stood on the top for his eighth time, waiting for the others. Unable to make it back to the South Col, they spent a cramped night in a tent at 27,500 feet. Apa and another Sherpa made it back to Camp 2 the next evening while the rest of the team took an additional day to descend. Several of our Sherpas asked me to see Apa because he had been snow blinded earlier in the day. When I got to his tent he looked like he had wandered around some city park. He hopped up offering me his seat, and went to fetch me a cup of tea! Sight returning, he wouldn't let me look at his eyes, choosing instead to chat and laugh with his friends."

Dave and I now had the opportunity to chat with one of our new Sherpa friends and to try to understand how such high achievement could come from such humble roots. The evening after Dave's hike, Mingma Sherpa again cooked us a delicious supper. After that, by the light of a battered kerosene lamp, she spoke of her life married to a climbing Sherpa, her many months of solitude while he was away, the challenges of raising her two boys largely on her own, and the other obstacles faced by the residents of her tiny village

"Sherpa life no good," she said shockingly as the light of the lamp etched shadows in her weathered but vibrant face. "Sherpa life … hard."

> *You are too weak. You will get ill again, or you*
> *will slip on the ice and fall and kill yourself.…*
> *You take too many risks.… You are a daredevil.*
> *You care nothing about me or the children, or*
> *what happens to us if you die.… But you are mad.*
> *You will kill yourself on this mountain.*
> *You will die.*
>
> — Tenzing Norgay's wife, Ang Lahmu, reacting to
> Tenzing's decision to go back to Everest in the spring of 1953
> with the British, after his experience with the Swiss
> in the autumn of 1952, *Man of Everest*
> (Tenzing summited with the British that spring.)

High-altitude expeditions have both helped and hindered the age-old Sherpa culture. On one hand, health and educational standards and facilities have improved immeasurably, but on the other, the steady stream of Westerners into the once isolated region has created untold other problems. Perhaps the most culturally devastating of these effects is how some of the Sherpas now perceive themselves. Once proud of their rich heritage and Buddhist culture, some of them now look at visitors toting climbing equipment worth more than their entire worldly belongings, and ask themselves the inevitable question: "How come I don't have that?"

This economic gap has also created inner resentment in some of the Sherpas. In comparison to the majority of Nepalese, the Sherpas are financially wealthy beyond measure. However, compared to the trekkers and climbers who frequent Nepal by the tens of thousands every year, some Sherpas feel they are financial underdogs. Some are apologetic of their possessions and living conditions. Many do not perceive how so much wealthier they are spiritually than the vast majority of those in the West. Buddhism has for centuries brought them a sense of personal peace, community, and belonging that is rarely found in the developed world. Now, although they remain committed to their culture and their spirituality, I believe many Sherpas are struggling to find a balance between the externally oriented West and the internally oriented East. Some would like to have more money and creature comforts, but this is contrary to the Buddhist philosophy of inner enlightenment. Thus, they are now in conflict with their own values. The apparently harmless act of kindness of giving candies to Sherpa children, for example, has resulted to increasing incidences of dental problems. The local hospital in the Sherpa village of Khunde, from which Ang Temba, our Sirdar, hailed, has seen a rise in the frequency of such traditional "Western" problems as ulcers, mental illness, depression and alcoholism. Thus, as in any culture, all is not well in this paradise either.

Mingma's words unsettled us. To a degree, we felt personally responsible for contributing to the very cultural and economic conflict she now had in her life. At the same time, we knew we were paying her (or more accurately Colliers and Lotus were paying her), to feed and lodge us. This money would be used to feed and clothe her and her family, keep yak dung heating her tiny Himalayan home and help pay for her to fly to Kathmandu from time to time to go to market there. Thus, there was a trade-off. Did the positives outweigh the negatives? That is a very difficult question, and I do not have the answer. However, I do feel in part responsible for the erosion of her culture.

The life of a Sherpa mountain man is, I suppose, something like that of a sailor. When things are good with him he is away from home much of the time and not often with his family.

— TENZING NORGAY,
Man of Everest

Our time in Dingboche was brief. The last thing I wanted to do was miss a potential summit window on Everest. I couldn't afford to miss that opportunity, yet it was just as important to rest. So, after a wonderful day with Mingma, on May 16, Dave and I started trekking back up the valley toward base camp.

We didn't get far before we were met by bad news. During a 10 a.m. radio call with base camp, we learned that Camp 2 had apparently suffered severe damage in a wild wind storm the previous night. Five climbers on the north side of Everest had apparently died at about the same time. The exact extent of the damage on our side of the mountain was not yet known, but there had been no loss of life. Nevertheless, as echoes of the '96 disaster reverberated down the Khumbu, the e-mail and satellite telephone calls from sensation-seeking Western media, concerned friends and families, were apparently already pouring in to base camp. Unaware that Everest straddles Tibet and Nepal, some people were apparently concluding the deaths had been on our side of the mountain. Speculation and misinformation was running rampant.

"The media crush was overwhelming," Steve remembers of that time back in Colorado. "After having left the expedition in Kathmandu, it was kind of like the kid had gone away to college, had got a job and now was out on his own. I was just another voyeur looking in from the States. I'm a terrible spectator ... But when people died on the north side, it pulled me back and kept me from being a spectator."

Back on the trail to Everest, I felt disheartened. The north side of the mountain might just as well have been on the moon. Although the expeditions there were only a few miles away, thanks to the nuances of radio signals, people half a world away could reach them by satellite telephone easier than we could by radio. Visions of the avalanches that had obliterated our two high camps on the north side during our second expedition to Everest in 1994 flew immediately into my mind. Fortunately, those camps had not been occupied at the time.

"Damn!" I thought to myself. "Just when we needed a little good luck."

> *[The Western Cwm] was not so silent now,*
> *but filled day and night with the sound of the wind.*
> *Sometimes we were not actually in the wind:*
> *we would only hear it as a roaring on the peaks*
> *far above us. But then it would come down.*
> *It would hit us, not like moving air, but like*
> *some sort of terrible wild animal let loose by the gods,*
> *and until it stopped we could not move or work*
> *or do anything except barely keep alive.*
>
> — TENZING NORGAY,
> *Man of Everest*

With just two weeks left before our climbing permit expired on May 31, I knew that a setback as substantial as the loss of our Advanced Base Camp could mean the end of our summit chances on Everest. Strategically, it was a critically important camp and if it had been destroyed, it would take at least a week or more of work to reestablish it. That would put us to May 23 at the earliest before we could even begin a summit attempt.

That was almost too late. It would still take several days to properly clear the mountain of our tents and equipment after that in order to be down to base camp by the beginning of the monsoon. After that, mild temperatures and snow accumulations in the Icefall would make it unsafe to climb in, and virtually impassable. We were running out of time.

I remember sitting on the hillside after that radio call and looking out over the Khumbu Valley. It was a wonderful morning, cool and crisp, and I looked out again on a gloriously beautiful panoramic view, but I did not see it. I felt deflated and violated, like someone had just stolen something intimately important from me. They had taken away my dream.

"She's [Everest] not done with us yet," I said to Dave. "She's lashing out in anger. Maybe no one will summit this season."

It was a rare moment of pessimism. Quickly, I tried to steer my thoughts back to something more positive. The reality was we were still at least a day's walk from base camp. It would take me another day to get to Advanced Base Camp from there, even if I was in top form. Clearly, there was nothing I could do today. The situation was completely outside my control. That, in a sense, was liberating.

I resigned myself to taking one more step up the hill toward base camp. On the positive side, I didn't have to expend energy reestablishing Camp 2. For that, at least, I was thankful. Perhaps there was a reason I was below base camp. Perhaps I wasn't supposed to be there.

"You are to report to base camp for 9 a.m. tomorrow morning," Jason told us emphatically over the radio. "We will need all the manpower we can muster."

We started up the trail again. A few hours later, I was snapped from my thoughts by a team of yaks bearing wildly down on us. I jumped to the side of the trail in just enough time to keep from being run over. The yaks were carrying the gear of our last trekking team as it descended back to Lukla.

Seconds later, the trekkers appeared. They greeted us like a couple of heroes, hugging us warmly. I felt about as far from a hero as you could get. One of our key camps was damaged, possibly destroyed, our expedition was fast running out of time, and I wasn't even on the mountain.

They didn't care. We exchanged stories, posed for pictures, and even shared water bottles. I felt like someone had just popped me into a toaster — I could feel my insides warm up as the electricity coursed through me.

There is something special about the human touch. When you haven't had anyone hug you in a long time, you savor it like fine wine. You soak in the moment, holding onto it as long as you can.

I remember a special chat with Paul Braun. He is a real estate broker for Colliers, and among his many amazing physical achievements, he had run the grueling Angeles Crest Endurance Run — 101 miles over the California countryside, some 22,306 feet up and 26,210 feet down. I had met him at a speaking presentation for Colliers in San Diego some months before when he'd picked Jamie and me up at the airport. Before we'd even been in his vehicle five minutes, he'd shoved a notepad and pen into my hand and said:

"Here. Write down the titles of the finest five books on Everest and adventure that you know."

Paul was a keener. Like most parents, he had struggled to find a balance between the demands of his professional life and his family. I'd had a good feeling about him, like I'd see him again.

Sure enough, there he was, looking surprisingly strong despite what must have been for him and the rest of his party an arduous journey to and from base camp.

"I've had no problems," he said proudly. "It's been absolutely great."

A particularly humorous moment happened a few minutes later. One of the trekkers, Paula O'Keefe, a Lotus employee from Dublin, Ireland, wanted to take a photo of me with some of her trekking companions. After six weeks or so on Everest, you're not the prettiest sight in the world. I was dressed in the one-piece fleece body suit I'd worn day-in and day-out almost that whole time. It came complete with a variety of zippers so I could answer the call without disrobing. Each of these zippers

> *Like most parents, he had struggled to find a balance between the demands of his professional life and his family.*

had a large, brightly colored pull-tab attached to it so, if necessary, I could quickly find it in the dark with bulky mitts on in the event of an "*emergency.*" Two of these pulls tabs were positioned at the height of my, well … unmentionables.

Paula was all set to take the shot when suddenly she paused, looked up from behind the camera with a big grin on her face and said with all the Irish brash she could muster:

"Now Alan, this photo may go on Lotus's website. Mind your dangly bits!"

The entire trekking party, including Dave and I, exploded in laughter.

The entire meeting took no more than about 20 minutes, but it definitely was a diamond in my day. It was something of a turning point in our fortunes on the mountain too. By evening, Dave and I had learned by radio that damage to Camp 2 was not as extensive as we had previously feared and that things could be repaired within just a few days. We were still in the game.

"Take as much time getting back to base camp as you want," came back the reply from Jason.

I was relieved, but still realistic. We couldn't afford any more delays. If we got even one, it would probably mean the end of our expedition.

That evening, Dave and I overnighted in the tiny Sherpa enclave of Gorak Shep, the last outpost of civilization before base camp. After watching a beautiful sunset, we ate at one of only two small Sherpa lodges there, drank orange soda pop until we were bloated and burping, and lounged in the warmth of the yak-dung fire by a central stove. Our host was Tshering Sherpa from the village of Khunde, some distance away. He knew Ang Temba very well.

I felt an immediate sense of sanctuary in Tshering Sherpa's presence. Although we'd heard horror stories about visitors getting sick from the terrible hygienic standards in Gorak Shep, I knew somehow that we would be okay. I was back in the company of the Sherpas.

That night, I stepped outside the lodge to brush my teeth. What an amazing place this was. There we were, tucked in amongst hills of barren boulders and windblown sand, literally in the highest high-altitude desert on Earth, yet surrounded by the highest mountains too. The galaxy of stars above me was unbelievable. The nearest true electric light was hundreds of miles away.

Slowly, I savored the sight, listening to the sounds of Tshering Sherpa, his wife, and companions cook up meal after meal of boiled potatoes, fried eggs and spicy noodles for a lodge full of tired trekkers. In silence, I looked up at the mountain majesty that surrounded me and for the first time in the expedition, I was filled with a sense of wonder and peace. I absorbed it through my pores and felt it penetrate to my soul.

"Oh, Alan, it will be all right," I said to myself, thinking of the words Ang Temba had shared with me years before. "Even if we don't make it to the top, I will at least have experienced this. It's beautiful and it's here."

A Pact is Formed

*Until one is committed there is hesitancy, the
chance to draw back, always ineffectiveness.
Concerning all acts of initiative (and creation)
there is one elementary truth, the ignorance
of which kills countless ideas and splendid plans:
that the moment one definitely commits oneself,
then Providence moves, too. All sorts of things
occur to help one that would never otherwise
have occurred. A whole stream of events issues
from the decision, raising in one's favor all manner
of unforeseen incidents and meetings and material
assistance, which no man could have dreamt
would have come his way.* — W.H. MURRAY,
Scottish mountaineer

THE NEXT DAY in Gorak Shep was a gloriously sunny Saturday
morning. Just after 10 a.m., Dave and I set out to hike up the
nearby trekking peak of Kalapatar, an 18,300-foot tall "hill"
that on a clear day offers the most breathtaking view of Everest
in the world.

The day was magnificent, not a cloud in the sky, surprisingly
warm and with only a slight wind at our altitude. In less than
an hour, we were perched on the summit, hunkered down
against a frigid blast, but gazing up at the most awe-inspiring
sight I've ever seen —Everest from head to toe. Before us stood
the world's tallest pyramid, massive and imposing in her
blackness and absolutely chilling in her immensity. From the
peak tore a plume of snow projecting easily half a mile in the

jet stream wind, but looking so deceptively close, you'd swear you could reach out and touch it.

> *She was a mother hen, and the other mountains*
> *were chicks under her wings.* — Tenzing Norgay,
> *Man of Everest*

I knew that as long as the winds continued at the speed they were raging, the summit was untouchable. So close and yet so far, I thought. It would take a tremendous effort to return to base camp, pick my way through the Icefall yet again, slog slowly up the Western Cwm, climb up onto the steep ice of the Lhotse Face and eventually to the South Col at 26,000 feet. I could see the whole route in my mind's eye and most of it with my physical eye too. I wondered about that unknown stretch of snow and ice above the South Col. I knew that was the "Death Zone." It looked the same as the rest of the route, but it was exponentially more dangerous. There, the stakes of the already high-stakes game became even higher, especially now that Doug could not venture above base camp. He had taken advantage of the lull in climbing activity to descend down the valley for a quick visit with his wife and two daughters who'd flown all the way from Colorado to see him.

I was to learn later that that descent had been something of a summit for Doug:

"Kami Tshering and Pema Temba, two of our Sherpas, accompanied me for the first 15 miles to their village of Pangboche. We left just after lunch and these guys bloody flew down the hillside. Believe me, when it comes to walking (I had to jog to keep up) across rough, rocky terrain, these men are professionals. With baseball caps and backpacks flying, they ran down the terminal moraine. I watched in absolute amazement and understood, for the first time, the grace and elegance that ballet has always tried to capture. In the long shadows of evening, we rounded the corner into the Pheriche valley and smelled the first scrub juniper, unbelievably sweet after seven weeks on the glacier. An hour after nightfall, we

"As always on an odyssey such as this, an inward journey has accompanied the outward."

– Dr. Doug Rovira

FROM EVEREST TO ENLIGHTENMENT

marched into Pangboche where I spent the night in Kami's home. Having consumed some sort of alcoholic beverage in each of the towns we had passed on the way down, I was feeling no pain.

"I met Lucy and the girls in Namche early the next afternoon. My daughter, Elizabeth, 7, and Madeline, 10, are great campers. As the only Caucasian children in the valley, they are often the center of attention. They've had no problems with the altitude and have remained healthy and happy. It was wonderful beyond words to be reunited with my family after two months. Madeline regaled me with stories and Elizabeth peppered me with questions. Most days, we could catch a glimpse of Mt. Everest with a huge snow plume blowing off the summit. I loved introducing them to friends I'd made along the way and, most of all, enjoyed reading them to sleep at night....

"The summit is not to be for me this time. I'm disappointed, but far from defeated. As always on an odyssey such as this, an inward journey has accompanied the outward. By moments, I have glimpsed truth — in the wind on a distant summit, in the last words of a child as she slips into peaceful slumber and dreams, dreams I'll never know, with two dark-faced men walking in the long shadows of evening. In precious few moments, I have glimpsed truth."

While Doug was gazing up at Everest from below us in Namche Bazaar, Dave and I were face to face with the mountain on the top of Kalapatar.

"My God, that's *big!*" Dave hollered through the howling blast. "It's immense."

The prodigious mass that is Everest seems to hang in the heavens. It is supported aloft not only by an imposing base, but by some unseen, yet unmistakable force. No photograph, film, or videotape I have seen comes close to capturing its magnitude. It is indescribably huge and its preeminence has as much or more to do with its spiritual dimension as its physical dimension. It transcends the physical and is simultaneously metaphysical. There is such a presence to the peak that it speaks directly to your soul. There, it moves and touches you, deeply.

The prodigious mass that is Everest seems to hang in the heavens. It is supported aloft not only by an imposing base, but by some unseen, yet unmistakable force.

Quickly, Dave and I descended to Gorak Shep. By noon, we were ordering ourselves up as many plates of potatoes as we could hold down, preparing for the struggle ahead. Every time I felt like I couldn't take another bite, I remembered how huge Everest was, how much energy I would need to climb her and return safely to base camp. Then, I'd force down one more mouthful. It was wonderful to relax in the soothing rays of the sun outside one of the lodges and sip as much Sherpa tea as we could stomach. Life was great, I thought.

Suddenly, my moment of bliss was interrupted by a radio call from base camp:

"If you're not here this afternoon," a voice said, "we could make decisions that might adversely affect your summit chances."

Instantly, I felt the rage of only a few days before welling up inside me. I snapped the radio to my mouth.

"Only a few short hours ago we were told to take as much time as we wanted. We have all agreed what the mission of this expedition is. Are you saying you now intend to abandon that mission?"

Silence.

We agreed to talk again in a couple of hours when tempers had had a chance to cool down. The last thing I wanted to do was burn myself out climbing Kalapatar, hiking up to base camp in one day, and then leaving the next day for the summit. While other climbers might have thought that to be reasonable, I knew that in my now physically weakened state, it was unrealistic. To reach the summit of Everest, I knew I would have to parcel my energy out carefully. I could not afford to squander it unnecessarily, and especially not on something as unnecessary as anger.

Until returning from Everest, anger had always been one of my biggest weaknesses. It is, in some ways, a manifestation of my passion, the dark side to the bright side of my otherwise upbeat, high-energy personality. Through meditation, I have learned how to create peace within myself even amid tense situations and thus manage my anger, but I remain ever-susceptible to it. Sometimes I manage it. Sometimes it manages me.

My father, whom I consider to be an outstanding strategic thinker, would not have been impressed. My mother, a kind and sensitive woman, would not have been too proud either. Yet we are who we are, warts and all. Most of the time we are at our best, but sometimes, we are at our worst. This was one of those moments.

At that moment, we could have used a mediator. Steve would tell me later of another moment of conflict in his Everest experiences during which a Sherpa stepped into the middle of a very heated argument as well.

"He was the Sirdar (head Sherpa) for another expedition," Steve says, "and he had been deformed as a child. But he was very intelligent. He saw what was happening, interceded and got everyone to come to an understanding. The guy was a true master of diplomacy. He had no education, no training, but it was a lesson a few of our political leaders could take note of."

We are who we are — warts and all, most of the time at our best, but sometimes at our worst.

Dave stepped in as my surrogate Sherpa. He said he shared my frustration with the sudden change in the schedule and encouraged me to hang in there. For a moment, I sought refuge inside the lodge. There I was surprised to see two of our Sherpas, Kami Tshering and Pema Temba, enjoying a cup of tea with the proprietor. They too were on their way back to base camp after descending down the Khumbu Valley with Doug to spend time with their families. Unlike me, however, they hadn't the slightest hesitation about returning to base camp that day. It was a walk in the park for them.

I greeted them as warmly as I could considering my emotional state, but then, as if providentially, Kami took me quietly aside. What he said instantly shifted my focus from inside to outside.

"You will use oxygen?" he asked gently.

"Likely I will," I said, "but I will decide that very soon."

"Good," he said. "It is necessary."

There was a long pause. Kami took a sip of tea and turned and looked me straight in the eye. He seemed to look through me then, as if connecting to something inside me of which not even I was aware. I had never seen him look at anyone that way before, but I suddenly felt a deep connection to him. He was speaking to my soul. What he said next profoundly affected me:

"1991 … no summit," he said in a dulcet tone. "1994 … no summit."

Then, in a fashion very uncharacteristic of a Sherpa, he leaned forward:

"1997 … very important … summit."

In that instant, with those few words, I knew he understood why we were there. More importantly, he understood how necessary it was for me to give it everything I had. He understood completely.

I bonded with Kami at that moment. I felt different about him than I had about others who had questioned my oxygen decision. He questioned it too, obviously, but it was that look in his eyes and those simple, but powerful words. A huge boost of energy coursed through me, as if from a Supreme source.

I did not know it then, but the Sherpas had decided that Kami would accompany me on my summit attempt. To that point, I had hoped to climb with Lhakpa Tshering, who had summited with Pat Morrow in 1982 when Pat had become the second Canadian to climb Everest. I was to learn later that Lhakpa had chosen to climb with Jamie and Jason, apparently believing I was unsafe because of my decision to attempt Everest without bottled oxygen.

If I had known that then, it would have dampened my spirits considerably. I would also have instantly changed my position. When a Sherpa thinks one of your decisions is unsafe, that is a clear sign something is wrong. Of course, it never feels good when someone you respect does not consider you up to a challenge. It is worse still when they decide they wish to separate themselves from you because they believe you to be a potential liability. We all have personal pride.

That didn't matter then. All that mattered was that Kami and I had formed a pact. He would stay the course with me. I sensed that, beyond words. He was committing to me and

It never feels good when someone you respect does not consider you up to a challenge.

when a Sherpa commits to you to climb Everest, he is committing with his life. He understands the stakes of the game and he throws his dice in with yours. It is a gamble for your lives, and it is amongst the biggest commitments you can make in life. When you commit to marriage, you are committing for life, but when you commit to climbing to and from the top of the world, you are committing *with* your life.

Kami had first summited Everest in 1993 with the first British woman to climb the mountain, Rebecca Stephens. He had been with our expedition in 1994, and thus I knew he was very experienced, as all the Sherpas are. Rebecca had called him "a prince." I would learn why.

So, there we were, a Sherpa and a Canadian, united by a common dream, mine to make it safely to and from the summit and Kami's to ensure my safety in doing so. The oxygen debate suddenly became less important to me then. Now I was looking into the whites of the eyes of the man who would accompany me on my quest. He had to know he could count on me and me on him. He could and I could. It was powerful.

A few minutes later, I walked outside and radioed to base camp.

"Kami and Pema are leaving now to join you in base camp," I said. "Dave and I will join you tomorrow, as previously agreed. Let's do the dream."

The climber apologized for his previous behavior. We reconciled. The past was forgotten.

Instinctively, I knew I had to stay out of base camp as long as possible. My body needed just a few more hours of the air at lower altitude, even if it was only about 800 feet lower. I felt like I was dying in base camp. I could breathe easier in Gorak Shep. Besides, there were fresh faces there, trekkers from all over the world. They brought a wider perspective to my ever-narrowing perception.

With this decision behind me, I slept like a log that night. When I awoke the next morning for the hike to base camp with Dave, I could already feel the anticipation and anxiety of an impending summit bid starting to build inside me. It reminded

When you commit to marriage, you are committing for life, but when you commit to climbing to and from the top of the world, you are committing with your life.

me of the jitters I used to get just before competing as a gymnast. Inevitably, I'd find myself wondering at the last minute why I had chosen to put myself through such discomfort.

Now, as then, I knew why. I felt anxious, but it was right. Together with Dave and a new friend, a Scottish trekker by the name of Mark Litterick from Glasgow, we laughed and joked as we hiked our way slowly to the door of my dream, cracking jokes and cajoling one another. There is something marvelous about the Scots. I have yet to meet one who wasn't a character. Mark was no exception — high spirited, witty, and superb company. He had been sent to cut the tension, I think.

We took a new route to base camp that morning, up the moraine of a ridge that hung below base camp, but which afforded us a bird's eye view of that little tent village I had called home for over a month. It was an exciting time, a time I will not soon forget. I remember looking down into camp and thinking, "Well, in 10 days or so, I'll know one way or the other."

By noon, we were there. We were greeted warmly by the team, some of the Sherpas, our entire support staff, and even our Nepali liaison officer, Buddhinath "Booty" Bhattarai. After lunch, a shower and a shave, I began to pack for the summit. Painstakingly, I went through my gear and tried to eliminate every possible ounce of excess weight that would not be needed on summit day.

Not everyone on our team was fortunate enough to be packing for the top. Doug had noticed what he called "fluff" clouding the vision of one of his eyes. Upon closer examination, we determined it was not a piece of down from his sleeping bag. It was retinal hemorrhaging — a bursting of the tiny vessels in the eye from exertion in the reduced air pressure of high altitude. If he tried to climb higher, he might go blind.

"And so I sit here at the foot of the highest mountain on Earth," he wrote home to friends, "enjoying the warmth and 'rich air' of 17,300 feet, ambition in one hand, common sense in the other...."

To make the best of a bad situation, Doug busied himself by helping out in base camp however he could. In a daily display

> *"And so I sit here at the foot of the highest mountain on Earth,"* he wrote home to friends, *"... ambition in one hand, common sense in the other...."*
>
> – Dr. Doug Rovira

of teamwork that even caught the Sherpas by surprise, he helped one of our kitchen boys, Padam Bahadur Limbu, fetch water from a melt pool several hundred yards away on the glacier.

"One morning I followed Padam, ignoring his protest, with the second jug," Doug remembers. "We had to break the ice to fill our eight gallon jugs. Then he helped load the 66-pound container onto my neck and back. At first, I didn't think I could stand. Holding the tump-line next to my ears, I barely staggered across the loose rock back to camp, wondering how Padam does it 12 times a day. On the way, Sherpas from other camps were hooting and hollering to Padam, surprised to see a pale face carrying water. The work seemed basic and helpful so I continued to carry water in the morning. After several days, I asked Padam about the jeering — was I doing something inappropriate?

"Padam smiled and said, 'No, it is nothing like that. They say that one who carries water is brother.' To be called 'brother' by these people is one of the greatest compliments of my life."

As Doug and Padam shouldered their loads, the wind on the summit began to diminish. The howling gale started to sputter and the weather forecast looked guardedly optimistic. If we were to summit and be down off the mountain by the start of the monsoon, it was now or never. Our gun was loaded. All we had to do now was pull the trigger.

That night, after a late supper, I pulled my sleeping bag over my head and turned in in my tent just after 9:30 p.m. I slept fitfully, like a cat perched apprehensively on a tiny ledge between the past, the present, and the future. My mind raced with the possibilities of what might lie ahead....

> *One sees great things from the valleys;*
> *only small things from the peak.* — G. K. CHESTERTON,
> British essayist, 1874–1936

21

Decision Points

We promise according to our hopes,
and perform according to our fears.

— FRANÇOIS DE LA ROCHEFOUCAULD,
seventeenth-century French writer of epigrams

IT WAS A LONG, SHORT NIGHT, the kind that seems
interminable, but ends sooner than you'd like.

At 3:45 a.m., I was stirred from my unsettled slumber by
the alarm on my watch. To ensure I heard it, I'd tucked it
under my hat. At first, I fumbled around in my sleeping bag
trying to find the darn thing so I could turn it off, but finally
after some frustration realized it was on the top of my head.
I laughed at myself.

After pulling on my climbing suit and boots, I picked up my
pack, went to the loo and then stumbled my way across the
rocks to the kitchen tent. There, I managed to force down a
few cups of hot tea. One of our support team Sherpas, Ang
Dawa, was there to greet me. He was one of our cook boys, but
a boy he was not. He was an amazing man. Even at the
ungodly hour of 4 a.m., in the dark at 17,000 feet in a freezing
cold tent on Everest after weeks of work, he was still cheerful.
A broad smile of glowing white teeth shone out at me through
the darkness. By the light of a kerosene lamp, he made me a
breakfast of boiled eggs and noodles with all the care a loving
mother would give a son.

During the expedition, Ang Dawa had endeared himself to the entire team, not only because he was a workhorse, as all of the Sherpas were, but because he was especially kind and gentle. No matter what the hour, the weather, or the circumstances, his demeanor never changed. He was the epitome of peace and reassurance. A light seemed to shine out from his eyes. He was a wonderful person — soft spoken, humble, and warm.

At the appointed hour of 5 a.m., I was joined by Shyam Pun, our cook from Advanced Base Camp, who was to accompany me back to his haunt at 21,000 feet in the Western Cwm to feed us prior to our summit bids. A small party of well wishers, among them Dave, Pema Temba, Bruce Kirkby, Mark Litterick and our Nepalese liaison officer, Booty, was there to see us off. Jeff Rhoads had decided to stay another day in base camp to greet his wife, Kellie, who was to arrive that day with a private trekking party she was leading. As my plan was to climb to Camp 2 and then rest a day there, Jeff would skip the rest day and join me in Camp 2 on the beginning of my climb to Camp 3 two days later. It was all coming together.

By the first rays of the gray Himalayan morning, Shyam and I set out from base camp. I had gone no more than four steps when the unimaginable happened. In mid-cough, I suddenly heard a popping sound on the left side of my chest. In seconds, I was doubled over in pain, clutching my side and groaning in agony. I felt the burning sensation I knew only too well from my experience as a gymnast, the tearing of a muscle.

Because there is about one half the atmospheric pressure in base camp that there is at sea level, the chest cavity can expand more than it conventionally does during inhalation or coughing. Because the dry, desert-like air at high altitude stimulates the body's coughing response, this can put substantial stress on the chest muscles used in breathing. The result is that the intercostal muscles, the ones between the ribs that aid in respiration, can actually tear when you cough or breathe strenuously.

This is what had happened to me. I felt like someone was stabbing a white-hot poker into my side and twisting it with everything they had. Wheezing wildly, I hung over the rocks in front of my teammates in pain and anguish.

"Christ! What timing," I said to myself. Then I became angry.

"No damn way!" I thought. "No damn way! To hell with it. To hell with this whole damn place. This is just madness."

A second later, something inside me changed. I'm not sure how or why; it just did. I moved to solution, or at least to temporary damage control.

"Bruce," I forced out between struggled breaths. "Do you have any pain killers?"

He disappeared to his tent. Ang Dawa put his arm around me. He had watched me innumerable times during the expedition try to clean out my blocked sinuses by hanging my head over a bowl of steaming hot water in the kitchen tent. He knew what I'd been through to get to this day.

In a minute, Bruce reappeared. In one fluid, sweeping motion, he tossed me a bottle of Advil. To catch it, I had to stand up suddenly. Once again, my chest burned.

"Thanks buddy," I said, wincing. "You're a Godsend."

I could do one heck of a good TV commercial for Advil, I'll tell you. I popped a couple of tablets, wrapped my side with a stretch bandage and pulled my left arm across my chest as a splint. I remembered how Laurie Skreslet had climbed Everest after suffering broken ribs when he'd fallen into a crevasse in the Icefall pulling out a fellow climber in 1982.

"If Skreslet can climb this thing with a broken rib," I thought to myself, "I can climb it with a torn muscle."

> *"This is the time you must do it," I kept telling myself. "You must do it or die."*
>
> *… we will go to the top together. We will get there. We must get there. I must get to the top or die.…*
>
> — TENZING NORGAY,
> *Man of Everest*

"To hell with this whole damn place. This is just madness."

Ang Dawa helped me. With a look that communicated sensitivity and courage, he quietly sent me on my way. Slowly, listing to one side like a limping sailboat, I bore into the wind and headed into the Icefall.

The first 20 minutes were terrible. The bad news was it hurt like hell. The good news was it only hurt when I breathed. After a while, however, the Advil began to take effect and although I was still in a great deal of pain, I was at least able to function. I was grateful for the compassion I'd received in base camp, and for the medical research that had led to the development of painkillers.

Shyam and I had climbed for about an hour when to my chagrin, we came upon a collapse in the Icefall. My heart sunk.

Was I really not supposed to be in here today? Was someone or something trying to give me a message? Or, was that entity just testing me again?

Thank goodness for Shyam. With all the composure only years of experience can give you, he carefully picked his way through the melee of fallen ice blocks and regained the route about 20 minutes later. Above and below the collapse, he made sure he held all the ropes taut on the ladder bridges so that when I crossed, I had the maximum degree of stability. It made a huge difference to know he really cared.

It took Shyam and me four hours to reach Camp 1 above the Icefall, a very slow time. There, we huddled together in the vestibule of our lone expedition tent and shared a few boiled eggs. I was grateful for such luxuries. Without a replenishment of critically needed calories, after the nausea of the early morning start, I would likely never have gotten beyond Camp 1. I tried to remind myself not to linger there, for with every passing hour the risk of avalanches and serac falls increased. I remembered a story Doug had told me about a frightening night he had spent there:

"I was awakened several times by the wind slapping the tent.... A huge ice avalanche broke off the west shoulder of Everest and roared for what seemed like a whole minute. I was sure it would crush my tent, but when I could trace its path in the morning, it was over half a mile away!"

I didn't want anything like that to happen to us, so half an hour later, we were off again. Shyam joined a Sherpa from another expedition on his way to Camp 2 and we agreed to meet again at Advanced Base Camp. For the next hour and a half, I climbed alone. With every step, I knew I was coming closer to the dream, but without knowing if the winds would cooperate, I also knew that one way or the other, this was the last time I would take these difficult steps.

The Cwm, as usual, became progressively hotter as the sun rose. "The endless hill," as the stretch from Camp 1 to Camp 2 had been dubbed, proved to be just that that morning. I plodded my way interminably upward.

> *… mostly there was only a great snowy stillness,*
> *in which the only sounds were our own voices,*
> *our own breathing, the crunch of our boots, and*
> *the creaking of the pack-straps.* — TENZING NORGAY,
> *Man of Everest*

I had to face myself — and my own inadequacies.

Those 90 minutes were amongst the most important of the expedition for me, if not some of the most significant in my life. It was a time when I truly melded to the mountain, assessing where she was, and most importantly, where I was relative to her.

There was no longer any room for idealism or unrealistic expectations about climbing Everest without bottled oxygen. Now, I had to face myself, and my own inadequacies.

By the time I reached Camp 2 at 11 a.m., I knew it would be foolish to attempt Everest without the use of bottled oxygen. My watch told me I simply wasn't moving fast enough. In fact, I was slower and weaker than I had been before. It was disappointing, but it was the harsh reality. I could not argue with the facts. They were as obvious as the watch on my wrist. Stopwatches don't lie.

Although some 700 people have climbed Everest using bottled oxygen, only about 70 have managed to do it without. Austrians Peter Habeler and Reinhold Messner first climbed the mountain without supplementary oxygen in 1978. All the scientific data at the time indicated it was impossible to climb Everest without bottled oxygen. "You will go up sane men," they were told, "but come down mad men — if you come down at all."

In one of the most courageous ascents of Everest ever recorded, Habeler and Messner defied the skeptics and proved them wrong. Although both men came close to dying during the summit bid, which saw them crawl on their hands and knees the last few feet to the top, it was the descent that proved the most potentially lethal. Habeler sprained his ankle so badly in an avalanche he thought it was broken. Messner went snow blind after he spent too much time with his goggles raised on the summit. Miraculously, the lame managed to lead the blind back to the relative safety of the South Col and history was made. Habeler wrote about the epic struggle in his book, *The Lonely Victory*. I believe it is one of the finest books ever written about human achievement. It moved me to tears.

In an appalling illustration of the pervasiveness of negativity in the world, however, some die-hard doubters still maintained Habeler and Messner had "cheated." In a way, they had. They had cheated death.

To climb Everest "without gas," as they say in climbing circles, remains perhaps the crowning physical achievement on the planet. To accomplish this amazing feat, you have to be fit, healthy, determined, experienced, and above all, quick! I was certainly fit, determined, and experienced, but unfortunately, I was far from healthy or fast.

At 11 a.m., I plodded into Advanced Base Camp, my side aching, but my spirits still high. After a light lunch, I rested the balance of the day in my tent. I felt good, but tired. Around 5 p.m., Jamie and Jason started testing oxygen masks. It was then that I told Jason of my decision to climb with gas.

"I wasn't gleeful in the sense that I had 'won' and Alan had 'lost,'" Jason remembers, "— to the contrary. I was encouraged at his potential now to *really* make the summit. I was happy for him, for the team, and for everyone on the mountain. I was

"You will go up sane men," they were told, "but come down mad men — if you come down at all."

truly worried about his safety, the safety of our team, and the safety of others on the mountain if he was to make the climb without oxygen.... They [the other expedition leaders on the mountain] were all concerned that Alan might create issues for them on the mountain, and they all wanted to avoid them.... So, I worked closely with them to assure them that we had a safe team, and would do all of the things we could do to avoid issues that unnecessarily increased the danger or likelihood of having an accident. All the leaders vowed to work together, and Alan's insistence to climb without oxygen somewhat compromised my ability to coordinate things with the other teams.... Once Alan agreed to use gas, I was welcomed and brought in more on things, which was of great benefit to our team and Alan's subsequent success on the mountain.

"... maybe we were all a bit 'shell shocked' by the accidents the year before on Everest [the disaster in the spring of 1996]. It wouldn't be an easy thing to go through that kind of thing again when we returned home, much less if it meant losing a good friend like Alan.... [I tried to see] the larger picture."

Within half an hour, I had chosen a reasonably comfortable oxygen mask. It felt strangely claustrophobic to be wearing it, like I was in my own little world. I knew then how fighter pilots and astronauts must feel behind their masks. You were somehow detached from your environment.

The most unsettling aspect of wearing a mask was that you could not easily see your feet. Rather than simply glancing down, you had to consciously crane your head forward, rather like having to bend all the way over just to see if your shoes were tied. This visual impediment, more than anything, was the most frightening part about wearing a mask. If you cannot see your feet, as a climber, you cannot see the ground, and if you cannot see the ground, you have no way to anchor your world. It can also mean you've fallen.

Given my chest muscle, my persistent head and chest cold, my physiological and psychological deterioration, and the still fierce summit winds, I knew I was only going to get this one chance to climb Everest, if she allowed us. So, I resigned myself to the use of the mask and spent quite a bit of time getting accustomed to it.

Later that evening, we talked to base camp on the radio. I was aghast to learn that Jeff had suddenly fallen sick. Apparently, he was running a fever and his throat was very sore. We told him to hang in there and see what the next 36 hours brought. I still wasn't scheduled to leave Camp 2 for another day anyway, so there was still time. Nevertheless, he sounded understandably anxious.

Jamie and Jason were to leave early the next morning for Camp 3. So, after bidding them good-bye, I headed off to my tent.

In the back of my mind, I began to weigh my options. I knew I might need to accompany a Sherpa and make a summit bid without Jeff, if necessary. Because I had climbed a fair amount with Jeff, this prospect did not excite me, but I knew my own decisions had led me to where I was. I would have to accept the outcome of my decision.

That night, I prayed the winds would subside and Jason and Jamie would have a safe trip to and from the summit. The next day, May 20, the weather forecast called for a potential reduction in the summit wind speed two days hence on May 22. So, Jamie and Jason decided to wait another day in Camp 2. At this point, a miscalculation of a single day in the weather might easily eradicate our summit chances. So fatigued were we all, so strung out from the physical and psychological strain of the previous weeks, that we could not afford to make one strategic mistake. If we moved into Camp 4 at 26,000 feet too early and were forced to wait it out there at the bottom of the "Death Zone," we knew it could lead to the end of our dream. We'd waited almost three weeks for the winds to subside. We could wait another day. Nevertheless, the urge to "go for it" was almost overpowering.

About noon, I spoke on the radio to Jeff in base camp. Things didn't look good. He said his throat was so badly swollen he was incapable of swallowing.

"The doc says it's some kind of infection or something," he reported.

Everyone knew we had all reached a decision point. If Jeff couldn't join me, I had a choice — I could wait one or two more days and gamble that his condition would improve or I could team up with Jason and Jamie and together, all three of us could launch a combined summit attempt with as many of the Sherpas as we could.

A long period of intense discussion followed in Camp 2. There, at the head of the Western Cwm, in full view of the massive Lhotse Face and the towering summit pyramid that hung above us, we struggled to come to one of the most difficult decisions on the expedition.

Since Jeff was my climbing partner, I was given the unenviable task of talking things through with him.

"What do you think?" I asked over the radio.

"Don't wait for me," he said in a raspy voice. "Your summit chance is here. That's what we came here for. If you decide to go for it, though, hold back a Sherpa so that if I can kick this infection in a few days, I still might have a chance at the summit with him."

"Roger," I said. "We copy. Stand by for more information."

More discussion ensued.

The feeling in Camp 2 was mixed. Some felt that if we held back any Sherpa firepower now, the first summit team might not make it to the top. Then, after the fact, we'd all be faced with "we should haves." Others felt that in return for busting his butt to help get us into position for a summit attempt, Jeff was at least due a shot himself, even if only with one Sherpa.

Back and forth, back and forth, we hashed it out. If we didn't leave a Sherpa behind for Jeff, it was argued, some of us could be seen as selfish, egocentric bastards who said they cared about the team and "worked together," but in the end, showed otherwise by denying him a shot at the summit. If we went with every Sherpa we had and didn't make it, everybody would lose. Jeff wouldn't even get his chance either.

Our "best," we decided, (knowing full well the relativity of the term under the circumstances) was to give it everything we had — every man still standing, every Sherpa capable of the climb, every bottle of oxygen we could get into position, every available tent, sleeping bag, and remaining ounce of food and combine it all with all the courage and commitment we could muster.

> *"Because we must try again," I said.*
> *"We must try everything."*
>
> — Tenzing Norgay,
> *Man of Everest*

I called down to Jeff and told him what we were thinking. In one of the most amazing displays of maturity and commitment I have ever seen, he supported our position. He was deeply disappointed, we could tell, having himself also been beaten back by Everest twice before, but he knew the reality of what we were facing.

"Get your butts up there and go for it," he said courageously. "But come back safely."

That was all he said.

I sat on a rock in Advanced Base Camp with the radio clutched in my hand and hung my head. I felt like someone had let the air out of my body. I was limp and lifeless. I tried to distract myself by sorting my summit gear for the third time, checking, double-checking and triple checking every little detail. It was nothing more than busy work really, but it was necessary to get through the moment.

That night, as I lay in my tent, I tried to put the whole uncomfortable situation out of my mind. Tomorrow, we were to climb to Camp 3 on the Lhotse Face. From there, if the winds and weather looked favorable, we would head up to Camp 4. From there, without so much as pausing to sleep, we would mount our summit bid after a few hours rest. If I hoped to pull this off, I had to put the past behind me and focus on the future. More to the point, I had to focus on the present, now!

About 2 a.m., I awoke alone in my tent with a sore throat. Everest was shaping up to be the biggest battle of my life — surprise, surprise. To survive, I knew I'd have to run it out so far beyond where I had previously been in my life that I'd lose sight of where and who I'd been. To get to the summit, I'd have to undergo a personal metamorphosis; the way a caterpillar enters into a chrysalis and later miraculously emerges as a butterfly. While in this transcendent state of suspension, however, there were many potential predators ready and eager to devour them.

There was no question that, metaphorically speaking at least, I was crawling on my belly like a caterpillar. Now, wrapped in the down chrysalis of my sleeping bag, I hung in suspension aside the world's tallest mountain. There, I awaited nature's transformation, my own.

Fear and dread are my life insurance.

— ERHARD LORETAN,
Swiss mountaineer, pioneer of many bold
new routes, methods and rapid ascents
in the Himalayas

22
To the
Edge of the Dream

I will lift up mine eyes unto the hills,
from whence cometh my help. — PSALM 121:1

THE ALARM ON MY WATCH sounded in Camp 2 at 4:45 a.m. and once again, I fumbled in the dark to find it amid a groggy stupor.

No matter how long you sleep at high altitude, you never awaken refreshed. The partial pressure of oxygen in the air above 17,000 feet is not enough for the body's cells to regenerate. This means that regardless of how long you've been asleep, reentering the world is always unpleasant. Usually, the first thing you do is cough. If you've got any respiratory infection, you usually then start to cough up phlegm and try your best not to gag on it or vomit. It really can be a rude awakening.

After crawling out of my sleeping bag, I staggered my way to the kitchen tent. There, I awakened Shyam, our Camp 2 cook, who rose as he always did with a smile on his face.

"What want breakfast?" he inquired in broken English.

"The usual will be great," I replied, knowing that I'd be lucky to hold down tea.

I was grateful for Shyam that morning, as I was every morning I was in Advanced Base Camp. He was always so cheerful, no matter how badly he too was feeling. That is perhaps one of the greatest things about a high-altitude expedition. Everyone is feeling about the same, rotten. In the morning, no one feels strong, well rested, alert or particularly ambitious. We're all just trying to get going. Coffee is of little help. You need "Everest Expresso," the equivalent of high-octane intravenous caffeine, to really jump-start a body at altitude. Unfortunately, we often don't have any, at least not any of the fresh ground variety. I don't drink coffee. My brother, Eric, says: "Don't put any stimulants into Alan. He's stimulated enough already." At altitude, however, I could use it, especially in the mornings. In the mornings, I usually feel putrid.

That morning, I went through my usual bout of nausea, coughing, hacking, spitting, and near-gagging until Shyam had successfully put food into me, and I set out with Jamie and Jason at 6 a.m. for Camp 3, about 3,000 feet above. After hugging Shyam good-bye, our trio made its way slowly across the Khumbu Glacier to the head of the Western Cwm and up a series of massive ice benches that rolled their way to the base of the towering Lhotse Face.

There was an air of excited anticipation in the air, but it was tempered with the reality that we weren't sure what the summit winds would do over the next few days. So, we climbed slowly to the base of the face, making sure we did not waste any precious energy in the process. We had no way of knowing if we'd have to turn around in the next day or two from Camp 3 or 4 above, descend all the way down to Advanced Base Camp to await favorable winds, then make another try if we got a chance.

One thing was clear. We could afford a delay of only one or two days. If we had one longer than that, we wouldn't get a shot at the summit. We'd have to go home again, this time without even having had a chance to make a bid on the peak. I tried not to think about what that would mean.

Slowly, we plodded up the face. I was impressed again with the steepness and hardness of the ice. It reminded me of the many hours I had spent on similar "ground" in the Canadian Rockies, where the cold and dry air makes the ice almost as hard as rock.

FROM EVEREST TO ENLIGHTENMENT

This experience, really, was nothing like being in the Rockies, however. For starters, there was anchored rope all the way up the route. A fairly steady stream of climbers was spread out along it on their way to Camp 3 and beyond. It was not crowded, however. Reports of crowding on Everest, in my experience, are exaggerated. There certainly are other climbers around you and on rare occasions, there can be bottlenecks, but Everest is a huge mountain. Even a horde of climbers quickly gets spread out along the route the way a pack of marathon runners does only a few miles after the start.

Knowing the unpredictability of the summit winds, I tried my best to conserve energy, relax, and enjoy the experience. The view from the Lhotse Face was breathtaking. I could see all the way down the Western Cwm to the edge of the Icefall. From there, the world below disappeared into cloud. One of the greatest pleasures of climbing at high altitude is that the clouds we spend so much time looking up at at lower altitudes we often look down on from far above on high peaks You definitely see the world from a whole new perspective.

Lower on the mountain, Jeff's perspective was very different from mine. He had made a courageous attempt to reach Camp 2, and at a point just a little higher than where I had vomited my first time through the Icefall, he had ground to a halt.

"I hit the wall in the Icefall. I was puking, couldn't breathe, coughing. I felt like I was tearing my tissue apart.... It was the worst timing in the world. I was just totally crushed I couldn't be there [on the summit attempt]. It was like a slap in the face. I was totally bummed and depressed, but that's the way that mountain is. Nothing's over until it's all said and done."

It wasn't done yet, in fact, we'd hardly got started on our summit attempt. Our little party, without Jeff, pulled into Camp 3 shortly before 11 a.m. As always, it was a great relief to get there because although the climb from Camp 2 to 3 is straightforward, it is physically demanding. Many were the moments when I'd find myself panting heavily on the steep face, head down, chest heaving. Your goal is always to ensure

Reports of crowding on Everest, in my experience, are exaggerated.

you keep from overexerting yourself, but even that is a bit of a joke considering where you are. Unlike climbing at lower altitudes, there is always a delay between the moment you overdo it and when the body suddenly realizes you have. A few seconds after pushing out a few quick steps to get over a steep section in the ice, for example, you suddenly find yourself struggling for air and vowing never again to let your ambition exceed your body's ability to process oxygen. The reality is that it is never exactly clear where that line of demarcation is and, unfortunately, the only way of determining where it is is to cross it. On Everest, the energy equation is simple — if you overextend, you pay. And, once the energy is used, you cannot recover it by taking a break. Once it's gone, it's gone. As you struggle upwards, the gas gauge only goes one way, down.

Camp 3 is a spectacular perch. It is the one place in the world where you must never sleepwalk.

Because of the wind storm only a few days earlier, one of our expedition's two tents in Camp 3 was badly blown in with snow. So, Jason and Jamie got permission from another team to occupy one of their vacant tents nearby. I took up residence in the only tent still standing in our camp.

Camp 3 is a spectacular perch. It is the one place in the world where you must never sleepwalk. Ten inches outside your tent door is a 3,000-foot drop to the Khumbu Glacier below. The last thing you want to do is venture out of your tent unprepared.

I pulled one of these foolish maneuvers a few hours after arriving in Camp 3 that day. A friend and fellow Calgarian, Karl Nagy, surprised me when he appeared in camp. He was a member of a commercial expedition that was climbing Mt. Lhotse. I was so overjoyed to see his face that rather than taking the time to don my harness and clip into the anchored rope, I just grabbed my ice ax and climbed a short distance down to greet him.

Jason and Jamie instantly chastised me for being so stupid, and rightly so. Jason instructed Karl to escort me back to my tent where Jason told me in no uncertain terms to stay where I was and not be so foolish again.

Jason and Jamie were right. I was lucky to get away with it. It was a rare lapse in judgment, and on Everest your first mistake can be your last. I might have jeopardized the entire expedition, not to mention my life.

It was great to see Karl's smiling face, bushy beard and hear his booming voice. I knew that he, almost as much as Laurie Skreslet, Bill March, Pat Morrow, John Amatt, Sharon Wood and other leading Canadian climbers, had helped drive my Everest dream. One thing was sure, were it not for the hours Karl and I had spent on long and difficult ice climbs in the Rockies, I would not have been able to move on to higher ground.

By mid-afternoon, the temperature inside my tent was well over 100 degrees. The severe ultraviolet rays at 24,000 feet created a pressure-cooker surpassed in intensity only by the one on the floor of the Western Cwm below. To make matters worse, I had to operate a stove inside the tent to melt water and prevent dehydration. So, I lay naked in my tent in a full sweat, toweling myself off and praying for sunset. Within minutes of its arrival, I knew, the temperature would plummet to well below freezing and I would have to scramble for my down parka.

No other physical activity I have experienced demands such a high degree of adaptability and tenacity as does high-altitude climbing. In a typical day, you have to be able to function in temperatures from 30 or 40 below zero to over 100 above, and be able to switch gears quickly. This means that if you're climbing in the heat of the day but plan to be out after sunset, you must always carry extra clothes, even if you're soaked to the skin with sweat. It's like flying from the Caribbean to the Arctic in a couple of hours. Proper hydration is critically important because of the baking heat during the day, the dryness of the mountain air and the extreme exertion of climbing with a pack on steep ground in a hostile environment. If you want to get up Everest, you must endure these kinds of conditions, not just for hours, as might be the case in a marathon, triathlon, or Ironman competition, or even for days in the case of a multi-day adventure race, but for months. That is perhaps why Everest has been called, "the ultimate physical challenge."

As the sun beat down on my slightly inclined tent, I lay down on my sleeping pad, slithering on my sweat toward the door. Wouldn't it be hilarious, I mused, to read the headline: "Naked climber slides to his death on Everest." The manufacturers of anti-perspirants would have a field day. I could see the slogans: "Our product can save your life. Make sure you stay dry everywhere you go, even on Everest."

By 8 p.m., after sunset, my tent had turned into a freezer. I took refuge in my sleeping bag, which I had been careful to keep from getting soaked with sweat during the day.

That night, I slept for the first time on bottled oxygen. Using the lightest flow rate, about one quart of oxygen per minute, I dozed off and on, in spite of feeling slightly claustrophobic. Sleeping masks are much smaller than the ones used for climbing. Fortunately, they are therefore less obtrusive. The only catch is that your warm, moist exhaled breath quickly condenses into water when it comes in contact with the cold mountain air. If you lie on your back, this creates a steady stream of droplets that fall onto your face from inside the mask. I counteracted this by burying my face into the warmth of my sleeping bag, but that, of course, only added to my feeling of confinement.

> **"Naked climber slides to his death on Everest."**

I reminded myself again that, if all went well, this whole ordeal would be over in just a few days. That philosophy is easy to articulate, but not so easy to practice, especially when you're forced to get intimate with a freezing cold, titanium oxygen tank. I took comfort in the fact that at least it didn't snore.

I knew that if things went according to plan, I would begin my summit bid the next morning. If the weather held and the winds diminished, we would only rest, but not stay overnight, in Camp 4. From there, we would move continuously to and from the summit if we could. That meant we'd be going from Camp 3 to Camp 4, on to the summit and back down to Camp 4 without sleep. The push would last some 30 continuous hours.

The next day, May 22, I arose bleary-eyed at about 6 a.m. and went to work preparing breakfast. I knew from my previous unhappy experience "bonking" en route to the Yellow

Band, that if I was to climb successfully through it and on to Camp 4, I needed to put down more calories this time than sugar-free apple cider. So, I went to work stomaching a mixture of macaroni and tuna I'd prepared the night before. First, I thawed out the whole frozen works by heating it over the stove, then I washed it down with as much hot chocolate as I could.

Meals at high altitude can take up to three hours to prepare, depending on circumstances. The first step is to gather snow or ice to melt. This usually means you have to leave your tent, burrow around outside with a shovel, and fill some kind of a bag, often a stuff sack, with as much snow as you can. Then, like a squirrel storing nuts, you return with your little bag to your nylon lair and progressively dig out cups full of snow from the bag. You then dump this snow into the pot on your stove.

It takes a surprisingly large quantity of snow to create as little as a quart of water. The melting process is very slow. At extreme altitudes, the kind you get on Everest, it's best to keep your stove in the vestibule of your tent, where it doesn't consume what little oxygen you have already during the burning process. In high winds, you've also got to be careful to ensure no part of the tent touches the stove or it could melt your only source of shelter. Making a meal can not only take a long time, it can also require constant attention, the kind of focus and concentration an exhausted climber doesn't have.

Many an expedition has ended prematurely when a lit stove fell over and melted a tent, or worse still, a fuel cartridge of propane/butane was improperly fitted to the stove and suddenly ignited and exploded. This occurred on the north side of Everest in May 1986 when Canadian Sharon Wood had just returned from the summit after becoming the first North American woman to climb the mountain. There, together with her fellow summiteer, an equally exhausted Dwayne Congdon, they improperly fitted a gas cartridge to their stove and as soon as they tried to light it, it exploded, burning a hole the size of a football in the roof of their tent. To save themselves, they instantly jettisoned the stove — their only method of creating water, out the tent door to prevent from being burned

The push would last some 30 continuous hours — rather like childbirth.

themselves. The stove fell thousands of feet to the Main Rongbuk Glacier below. Miraculously, Sharon and Dwayne somehow survived the night without dying of high-altitude sickness caused by dehydration. Even more amazingly, the next morning they still managed to safely descend without falling or collapsing from fatigue.

Knowing this, I was extra careful with the stove that morning. I didn't want to jeopardize my summit chance by having it explode, literally, in my face.

"By 8:15 a.m., all three of us were ready," Jamie recalls. "Jason and I already had our oxygen sets on and running, so Alan quickly donned his. Together, we made our way to the anchored rope leading up the Lhotse Face towards the Yellow Band."

It was amazing the difference a little oxygen made to my climbing strength. In no time, I found myself passing other climbers on the anchored rope, a few of whom were climbing on oxygen themselves. Most of the climbers had decided not to start using gas until they reached Camp 4, due as much to financial and organizational constraints as to personal preference. I was thankful Jamie and I had taken the time with Colliers, Lotus, and our other sponsors to ensure we had sufficient capital so Steve could secure enough oxygen and personnel to do the job as safely and efficiently as possible. I was also thankful, in retrospect, that I had finally decided to use bottled oxygen. Starting on oxygen out of Camp 3 was clearly an advantage. Considering we were climbing into the "Death Zone," that was reassuring.

Above us, a steady stream of climbers laboriously made their way higher. This was really the only time during the expedition when I felt like things got a little crowded. I was afraid that if someone above me on the anchored rope fell, he or she might pull out the entire section of the line and, in doing so, everyone on the rope could fall too.

"This isn't a pristine Rocky Mountain experience," Jamie remarked from beneath his mask.

Fortunately, no one fell. As we approached the Yellow Band, I seemed to be moving faster than anyone else in our party, due in large part to the fact that Jamie was stopping frequently to shoot videotape, as he had been during the entire trip. It was an amazing feeling for me, having labored during most of the expedition. For the first time, I began to feel that being on Everest was actually fun. It was positively joyous to be passing some of the strongest climbers in the world, among them professional guides, knowing that maybe all those thousands of lonely training hours were finally paying off. For the first time, I felt like a mountaineer instead of a pitiful, puffing weakling. It was a huge boost.

In a little over an hour, we reached the Yellow Band. There, I paused at the base of the anchored rope to prepare to ascend a 10-foot high rock step at the base of the band. Jamie quickly caught up and prepared to shoot me as I did so.

Using two jumars, one in each hand, I did my best not to haul myself hand-over-hand up the anchored rope but instead, to actually climb the rock band, using my jumars only to stop me if I fell. It was exhilarating.

"My God!" I thought to myself. "I'm actually climbing the Yellow Band," a feature I had read and dreamed about since I was a boy, something famous in the history books. What a thrill it was to be moving in the footsteps of Sir Edmund Hillary, Laurie Skreslet, and Pat Morrow. We were actually doing it.

Scaling the Yellow Band was surprisingly challenging, especially while wearing those sharp-pointed steel crampons we attach to the bottom of our boots to get purchase in the ice and snow. Since there was very little snow on the ledges and next to no ice, it was easy to see how someone could lose their footing here, fall, and tumble all the way down the Lhotse Face. In addition to the challenge of climbing on relatively bare rock in crampons, I also had to deal with the fact that most of the anchored ropes had obviously seen better days. Some of them looked like they had been there for several years although it was, of course, impossible to tell. They were tattered, torn, and worn by the elements.

To cope with the stress of this uncertainty, and the thousands of feet of air beneath my heels, I remembered the ladders in the Icefall and focused on my feet. They were sometimes difficult to see from beneath my oxygen mask so I had to practice positive self-talk to stay in control. The cool sensation of the flow of pure oxygen danced across my cheeks. This, combined with the gentle hissing sound of the gas being released from its tank gave me a feeling of surprising security. I knew, however, that that security was false. There was nothing secure about my situation. With every passing minute, my tank was emptying. Outside my mask, just a quarter of an inch from my skin, was the bottom of the "Death Zone" at 26,000 feet.

Our goal that day was to get to Camp 4 before we ran out of oxygen, a feat that in theory should be straightforward. Each tank of oxygen normally lasts six to eight hours at low flow. That day, things went smoothly. We crested the Yellow Band after some exertion, climbed across a long snow slope into a "corner" gully on the Lhotse Face and immediately made a hard left toward the right side of the Geneva Spur, a huge outcrop of rock that separates the face from the South Col.

The spur was massive, much bigger than I had imagined. Everything on Everest is on such a huge scale that it's often impossible to tell how big things are from photographs. The Lhotse Face, for example, absolutely dwarfs you in Advanced Base Camp, as does Everest's towering Southwest Face above. You feel like you've entered "The Land of the Giants" and you have. It's impossible to feel the least bit important there, or anywhere on Everest. What you do feel is humbled, privileged, and anxious. If you mess up, the outcome is clear — you'll go for "the Big Ride" down that great white highway in the sky.

Slowly, we made our way across the right side of the Geneva Spur. It was spectacular. It loomed before me. The rock was black and surprisingly solid and thanks again to anchored rope, we jumared our way, along with a few dozen other climbers, to a sloping rock ramp traversing a ridge about halfway up it.

When I reached the ridge and turned the corner to the right, my whole perspective on Everest changed. I could see straight into the South Col, the world's highest mountain pass. Above me, stood a sweeping triangular-shaped face spreading down and outwards in a huge fan from the South Summit of

With every passing minute, my tank was emptying. Outside my mask, just a quarter of an inch from my skin, was the bottom of the "Death Zone."

the mountain to the Col. Below me were thousands of feet of empty space all the way down the Lhotse Face into the Cwm. Only one word described it — overwhelming.

The triangular face was riddled with snow chutes, outcroppings of rock, and cement-hard blue ice. It was obvious how people perished here. A savage-looking plume of snow blasted from the South Summit, above which I knew lay the last 100 vertical meters of ground to the top of the world. Above that, there was nothing ... nothing but space ... all the way to the moon.

The wind was gusting across the Col at up to 40 miles an hour. Jamie and I were buffeted from time to time by its force, but I hardly noticed it. I was so struck by the scene, the football field-sized bench of rock, snow, and ice that was the Col, the gigantic triangular face above it and the terrifying height exposure below, that I could hardly believe I was there. Here, everyone from Hillary to Habeler and Messner, from Burgess to Bonington, had left for the summit over the decades. Others had never returned. I was approaching a very historic spot, the launching pad of dreams.

Above that, there was nothing ... nothing but space ... all the way to the moon.

> *I think the South Col of Everest must be the coldest and loneliest place in the world.*
>
> *I have been in many wild and lonely places in my life, but never anywhere like the Col. Lying at 25,850 feet between the final peaks of Everest and Lhotse, it lacks even the softness of snow, and is simply a bare, frozen plain of rock and ice, over which the wind roars with never a minute's stop.*
>
> — TENZING NORGAY,
> *Man of Everest*

If there is one place where there is an inordinate accumulation of equipment, not necessarily garbage, but equipment, some of it very old, it is the South Col. If you're lucky enough to make it back to the Col alive after your summit bid and one of your 12-pound oxygen tanks is empty, ethics and the environment behoove you to carry it down the mountain. However, it takes so much effort to take a single step here that to carry such a burden might well cost you your life. The result is obvious. Climbers leave them behind.

For our part as an expedition, we left almost nothing behind. On my summit day, I was unable to retrieve a few spent oxygen cylinders that I left behind in the snow higher on the peak and thus, I contributed to the problem. I did come back alive, however. I can celebrate the fact that I did not leave my body behind as well as one or two tanks.

I will long remember my thoughts as I approached the South Col. For the first time on our expedition, I realized we were no longer ferrying loads back and forth, getting into position. Now, we were finally in position. Now, I was staring at the very spot where Laurie Skreslet had stood 15 years before me. It was almost unimaginable to think there was no longer any imagining to do. You really could shoot for the stars from here. In fact, it seemed you could almost reach out and touch them, even in broad daylight.

You really could shoot for the stars from here.

I "hurried" to make my way across the remaining part of the Spur to the Col, as "hurried" as you can be when almost two-thirds of the world's oxygen is beneath you. The ground was straightforward, like walking across a slightly outward sloping ramp of rock. The exposure here, however, was anything but straightforward. My heart fluttered. I stayed clipped into the anchored rope as much as possible, although it was tattered and fraying in many places.

About 20 minutes later, we pulled into the Col. There, we found about half a dozen of our Sherpas quickly erecting tents on the rocky landscape in the howling wind. It was 12:45 p.m., under bright sunshine.

> *Sherpas have set up the highest camps on every major climb in twentieth-century Himalayan history, and in many cases, after that, we have gone on with our clients to the top ... we consider it is our duty to take care of our clients.*
>
> — TENZING NORGAY,
> *Man of Everest*

At Jason's insistence, I crawled into the first tent and started laying out our sleeping bags and mattresses. Jamie hung around outside for a few minutes shooting precious videotape, then joined me. At last, we were together on the South Col.

Everyone knew we wouldn't really be sleeping here, only resting before leaving at around midnight for the top. We only had one problem. Unless the winds diminished, it was doubtful we'd be going anywhere but down. That prospect, like all of the unhappy ones I'd contemplated during the seven or so weeks of climbing to that point, did not inspire me. Were we ever going to get a shot at this? Was Chomolungma going to deny us again?

"Christ!" I muttered to Jamie. "If this wind doesn't stop, we may as well go home. When the sun sets, an ice box will seem like the Caribbean here."

"Let's try not to think about it," he said.

Jamie said we should wait until 9 p.m. and if the winds hadn't come down enough by then, we'd decide whether to go down to Camp 2 or 3, or to hold here for a day.

"How keen would you be to come all the way back up here from 2 or 3?" I asked. "Do you honestly think we could all do that and still have enough left to make it safely to and from the summit?"

Jamie didn't answer. That, I knew, was an answer.

> *It was getting dark, and the cold and wind were indescribable.*
> — TENZING NORGAY,
> *Man of Everest*

Gyalbu, one of our Sherpas, started to brew liquids. I tried to relax.

It was impossible. The best I could do was close my eyes and pretend I wasn't there. I put in my earplugs, covered my eyes with my hat, and tried to think of some warm sandy beach somewhere. It was futile. The air, although thin, was so electric with anticipation that it seemed to shake the walls of the tent almost as much as the wind. To make matters worse, one of our

The air, although thin, was so electric with anticipation that it seemed to shake the walls of the tent almost as much as the wind.

Sherpas, Pema Temba, had not yet arrived. His presence, I would discover, was to be critically important to our summit bid and my subsequent descent.

Jason began to get concerned. He dispatched a few of our Sherpas to go and find Pema. Thankfully, a few hours later, they re-appeared with their friend. Everyone was relieved. At this point, a full-blown high-altitude rescue would have killed our summit chances. I was just glad he was safe. At about 26,000 feet, even the Sherpas start to struggle and the playing field between Easterners and Westerners begins to even. The higher you go, the "flatter" that playing field becomes.

At about 26,000 feet, even the Sherpas start to struggle and the playing field between Easterners and Westerners begins to even.

While we were awaiting Pema's arrival, Jamie and the others started passing me food. Pringles potato chips, something as I've said I would almost never eat at lower altitudes, went down as easily here as they had in base camp. I was thankful for any appetite, something I knew was a direct result of breathing bottled oxygen.

Jason hurried around directing the Sherpas and taking care of a myriad of last minute details. He instructed Jamie and me to put on a fresh tank of oxygen, to sit back, relax as much as we could, and prepare ourselves mentally for what lay ahead. I was thankful someone was taking care of the larger picture. Jason did a wonderful job.

"I was really dragging my ass to Camp 4," Jason remembers, "and I worked really hard when I got there. I wanted to personally ensure all the details were taken care of."

It was all I could do just to try to calm down. I am not by nature hyper in tense situations, but I'd never experienced this kind of pressure, whether atmospheric, psychological, physiological or emotional, before. As a gymnast, I was used to putting months of intense training on the line at a national meet, but here, I knew there was a lifetime of effort, and my life, at stake. I also knew that in the next 24 hours, that lifetime would be reduced to one day, one hour and one step, if the mountain allowed us to take any steps. The situation reminded me of the 100-meter final at the Olympic Games, 15 years of preparation that all came down to 10 seconds of performance.

The big difference here was that if you lost, you could die. The stakes were as high as you could get.

An hour passed, and another. Slowly. Slowly.

— TENZING NORGAY,
Man of Everest

As I lay on my back with the oxygen mask on my face, I thought of my parents, my three brothers, my friends, Steve, and my staff back home. And, I thought of dear Diane and how much I missed her. I had dreamed of proposing to her from the summit, saying, "I'm on top of the world sweetheart, and now I'm coming down to spend the rest of my life with you and the kids."

That, of course, was not how that dream had played out. It wasn't clear how the next 24 hours would either. Would I realize my Everest dream or would it be swept away by the wind?

I lay in the darkness, listening to the wind, and I thought, it must stop. It must stop, so that tomorrow we can go up.

— TENZING NORGAY,
Man of Everest

If you lost, you could die.

At 8:30 p.m., in the darkness of our crowded tent in Camp 4, I rolled over in my sleeping bag, turned on my headlamp and squinted at my watch.

Outside, the wind was still howling across the Col. It would be impossible to climb under these conditions.

Across the Threshold

That the supreme and those precious moments
of human living however much they may appear
to depend on the body and the senses, are primarily
experiences of the spirit.

— JAMES RAMSEY ULLMAN,
author of *Man of Everest*

TWENTY-MINUTES LATER, I was stirred from my half-slumber by a sound, or rather a lack of it. Something had changed.

I sat up and listened. My ears strained.

"What time is it?" Jamie asked, clearly wide awake.

"Shhh!," I said. "Ten to 9."

"Do you hear it?" I asked.

"Hear what?" Jamie said.

"The wind," I replied.

There was silence in the tent.

"Holy shit," Jamie said.

"You're not kidding," I exclaimed. "The wind has stopped! Hang on while I check."

Quickly, I turned on my headlamp. As the vapor from my breath swept through the beam, I peered around in the darkness at the three lumps of down beside me — the sleeping bags containing Jamie, Jason, and Gyalbu. Carefully, I reached over the mound that was Jason, pulled up the zipper on the tent door and stuck my head out into the darkness.

Outside, it was an eerie scene. The wind very definitely had stopped. My heart missed a beat.

"There's a full moon out here," I said.

I heard the rustling sound of Jamie sitting up in his sleeping bag.

"You're kidding," Jamie said.

"It's hard to fake a full moon buddy," I replied. "She's clear as a bell out here."

A strange sensation came over me. It was mysterious, like the moon. I'd had the same feeling four months before during my last 20-hour training day with Bruce in the Rockies. Late on February 21, as if on cue, the moon had also risen just when we needed it, lighting our way to a pass previously obscured in fog. I remember telling my physiotherapist, Patti Mayer, about it.

"We get what we need in life exactly when we need it," she'd explained. "And what you needed then was someone to light the way for you."

"But the world doesn't revolve around me," I'd replied. "If the moon rose for me, it rose for everyone else as well. I don't understand."

"Understand, Alan, that there is far more to life than what we see."

Nothing became clearer to me than that at that moment. It was so clear I could see it with my own eyes. Just 20 minutes before, our dream had been in jeopardy. Now, you could see all the way to the South Summit like it was across the street. The calming of the wind and the moonrise was a message from the mountain. It said: "Okay boys, here's your chance. But you'd better make your visit very brief, and you'd better conduct yourself with a great deal of care because my benevolence may not last."

For the first time since arriving in base camp, I felt like I had touched the inner core of the Mother Goddess. She was cold and foreboding, but at least she appeared to be giving us a chance. She had spoken.

We acted. Jamie and I acted like a couple of kids.

"Get the stove going, get the stove going," I said, near bursting with anticipation. "We might still be in the game."

Everyone stirred quickly. The Sherpas in the second of our two tents, Kami, Tashi, Lhakpa, Nurbu, and Pema, were

> *"We get what we need in life exactly when we need it."*
>
> – PATTI MAYER

already up. Elsewhere on the Col, we could hear the sounds of other parties preparing for their summit bids as well. There were about three or four other teams ready to go. The collective sounds of their coughing, gagging, and spitting echoed across the pass.

Two and a half hours later, at 11:30 p.m., we had melted enough snow, consumed enough hot chocolate and pounded down as much food as any of us dared. I was greatly relieved by a miraculous lack of nausea, a delight I had not experienced for weeks. What a treat it was not to feel sick. Things were definitely looking up.

Slowly, all nine of us on our team crawled out of our tents. Even in the moonlight, I still almost managed to commit the blunder of all blunders. I lost my balance putting on my crampons and narrowly missed stepping on the tube leading from my oxygen tank to my mask. Gratefully, the sharp points fell on either side of the tube, and all I did was compress my lifeline momentarily. How silly it would have been, I thought, to cope with all the complexities of getting to Everest and climbing to the Col and then mess up my summit chances on something so simple. But in any endeavor, it's the small stuff that can kill you, not the big stuff you're so careful to pinpoint in your planning.

> **It's the small stuff that can kill you.**

To reduce weight, I'd gone to great pains to purchase a special lightweight set of aluminum crampons specifically for summit day. By reducing the weight on my feet, I thought I'd have more energy for each step. Unfortunately, in the cold and rarefied air of the Col, I hadn't anticipated the extra concentration I'd need to put them on in the dark, particularly as they were new to me. Another lesson learned, almost too late.

Shortly after 11:30 p.m., all of us departed, on oxygen. There was a surreal sense to the scene. As the moon cast its rays over our shoulders from right to left, it lit up the entire triangular-shaped face like a huge white board. In my mind's eye, I traced out the route we might take with a mental magic marker — up one of these snow chutes straight ahead of us, over a rock outcrop or two above that, then diagonally right onto the southeast ridge at the point they called the "Balcony" at just under 28,000 feet.

The air was crisp and cold, about 30 below zero, practically sun-tanning weather for 26,000 feet on Everest. Conditions were perfect. But would they hold?

Slowly, we started taking the steps. Jamie, Lhakpa, Gyalbu, and Tashi quickly took the lead, then Kami and me. Jason and Nurbu pulled up the rear.

> *That is how a mountain makes men great.*
> *For where would Hillary and I have been without*
> *the others? Without the climbers who had made the*
> *route and the Sherpas who had carried the loads?*
> *Without Bourdillon and Evans, Hunt and Da*
> *Namgyal, who had cleared the way ahead? Without*
> *Lowe and Gregory, Ang Nyima, Ang Tempa, and*
> *Pemba, who were there only to help us? It was only*
> *because of the work and sacrifice of all of them that*
> *we were now to have our chance at the top.*
>
> — Tenzing Norgay,
> *Man of Everest*

The air was crisp and cold, about 30 below zero, practically sun-tanning weather for 26,000 feet on Everest.

The ice was hard. At first, it undulated in long, slowly rolling waves, but then steepened suddenly. It was far steeper than I had imagined, and there were no anchored ropes. They had stopped just below the Col and would not begin again until some distance above. I knew that if a single step failed to get purchase here, I'd fly down the face back to camp. This wasn't so unsettling at first, but as time passed and we climbed higher, the consequences of a fall became progressively more obvious. If you tumbled from here, by the time you reached the Col, your body would be going so fast it might easily rocket all the way down the Lhotse Face, a combined drop of easily 4,000 feet. Trying to stop yourself on this type of terrain using your ice ax would be next to impossible. If you weren't able to do it in the first few seconds, you'd pick up speed so fast you'd be history in no time.

I tried not to think about all the "what ifs." Instead, I concentrated completely on my feet, slamming my crampons down into the ice as if my life depended on it, which, of course, it did. I was disturbed every now and again when to my horror, my aluminum crampons, which apparently did not maintain their sharp points as well as conventional steel crampons, did not bite sufficiently into the ice. Suddenly, one of my feet slipped just a little bit, and my stomach jumped into my mouth.

"Damn," I thought. "Should have stayed with what I know. What a time to find out."

It was too late to change now. We were committed, as committed as you can be on any mountain. We were going for the summit.

About an hour above camp, Tashi and Lhakpa led us to the left of a rock spur and into softer, deeper snow beside it. At first, I was thankful to get off the exposure of the ice, but I soon began to labor inexplicably. Slowly, Jamie and the rest of the Sherpas began to pull away. As I had been climbing strongly on the previous days, this didn't make sense to me.

What's happening? Why can't I keep up?

In no time, it was taking me up to a minute to take a single, six-inch step. The snow, which was only a few inches deep, felt like bottomless quicksand. It seemed to swallow up my boots. To make matters worse, the wind started to pick up again too. Huge clouds of spindrift snow, like freezing dust devils, began to sweep wildly across the moonlit face, buffeting me from side to side and driving me periodically to my knees, as if in forced prayer. Add to this the fact that we somehow seemed to be off route and I began to become more than a little concerned.

"Where is the Balcony?" I asked Kami.

He looked back at me perplexed. Silence.

"Where is the Balcony?" I repeated.

Still no reply.

I was breathing too hard to discuss it. I put my head down and decided to continue. In places, I broke my own trail and in others, I followed in Kami's footsteps. I had no idea which way Jamie had gone. All I knew was I had to continue as long as I could.

In no time, it was taking me up to a minute to take a single, six-inch step.

My struggle went on for at least an hour. After a while, I became convinced we were off-route. Frustrated at my inability to communicate with Kami, I found myself panting uncontrollably, mouth hanging open, gasping for breath. Not only was I now sure we were off course, but suddenly, I felt like I was suffocating.

My throat was dried up and aching with thirst,
and some of the time, in the steep snow, we were
so tired that we had to crawl on all fours.

— TENZING NORGAY,
Man of Everest,
on his summit attempt with the Swiss, spring, 1952

"Kami," I struggled out between breaths. "Can you have a look at my oxygen?"

I was already tired. Above me, I could just barely see the outline of Jamie and Lhakpa, or so I thought, moving in and out of the spindrift. For a second, they would appear. Then, in the next, they would vanish like apparitions. I knew that if that was, in fact, them, they probably couldn't wait there for me. It was too cold.

At one point, I thought I saw another party of about 10 climbers, all of them on headlamps, move quickly by me and straight up another snow chute just off to my right. It seemed like they were where we were supposed to be. Something wasn't right. Was I hallucinating?

Something wasn't right. Was I hallucinating?

"Where is Jason?" I asked Kami.

"Jason go down," he replied.

"What do you mean?" I inquired. "Is he all right?"

"Eye problem," Kami said. That's all he said.

I was to learn later that within hours of setting out from the Col, Jason had overheated, stopped to take off a few layers of clothing and raised his goggles to cool off. Then he had turned on the speed to catch up to the rest of us above.

"Gradually, I began to notice that my vision was getting kind of blurry," he remembers. "It was pretty drastic. It was like looking through wax paper."

Apparently, the freezing wind had somehow frozen his right eye. Without both eyes to provide him with the depth perception so vital in climbing, he had been faced with a major decision.

"It was life-threatening to go on," he recalls. "My responsibility was to do exactly what I'd done — to lead the expedition. I realized Jamie and Alan had plenty of coverage, [Sherpa support] so I decided to leave."

Nurbu helped Jason down the rest of the face. It was a frustrating time for the man who had been the pillar of strength and good health throughout the expedition. He had given so much of himself to get Jamie and me to that point. Perhaps it was the mountain's way of saving him for another day.

"'God damn it!' I said to myself," Jason recalls. "Why is this happening to me? I take care of myself.'"

"He had to come down," Doug insists. "For him to have gone up would have been reckless."

Jason descended to Camp 4 and then on down to Camp 2 later that day. Within 24 hours, his vision had completely returned. He suffered no long-term health or vision effects whatsoever due to the wisdom of his actions. He is a highly experienced high-altitude mountaineer, and he made a sound judgment. Had he decided to continue, he might well have become permanently blind, if he'd come down at all.

At that moment, then, there was only Jamie and me and four of our Sherpas, Lhakpa, Gyalbu, Tashi, and Kami still going for the top. Jason was climbing down with Nurbu. Pema was waiting in support at the Col. I was laboring harder than I had in my whole life.

I glanced at my watch. It was 2:35 a.m. My altimeter read 27,160 feet. I remember the exact time and altitude because at that exact moment, on May 23, 1997, a powerful gust of wind blasted a cloud of freezing cold spindrift snow straight into my hood. It went around my neck about three times and went straight down my back.

In a second, I became an instant icicle.

Had he decided to continue, he might well have become permanently blind, if he'd come down at all.

We stopped, and for a few moments stood where we were, crouched over like animals against the fierceness of the wind. If it had not been so cold that the tears would have frozen before they left the eyes, I think that I might have wept. — Tenzing Norgay,
Man of Everest,
during Swiss Everest Expedition, autumn, 1952

"No oxygen," Kami replied.

"What?" I bellowed through the howling wind, starting to shiver.

"No oxygen."

Instantly, I was snapped from one reality to another. Kami had discovered my oxygen tank was empty. I'd probably been climbing without oxygen for at least an hour. That's why I hadn't been able to keep up. That's why I was struggling to breathe.

"Can you hook me onto my other tank?" I asked Kami as I motioned for him to dig into my backpack again.

"Sure," he replied

Slowly, I felt Kami tugging at my pack. Within seconds, though, I started to really shiver. Seconds after that, I was shaking uncontrollably. I could feel the cold penetrating to my core. I was in trouble.

In a second, I became an instant icicle.

My worst nightmare — freezing to death, high on Everest — cold, dark, frigid.

"K-K-Kami," I said as my teeth chattered, "I t-t-think we need to g-g-o down."

He didn't reply. He just kept monkeying with my oxygen tanks.

Finally, after what seemed like a lifetime, I said in a louder and now forceful tone:

"K-K-Kami. We need to go down N-NOW!"

It's hard for me to describe to you how frightened I was at that moment. Because of my terrible fear of the cold, my high susceptibility to it, and my inability to quickly recover once cold, I knew I could not mess around with this situation. It could kill me — quickly. A volley of scattered thoughts raced through my mind. One stuck:

"If you give up now Alan," I asked myself, "will you have given it everything you have? Will you look back on this moment with no regret? Can you live with it for the rest of your life?"

My reply was quick and sure, "Yes, I can. I can. It's over."

When you think you could die, it's amazing how quickly you let go of the past, all your work, all your effort, all those obstacles overcome. They vanish into insignificance, and for good reason. You must be totally reasoned at moments like that. If you aren't, the situation could quickly become *unreasonable*.

The wind was too much. The cold was too much.
Under our three pairs of gloves our fingers had lost
all feeling. Our lips, then our noses, then our whole
faces, began turning blue. Behind us the line
of struggling Sherpas had almost ceased to move
at all. There was only one sane — one even possible
— thing to do. That was to turn back.

I let go of my dream.

— TENZING NORGAY,
Man of Everest,
during summit attempt on Everest with the Swiss, autumn, 1952

If there was a moment of truth in my life, it was that moment. I decided my own fate and set a course toward my own destiny. The summit was deceptively close, but it might just as well have been light years away. I completely abandoned my hopes of reaching the top and was instantly at peace with my decision. I let go of my dream.

It is impossible, I kept thinking. We cannot go on.
And still we did go on.

— TENZING NORGAY,
Man of Everest,
during attempt on Mt. Nanga Parbat, 1950

I didn't want to die. I didn't want the skeptics to say, "There, I told you so. He took a risk and he paid for it with his life. He deserved it. He courted disaster and he lost."

Kami had other plans.

"Oxygen now?" he asked.

Slowly, I felt the cool flow of gas on my cheeks. I heard a quiet hiss behind me between gusts.

"You climb?" Kami asked.

Before I could reply, the words he had said to me that day in Gorak Shep came back to me.

"... 1997 ... very important ... summit."

"I'll t-t-try," I said.

Those two words, that willingness to give it just a little more, to squeeze out that last ounce of what I had when it seemed I had nothing, changed my life forever. I will never be the same man, not because of what I was able to do over the hours and days that followed, but because of who I became in the process — a changed man and a weathered soul.

I took a step. It seemed to feel okay, so I took another, then another, and another. I thought, "Well, if I'm able to move, maybe I'll be able to warm up. If I'm able to warm up, maybe, just maybe, I'll be able to keep from freezing to death on this mountain."

We had to move, or else freeze to death.

— TENZING NORGAY,
Man of Everest,
during attempt on Everest with the Swiss, autumn, 1952

It's fascinating in life to see what happens to us when we take a few steps.

It's fascinating in life to see what happens to us when we take a few steps. Because we're off balance and in motion, we take a few more ... and a few more. Pretty soon, if we can somehow stay on our feet, we start to cover ground, we break through our self-doubt and fear and we begin to discover one of the ultimate truths of life:

On the other side of fear is freedom.

I had to find that freedom. I had to. I didn't want to die.

Twenty minutes later, I began to warm up and started thinking more clearly:

"You take the lead," I told Kami. There was no sense in me, the weakest member of our two-man team, breaking trail and potentially jeopardizing the summit chances of both of us. "Can you?"

Without a word, Kami took over.

A few minutes later, we crested the southeast ridge and onto the "Balcony."

To my surprise, Tashi was standing there waiting for us.

"You okay?" he asked.

"Yes, better now," I said. "I got very cold down there."

"We go," he said without hesitation.

I looked around. My God, what a sight! Those Himalayan giants we had looked up at for weeks were now at our feet. Above us, I could see the entire upper part of the southeast ridge, the South Summit and beyond that, the main summit. It was as plain as day. So were the billions of stars in the heavens above. They shone out like beacons lighting the darkness of my chilled core.

What a dramatic change it was from the uncertainty and imprisonment of the triangular face. What a shift from looking face-first into the snow for hours wondering where the strength for the next step would come from.

Suddenly, the dream was reborn. I could see the headlamps of Jamie and the others above me, and I could clearly see our objective. I was looking up at the southeast ridge of Mt. Everest! We were within striking distance of the top.

But were we?

"How much oxygen do you have Tashi?" I asked.

"Three bottles." he replied.

"Really," I said. "Three bottles?"

"Yes," he said emphatically. "— two for me and one for you."

"Wow!," I thought. "Holy shoot! We might just pull this off! We just might. We just …"

"Kami, have you got any oxygen?" I asked before I got too far ahead of myself.

"Three bottles too," he said grinning from under his mask, "two for me and one for you."

Elation. Exaltation. Rapture.

Then quickly, reality:

"Tashi," I said. "It's 4 a.m. Even with enough oxygen, do we have enough time to do this safely?"

"No problem," he said matter-of-factly. "Still early."

I felt like someone had lit fire crackers and shoved them into my boots. I took off like a house on fire. No longer burdened by my fear, now I was determined to see things through. Summit or no summit, honor or dishonor, I was going to give it everything I had, short of my life. A weight had been lifted from my shoulders. My dream had been re-ignited.

Tashi would hear nothing of me leading. He was a Sherpa. In his view, I was in his charge and he was in charge. He'd been here three times before. This was my first time. He would lead, I would follow. Kami would follow me. That's how it would be, no questions asked.

I acquiesced, easily, and so off we went. We climbed smoothly like this, as a three-man machine, for about an hour, one step after laborious step, up the long ridge ahead. Off to my right, the sun began to rise over Tibet. It started as a faint gray, then the gray became pink, and the pink, orange. Finally, at about 5:30 a.m., the Himalayas exploded in light.

It was glorious. Dawn at the top of the world. I was standing higher than the top of all but one mountain on Earth. And, I was on *that* mountain and headed to *that* point! I started to feel euphoric, but immediately checked myself.

Skreslet spoke: "Don't celebrate until you're back in base camp, Alan," he whispered in the ear of my imagination, "and not a minute before."

I heeded his words, but it would have been so easy to let my mind wander. If there was one thing I couldn't afford to let my mind, or my feet, do at that moment, it was wander. This was no daydream.

I kept my head down. I focused on my feet. Every once in a while, I'd look up to see where Tashi was, then down between my legs to see how Kami was doing below me. I was closing on Tashi, but Kami was falling behind. So, I called out to Tashi to hold up a minute. He did.

I felt like someone had lit fire crackers and shoved them into my boots. I was going to give it everything I had, short of my life.

As we waited for Kami to catch up, I looked at my altimeter. It read 28,500 feet. It was amazing to see that number. I'd never seen a number like that on my altimeter before. It had an other-worldly feel to it. Was this actually happening? Was our altitude actually accurate or was I just imagining things? My altimeter had never been wrong before.

In base camp, Dave, Bruce, Doug, and Jeff had been monitoring our progress all night. Radio contact had been limited, but enough for them to know things seemed to be progressing reasonably well.

"It looked like you guys were going to do it," Jeff remembers. "I had to sit and listen to it on the radio. It was tough."

I knew we were only a short distance below the South Summit. If we could get there, I knew we would be able to see the Hillary Step beyond. That became my new objective, to see the Step, to fix my eyes on the feature I'd seen hundreds of times in books. I wanted to be there.

It was an endless ascent. Shortly after Kami rejoined us, we resumed climbing. False summit after false summit came upon us. For a while, I thought we might never get there. I began to become disillusioned. Then, I snapped out of it.

"C'mon Alan," I told myself. "All you have to do is be patient. All you have to do is take a step."

The weather was superb. It was a bright, blue sky morning. There was hardly a breath of wind, especially here on the lee side of the mountain. With the increased altitude, the temperature had fallen to about 35 degrees below zero, but in the heat of the moment, I hardly felt it. My sun ice suit was performing flawlessly.

The Southeast Ridge was spectacular. On my right, the mountain fell away from it 8,000 feet down the Kangchung Face into Tibet, creating a panorama of indescribable beauty. I didn't even look at the view.

It was one of the most dangerous places I had ever been on a mountain.
— Tenzing Norgay,
Man of Everest,
just below the South Summit of Everest, summit day, 1953

"Your moment of greatest strength is your moment of greatest singleness of purpose," Laurie had said. I remembered it, as I remembered him. He and my mentor, the late Bill March, came to visit me again then. They reminded me I was not to allow myself to become distracted. Distraction could mean death.

Unlike the triangular face below the "Balcony," in scattered places along the ridge, there was anchored rope along the route. Most of the time, I could clip into it, but like all the rope on the route, it was pretty tattered. The "security" of the fixed line was probably mostly in my head. One missed step here and it was over, and I mean over — over the edge and down, down, down, all the way to the bottom of the face. No one would ever see me again. I would disappear forever into Tibet.

My body really started to hurt. My legs burned and my lungs heaved. I wanted to give up. I just wanted the discomfort to end.

If I gave up now, I knew I would have to come back here again. I would have to go through all that fundraising, all those negotiations, all that training, all those trips between camps and all that sickness and discomfort. No way. No damn way. I would not be crushed. I would not be defeated. I would carry on as best I could, win or lose. I resolved to be patient.

At 7:15 a.m., after cresting a large snow cone, we finally stood on the South Summit of Everest. I could see clearly across the knife-edged ridge to the base of the Hillary Step. I could see the rounded snow ridge that led to the main summit beyond. We were here. We were 100 vertical meters from the top of the world. Jamie and the others, I reasoned, must be at the top already, or already on their way down from the peak.

I had planned to have a good rest on the South Summit, hydrate, and try to put down some food. We'd been going hard for almost eight hours. Now was the time to center ourselves physically and psychologically and prepare for the final push. But Tashi, once again, would hear nothing of it. He seemed impatient. He wanted to continue now.

"No waiting," he said. "No wait."

> **Distraction could mean death.**

It's amazing what can happen to people's personalities when they get within sight of a goal, and especially within sight of a summit. Some become gripped with summit fever, seduced by the desire to stand on top. I don't think that was what was happening to Tashi. I think he just wanted to get up and down as quickly and safely as possible. He knew that the longer we stayed in the "Death Zone," the greater the danger would become. We couldn't afford to linger here.

I do not tend to get caught up in these kinds of emotions. I am a plodder. I am so focused on the weather, my feet, my climbing companions, my hydration, my food intake, and how I'm feeling that I rarely get swept up in the moment. But when a Sherpa gets impatient, I pay attention. So, without stopping for more than two or three minutes on the South Summit, just enough for Kami to catch up again, Tashi forged ahead.

I looked out at the knife-edged ridge he was crossing. I'd had nightmares about it. On the right-hand side, there was that horrific, 8,000-foot drop into Tibet. On the left-hand side, there was a 6,000-drop into Nepal. Although the ridge looked to be as much as 10 feet wide in places, I knew that most of that width was nothing more than windblown snow. It had formed itself into a slab called a cornice that overhung the Kangchung Face. There was nothing underneath it but air. If I stepped three inches too far to the right, I could exit instantly through the cornice and fall more than a vertical mile and a half to my death. After that, the wind would fill in the hole through which I had fallen, and there would never be any evidence that I had ever even set foot there. I would simply vanish.

I am not very fond of heights.

Because of the deceptive nature of the cornice, I knew that in places, the actual line I had to walk along the ridge was only about one foot wide. The problem was, there was no way of knowing for sure from looking at the surface of the snow whether you were stepping into oblivion or onto the rock of the ridge underneath. So, I took the lesser of the two evils — I stayed to the left and followed the footprints of my predecessors.

But had they taken the right route? Would the weight of my body finally cause the cornice underneath me to collapse? Where was the ridge?

Even if I probed carefully with the point of the shaft of my ice ax, I had no way of knowing if I was on solid ground or not. The cornice was at least 20 to 30 feet thick in places and 10 to 20 feet wide.

No, I had to risk it. If I wanted the summit, I had to.

I have told you I am not very fond of heights. Imagine yourself standing there. How would you feel?

I am an experienced climber. I'm supposed to be used to dealing with extreme exposure. I am, but not *that* kind of exposure. It was the most horrendous piece of mountaineering terrain I have ever seen.

My legs began to shake. My grip tightened on the head of my ax. I was really afraid, probably the most afraid I've been in my life, except for that very morning on the triangular face.

"No mistakes here," I heard Skreslet whisper. "No mistakes."

I cranked my oxygen set up to maximum flow and ever so gingerly, took my first tentative steps out onto the snow....

My heart raced. The blood pounded in my ears. My breathing went shallow.

My past was below me. My future was above me. I was suspended between two countries, two summits and two possible fates....

That ridge ... where was that ridge?

It was the most horrendous piece of mountaineering terrain I have ever seen.

Half the Dream is Done

And today I know the path between tomb and towering heights is extremely narrow.

— REINHOLD MESSNER,
after he and Peter Habeler
climbed Everest for the first time
without the use of bottled oxygen, 1978

In a second, I was looking 8,000 feet down into Tibet.

STEP BY FRIGHTENING STEP, I made my way out onto the ridge. The snow seemed solid enough. I made sure my boots went exactly into the footprints of the climbers who had gone before me. My legs shook.

I'd gone about 15 feet when suddenly, my eye caught sight of a one-inch wide hole in the snow. In a second, I was looking 8,000 feet down into Tibet. I gasped in horror, then instantly, snapped my glance back onto my feet.

"C'mon Alan," I said to myself. "Don't look down guy. Whatever you do, *do not* look down! You don't want to go down. You want to go up. So keep focusing on what's going to get you there. Focus on your feet, man. Focus on your feet!"

I did, with everything I had. My concentration was probably enough to melt a hole in the snow. I knew the hole already there had probably been made by the shaft of the ice ax of a previous climber. I didn't want to make it bigger.

One shaking foot after another, I gradually made my way out onto the ridge. I'd gone about five more feet when, to my total amazement, I noticed a thin black line of anchored rope running along the snow on my right. Somehow, I'd failed to notice it before, perhaps because it was only about a quarter of an inch thick. Carefully, I raised my glance to follow it. To my absolute delight, the rope ran all the way along the ridge to the base of the Hillary Step. And, it was brand new!

You have never seen a guy clip into a rope faster. Without hesitation, I connected the line to my harness. Immediately, I breathed a huge sigh of relief, like I'd just overcome heart failure.

It was not until many weeks after the expedition that I learned that Jamie had placed that rope. He had taken the time to anchor the rope because he knew he and his Sherpa climbing partners would need an extra margin of safety on the descent. He knew we'd all have to traverse across that ridge on the descent. He also knew we'd all be tired.

Thanks to that rope, I safely and easily made my way across the remainder of the ridge. Ahead of me, Tashi quickly ascended the Hillary Step, a tricky little rock step about 30 or 40 feet high. At lower elevations, it would have been a walk in the park, but here, at more than 28,500 feet, it became an arduous challenge while wearing a bulky climbing suit, big boots, thick mitts, and a cumbersome oxygen mask.

Whatever you do, do not look down!

To get an idea of what this is like, next time you have the flu and a headache during the winter, put on every stitch of clothing you own, cover your mouth with a scarf, don dark goggles, heavy ski boots, snowmobile mitts and a snowmobile suit, put on a 30-pound pack, and head into your backyard on a bitterly cold day. There, see if you can climb your own back fence. What seems straightforward in principle is quite another in practice.

At the base of the Step, Kami and I waited for a party of climbers to descend from above.

"Climb! Climb!" Kami urged from behind me, his voice muffled beneath his mask.

"What are you talking about?" I said as the first of about 10 climbers started to slowly lower themselves down the Step on a rope. "Where?"

He pointed to the right of the Step. A wall of snow was caked to the rock, but it was impossible to know if it was sufficiently adhered to the rock to be safe to climb or even if there was anything solid underneath it besides air. My intuition told me there wasn't. I wasn't about to push the odds, especially here.

"You go," I said, my voice telegraphing surprise at his statement. "You go."

Kami did not reply. He just stared at me.

"Okay," I said. "We'll wait."

As the climbers slowly made their way down from above, I looked on in amazement. Most of them seemed very weak and hypoxic. One or two had a hard time just getting their boots to go between the many old ropes festooning the Step. It would have taken a little dexterity even at sea level, but obviously, they weren't at sea level.

I wondered what kind of shape I'd be in if I was able to make it to the summit and had to do what they were doing while descending. I didn't want to be as tired as they were.

Kami and I waited at the bottom of the Step for only about 10 minutes. Fortunately, there was just a slight wind, so we were able to stay warm. I was excited about the prospect of the summit ahead. We were almost there.

The last climber to come down was Jamie. Somehow, I knew it would be him. There was a kind of bizarre preordained sense to the whole day, like it was meant to be. I sensed Chomolungma was watching and orchestrating the whole thing, and I had very little to do with influencing the outcome. That outcome had already been determined long before we left the Col, although our journey to the top of the world had not been without its surprises that day, in my case in particular.

Jamie quickly rappelled down the Hillary Step. I was overjoyed to see him. I explained that my oxygen set had malfunctioned, that I'd become extremely cold, but that everyone was all right. He patted me on the shoulder, as if to say, "Well done."

Then, of course, I asked him the question anyone would ask in my place:

"What was the summit like?"

Jamie peered at me through his dark goggles. Beneath his mask, his words were muffled, but I will never forget them:

"It was wonderful," he said, "but it could have been more wonderful."

"What do you mean?"

"You could have been there."

Those words instantly etched themselves in my memory. They stay with me to this day. They galvanized into a dramatic realization, among the most powerful in my life.

It's not the destination that counts. It's the journey.

I had heard this phrase before, but it had never really registered with me. It did then, with powerful force. Not only is the journey important, but what's more important is who we share that journey with. It's who's tied into our rope, how much they care for us and how much we care for them. They'll anchor rope for us along the knife-edged ridges of life, or reach down and pull us out of danger when we are dangling over an abyss. That's the stuff of friendship. That's the stuff that counts. The rest is just details. If we think otherwise, we may need a reality check. We may need an "Everest Awakening." I got one that day.

At the bottom of the Step, Jamie and I didn't have a lot of energy for pleasantries. Besides, it wasn't exactly the kind of place you hung out and socialized. We were in peril even as we spoke. We simply shook hands and wished each other well. I hoped I would see him alive again. You could never take that for granted.

Before me stood the Hillary Step. What an amazing feeling it was to be standing at the base of it after all these years. Now, I could actually reach out and touch it. It did exist. It wasn't some figment of my imagination or some picture in a book. It was cold, hard reality.

I wanted to climb it. I wanted to see what lay above and beyond. I wanted the summit. I wanted it more than anything I had wanted in my life. There was no stopping me now. Now, we were going to stand on top. Now, we were going to do the dream.

The Step was no problem. I picked the least tattered and weather-beaten rope I could see, snapped my jumar onto it and hauled down on it with everything I had. I was past the point of caring. If it pulled, it pulled, and I died. Call me crazy, but I

It's not the destination that counts. It's the journey.

was beyond the point of worrying anymore. I wasn't arrogant or complacent. I was just resigned to fate. I wanted to meet this mountain on its own terms. I wanted to feel its force. I wanted to know its power. Kami followed closely behind.

Above the Step, all three of us — Tashi, Kami, and I — grouped together for the final steps to the summit. I could see the summit ridge rolling up and away to my right. There was nothing but blue sky above it. Carefully, I followed it along for 20 more minutes, 20 long minutes, until I caught sight of a brightly colored clump of tattered flags off to one side. My God! There it was. There was the summit of Mount Everest! There was the peak I'd been dreaming about for 39 years. There was the object of my fantasy, the focus of my passion. My already racing heart began to race even faster.

> *All those who had gone before us were in my thoughts*
> *... all the great climbers who had dreamed and*
> *challenged, fought and failed on this mountain,*
> *and whose efforts and knowledge and experience*
> *had made our victory possible. Our companions below*
> *were in my thoughts, for without them too — without*
> *their help and sacrifice — we could never have been*
> *where we were that day.* — TENZING NORGAY,
> *Man of Everest,*
> on the summit of Everest, May 29, 1953

A short distance from the top, I came across the only stone visible. It was a large boulder, about six feet long and about three feet high. Like everything around me, it sloped down to my left. At first, mesmerized as I was by the summit, I barely noticed it. Then my eye caught sight of a bunch of small pebbles sitting on top of it. Though I was hardly thinking at light speed, something inside me said, "These are for you, Alan. You may take them."

I hesitated.

"It's okay, Alan," I heard her say. "They're for you."

Mechanically, I zipped open a side pocket, reached down and scooped them up with my hand, and without even counting how many stones I had grasped, I carefully placed them inside my suit. Then I closed the pocket again and continued with those final steps.

> *I picked up two small stones and put them in*
> *my pocket to bring back to the world below.*
>
> — TENZING NORGAY,
> *Man of Everest*

Tashi got to the top first. Even from 100 or so feet behind him, I clearly saw his arm pumping up and down in jubilation against the sky. No other parties were with him. He was alone.

My God! We were doing it. We were almost on top of the world, and we had the summit all to ourselves. The weather was perfect, the wind was light and everything was right. Everything was exactly the way I'd imagined and hoped it would be every time I'd visualized it. My dream had not only come true. It had come true in almost every detail except one. Jamie was not with me.

"It's okay, Alan," I heard her say. "They're for you."

I could not do anything about that now. It was past. I shifted my focus to the present. I thought of my father and mother, Peter and Isabel, of my brothers Dan, Eric, and James, John McLernon from Colliers, Gloria Simpson and Jeff Papows from Lotus, Steve Matous, Dave Rodney, Bruce Kirkby, Jason Edwards, Jeff Rhoads, Doug Rovira, all the Sherpas, my dear friends Dale and Cathy Ens, Patti Mayer and Milan Hudec, Mike and Gisela Fuller, Rob Aikens, and, of course, Cal Zaryski.

I thought of Diane too. She was there, especially in my heart. I wished she was beside me. I felt her love.

> *At a time like this you think of many things. I thought*
> *of Darjeeling, of home, of Ang Lahmu and the girls.*
>
> — TENZING NORGAY,
> *Man of Everest,*
> during summit attempt in Swiss Everest Expedition, 1952

Then Skreslet spoke again, this time so loudly I almost looked around for him:

"Once in your life, if you're lucky," he said, "you get to make manifest what you profess to believe."

Through all those years, through all those setbacks, and all those "failures," Jamie and I had professed to believe we could climb Everest. Many had said we couldn't. Many had said we would die. But we *were* doing it. We were there! And so far, we *were* alive. I was just a few steps away from the culmination of my greatest lifelong dream.

Was this actually happening?

I took those last steps with ease. Kami followed within seconds. We all bear-hugged together on the summit. It was magic.

> *I waved my arms in the air, and then threw them round Hillary, and we thumped each other on the back until, even with the oxygen, we were almost breathless.*
>
> — TENZING NORGAY,
> *Man of Everest,*
> on the summit of Everest

I barely looked at the view. I just grabbed the radio and called out to base camp.

"Base, do you copy? Over."

"We copy loud and clear," Dave's crisp, clear voice came back as if he was standing right next to me. "This is Dave in base camp, Alan. Over."

I felt a lump welling up in my throat.

"David. Hobson here. Friday, 23rd May, 9 a.m. Half the dream is done. Over."

My voice started to crack with emotion.

"Alan, we are so happy for you. We are so proud of you. Congratulations my friend. You deserve it. This has been a long time coming. How do you feel?"

"I am here with Tashi Tsering, Kami Tshering, we're all on the summit. Over."

"That's absolutely fantastic, Alan. We're really happy for you. Great news. Over."

"Once in your life, if you're lucky, you get to make manifest what you profess to believe."

– LAURIE SKRESLET

24. Staggering immensity. The view of Everest from the summit of Mt. Kalapatar at sunset. She dwarfed everything around her, including our insignificant ambitions. (Photo: Bruce Kirkby)

25. The world at our feet. Kami climbing Everest's southeast ridge just below the South Summit during our summit bid. Mt. Lhotse is in the background. (Photo: Alan Hobson)

26. Sheer terror. The deadly knife-edge ridge between the South Summit and the Hillary Step. Not shown: The 8,000-foot drop on your right and the 6,000-foot drop on your left. The actual ridge is only a few feet wide. One misplaced step could be your last. (Photo: Jamie Clarke)

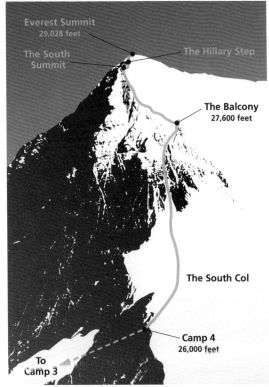

Everest Summit
29,028 feet

The South
Summit

The Hillary Step

The Balcony
27,600 feet

The South Col

Camp 4
26,000 feet

To
Camp 3

27. The penultimate peak. Kami cresting the South Summit. Note the overhanging slab of windblown snow, a dangerous cornice. If you step too far to the right, you fall 8,000 feet to your death. (Photo: Alan Hobson)

28. The route to the summit from Camp 4. Most of those who die on Everest die somewhere here, usually on their way down. Experienced climbers may celebrate on the summit, but they know that most of the danger, and the work, is still ahead of them. It truly "ain't over 'til it's over" in base camp.

29. "Half the dream is done." The author on the summit with Colliers and Lotus. It was a feeling of elation and anxiety. (Photo: Kami Tshering)

30. The view from the top of the world looking north into Tibet. We looked down on our two previous "failures" and knew what it had taken to get there. (Photo: Jamie Clarke)

31. Powered by Buddha. Lhakpa Tshering descending through the Icefall with a huge load. No crampons, no ice ax, and only a tumpline across the forehead to support the load. Strength, balance and endurance beyond human comprehension. (Photo: Bruce Kirkby)

32. Safe at last. Ang Temba (left), me, and my guardian angel, Pema Temba (right), moments after we emerged for the last time from the Icefall. Indescribable relief. (Photo: Bruce Kirkby)

33. Risky rescue. Carrying
Tsultrim Kalsang Sherpa
out of the Icefall. A massive
effort by climbers from
all over the world.
(Photo: Bruce Kirkby)

34. Half a face, but still
completely alive. Jason (right)
and Tsultrim (center) shortly
before the Sherpa's evacuation
by helicopter to Kathmandu.
He made a full recovery.
(Photo: Jason Edwards)

35. Nothing short of heroic. Jamie and Hugo (left) after the Mexican's rescue. (Photo: Jeff Rhoads)

36. A joyous homecoming. My mother, Isabel, a saint for having tolerated my risk-taking and strong will for 39 years, greets me as she always has, with open arms and a loving heart. Unconditional acceptance and support since I was a boy. (Photo: Peter Hobson)

37. A happy homecoming. (From left) Bruce Kirkby, Jamie Clarke, Gloria Simpson (of Lotus), the author, and Dave Rodney (who later summitted, May 13, 1999) upon arrival at the airport in Calgary. (Photo: Gloria Simpson)

38. The underwater equivalent of Henry Ford. San Francisco's brilliant submersible designer, Graham Hawkes (left) and the author in front of Graham's stunning prototype, Deep Flight I. (Photo: Karen Hawkes)

39. From the top of the world to the bottom. The 36,000-foot-deep Challenger Deep of the Mariana Trench. Deeper than Everest is tall. (Graphic: Rachel Moffat, Beyond Expectations, Vancouver)

40. James Bond meets Graham Hawkes. Graham's revolutionary "flying" submersible, Deep Flight I, during its maiden dive in the Pacific. (Photo: Amos Nachoum)

41. The key that could unlock the door to Earth's final physical frontier. Hawkes' stunning Deep Flight II design for The Ocean Everest Expedition. (Graphic: Hawkes Ocean Technologies, Richmond, Ca.)

"I also confirm the summit was achieved by Jamie earlier today with Lhakpa and Gyalbu."

"That's great, Alan. We're reading you loud and clear down here. We want you to be safe on your way back down. Over."

"Don't worry about that," I said. "I'll be doubly focused on that. Skreslet taught us all that. Now, we're going to take some pictures with the boys here. We're going to head down real slowly and all I'd like to say is ..."

I started to cry. My voice broke up.

"... if you're persistent enough, you can do the dreams. Over."

I wept openly in Tashi and Kami's arms. I just let it flow.

"Come on down back safe and we'll have a big party," Dave said. "There's Fanta (orange soda pop) waiting for you pal."

I tried to compose myself. It was hard. I just let go. I just let it all hang out. I couldn't speak for at least a minute.

Finally, I blubbered out some words....

"I'll be there to collect it [the Fanta] Dave. Love to you all and love to everyone who believed in the dream. Over."

I'd like to tell you that I had this magical moment of bliss on the summit. I'd like to tell you that I looked around at the view, savoring it like I'd savored the look on Diane's face the day she'd left in Pheriche, memorizing every color and curve of the face of Mother Earth, every nuance, every shadow, etching it indelibly into memory.

> *It was such a sight as I had never seen before and would never see again — wild, wonderful and terrible.*
>
> — TENZING NORGAY,
> *Man of Everest,*
> on the view from the summit

I didn't. Laurie, Bill March, Pat Morrow, Sharon Wood, Dwayne Congdon, and the other Canadians who had summited before me had hammered into me that you did not celebrate on the summit, that you didn't let go. If you did, you could die. If you let your guard down, even for a second, Chomolungma could whisk you away. She could punish you

"If you're persistent enough, you can do the dreams."

for your arrogance. You were, after all, standing on her heart. You were in her womb, her core. You did not laugh, cry, holler, or whoop it up like you were in some tavern. You were in the throne room of the gods. You maintained your composure and respect or you courted disaster.

I tried to control myself. I couldn't. I had to let go, if even for a moment. I prayed she would understand and allow me just this moment.

"Alan sounded like he should have sounded on the summit," Jeff recalls, "— pretty elated and emotional, but he understood what was ahead of him."

Tashi and Kami looked worried. They'd never seen me cry before. They wanted to ensure I was all right. I was, of course, but they had no way of knowing that. All they saw was this grown man crying, sobbing uncontrollably. The tears froze to my face.

You did not celebrate on the summit.

> *Is it the summit, crowning the day? How cool and quiet! We're non-exultant; but delighted, joyful; soberly astonished.... Have we vanquished an enemy? None but ourselves. Have we gained success? That word means nothing here.*
>
> — GEORGE LEIGH MALLORY,
> British mountaineer and Everest climber

My gymnastics coach, Ken Allen, of the University of Wisconsin in Oshkosh, came to me then too. He had taught me to finish one event and move on to the next. He had taught me to parcel off my feelings, to focus on the task at hand, and then to execute. It was time to move to the next event.

Summoning every ounce of emotional energy I had left, I pulled myself back into myself. I regained my concentration and started taking pictures. No matter what happened, they would prove we were there. I could look at them over and over again once I got down, if I got down. Now was not the time to celebrate. Now was the time to stay in control.

*I thought, No, we ourselves will get there — and can
do it! But if we do it, can we get down again?*

— TENZING NORGAY,
Man of Everest,
1952 Swiss Everest Expedition summit bid

We took our pictures. I remember a moment when I looked down at the summit flags. All of them were tattered, torn, and faded. They surrounded a beaten up weather instrument. Together, the whole sight looked a little junky, like it didn't belong there. That was the way I felt. I was intruding on an entity's inner space, an entity I couldn't even see, but who was unquestionably present.

I looked at the summit again, the highest geographical point on the planet. Oddly enough, it didn't seem sacred at all. It had been desecrated by man.

The summit of Mount Everest is a rounded snow fin formed into an arc. It's about 15 feet long, four feet wide, and four feet high. It slopes to a point from either side. Scoured as it is by the jet stream, it is often as hard as cement. That day, the snow was loose. We stepped easily into it, but we were careful not to step too far to the right....

On closer inspection of the summit, I was amazed to see a brand new red and white Canadian flag staring back at me proudly. At first, I thought Jamie had put it there. I learned later that it was fellow Canadian and Calgarian, Andy Evans, who had summited from the north side the day before. What a welcome sight it was, grand and glorious in its majesty. The maple leaf fluttered fairly in the breeze at 29,028 feet.

"Highest maple leaf on the planet," I thought to myself. "No doubt about that. No trees here."

I was only on top for 15 minutes. It was just a moment. People see the summit, but the mountaineer feels the mountain. I felt the mountain of effort it had taken to get there, the sacrifices, the setbacks, and the disappointments. The temperature was about 35 degrees below zero, the sky was a beautiful turquoise blue and there was almost no wind. But I didn't even really pause to feel or see it. Maybe it was my

**The summit
of Mount
Everest is
a rounded
snow fin
formed into
an arc. It's
about 15 feet
long, four feet
wide, and
four feet high.**

hypoxia, but as soon as the photographs were taken, I began to focus on the descent. I wanted to make this effort count. I didn't want to die descending. I didn't want to become another statistic, not after having come this far. I wanted to win. Winning meant surviving.

> *As we turned to leave the summit I prayed to Him*
> *for something very real and very practical —*
> *that, having given us our victory, He would get*
> *us down off the mountain alive.* — TENZING NORGAY,
> *Man of Everest*

Without taking a second glance back at the summit, at 9:15 a.m., we headed down. Quickly, we descended to the Hillary Step. Tashi led, as usual. He seemed to like it in front. Some climbers are happier there. Kami followed behind me as he had on the way up. There was a special feeling of security knowing I had two of the strongest Sherpas in the world with me. I knew I could count on them, and I would have to.

I wanted to win. Winning meant surviving.

The Descent from Hell

It's a round trip. Getting to the summit is optional.
Getting down is mandatory. — ED VIESTURS,
American high-altitude climber

AS A PRECAUTIONARY MEASURE, I took a tablet of dexamethasone. As I have said, it is a steroid climbers use to pick themselves up, rather like drinking an entire pot of coffee in one go, except you don't have to pee. It is frowned upon except in emergencies. Although I was still very much in control, I thought it was better to be safe than sorry. If it could add an extra margin of safety, I was willing to use it. I abandoned my ego and committed myself to my next mission, getting down safely.

Getting back across the knife-edged ridge to the South Summit was surprisingly straightforward. For some reason, I felt little fear. It was now known ground to me, and knowledge, as they say, is power. I just concentrated on putting my boots into the footprint holes as I had on the way up, and I didn't stop until I had gotten safely to the South Summit. There, we paused to rest and regroup and that's where I started to get cold again.

I don't know what happened. Maybe it was because I hadn't eaten anything of any substance besides small packages of PowerGel, a very high carbohydrate source similar in texture and taste to cake icing. I probably needed a lot more calories and until now, I hadn't noticed that I'd needed them. I had been too focused on making it to the top. Or maybe it was just the emotional relief of having achieved the peak and now my body was letting go.

Whatever the reason, I started to "bonk" again. I knew full well that most climbers who die, die on their way down from the summit. I also knew that bad weather could sweep in fast from Tibet and that because we were so high up, that weather would build silently from below.

I tried to pull myself back together, again. Within moments, however, I started to shiver.

I asked Kami if he could pull my parka out of my backpack. That would save me the energy and hassle of having to take it off myself.

He was in the process of putting on an extra pair of mitts. Apparently, he was cold too. So, I just lay down in the snow for a moment — a *big* mistake.

Within seconds, I went from shivering to freezing. When you're as tired as I was, with blood sugar low from lack of food, the world at your feet and it's freezing cold outside, all you want to do is lie down and have a little sleep. As I've said, it can be a sleep from which you never awake.

To conserve heat, I pulled my knees up against my chest and curled into the fetal position, face first in the snow. I tucked my chin tightly against my chest and pulled my bent elbows closely in against my sides. I knew Kami would help as soon as he could.

It's frightening how fast you can lose control on a mountain. Within seconds, I was shivering wildly, my speech was slurred and I knew I was in trouble again. Tashi was busy with his own challenges. Everyone seemed fine, I sensed, except me, but there was precious little I could do except try to warm up where I was.

It was impossible. My blood sugar was too low, I was too tired and now, I was too close to the snow. It was a recipe for disaster.

Those minutes on the South Summit haunt me to this day. I became even colder than I had been that morning and now, hours after my 2:35 a.m. moment of truth, I was faced with

Most climbers who die, die on their way down from the summit.

another one. Now, however, I was substantially more depleted physically, psychologically, and emotionally. My coping abilities were far less sharp.

... the coldness was so deep that it bit through even our warmest clothing into our flesh and bones.

— TENZING NORGAY,
Man of Everest,
Swiss Everest Expedition, autumn, 1952

"Come on Kami," I said to myself. "Get that parka."

If I appear as a weakling incapable of getting his own parka out of his pack, so be it. We all have moments of weakness and that definitely was one of mine. It was not only a moment of truth. It was also a moment of terror. I might easily have frozen to death there and still be curled up in a frozen lump for all eternity. If I could just use my body heat to warm up a little bit though, I thought, I might make it.

Here is my story. Here is myself. — TENZING NORGAY,
Man of Everest

We all have moments of weakness.

I thought wrong. Finally, I felt Kami burrowing into my pack. He pulled out my parka, pried off my pack and helped me into my down cocoon.

It was magic, like always. I cannot tell you how many times that jacket has saved my life. It was, and still is, one of the most indispensable pieces of equipment I own. I rarely go anywhere in the mountains without it, and I certainly go nowhere without it in the winter. It weighs almost nothing, packs down to a lump the size of a football and within minutes of being put on, it can capture enough body heat to bring you back from the brink. All I needed was a few minutes for it to do its stuff.

"We go," I heard Tashi say suddenly.

"No," I said as the words struck fear into my shaking body. "Just give me a minute here. I'll be okay."

"We go," Tashi said again.

This time, through the corner of my eye, I saw him gesture downwards, over the edge of the Kangchung Face. I pulled my head up out of the snow for a second and peered downwards.

Even though I was shaking so badly that I had difficulty seeing, what I was able to make out was enough to launch me to my feet immediately. Thousands of feet below us, there was a huge cloudbank sweeping in from Tibet. For the moment, we were fine, but in a few hours, we could find ourselves in a terrible storm.

With every ounce of will I had, I moved forward again. "Okay Tashi," I said, shivering. "We go."

> *Nothing mattered now except to get down out of that hell that was so close to heaven. We were in a race with the cold and the wind — and with death.*
>
> — Tenzing Norgay,
> *Man of Everest*

Thousands of feet below us, there was a huge cloudbank sweeping in from Tibet.

We did, slowly, and carefully. We got down off the South Summit, step by deliberate step, over the little rock step we'd come up below the penultimate peak, out onto the southeast ridge below, all the while conscious of the horrific exposure of thousands of feet only inches away from the soles of our boots. If any of us fell here, it would be over.

> *All that was in our minds was to get down, down and away from the cold, where a man could breathe, where he could eat and sleep, where he could warm his hands and his feet and his bones....*
>
> — Tenzing Norgay,
> *Man of Everest*

Just when I started to feel like I was warming up, I suddenly felt like I was suffocating. I checked the oxygen-flow gauge to my mask. It registered normal. I could feel the gas passing gently over my face and hear the hissing from the tank, but for some reason, I couldn't breathe. Within seconds, I was gasping.

I tore the mask from my face. Instantly, I could breathe. Kami and Tashi were not amused. Obviously, I was tired. The last thing they wanted was some white-faced rookie trying to descend Everest without oxygen. Heaven knows, it had been hard enough for me to climb up on oxygen. Now, as depleted as I was, I could be in grave danger if I tried to climb down without gas.

Tashi took action. Like a magician, he pulled a whole new mask out of his backpack. Within seconds, he had exchanged it for my old one. Moments later, I found myself breathing again. Likely, we deduced, the exhalation valve on my previous mask had frozen shut, thus allowing the carbon dioxide exhaled in my breath to build up in my mask to unhealthy levels.

Unfortunately, I quickly discovered that wasn't the problem. In minutes, I again began to feel like I was suffocating. The only way I could breath was to remove my mask every few minutes, take in some air from the outside, put the mask back on for as long as I could stand it, and repeat the process. The mask was on, the oxygen appeared to be flowing, but I felt like I was suffocating again. This went on for hours.

Unknown to me, the action of repeatedly removing and replacing my mask was slowly scraping the sun block from my skin. Imperceptibly, my face was gradually burning.

I wasn't the only one in difficulty. Because the bulky oxygen mask and glacier glasses or goggles weren't necessarily compatible, while I was having problems breathing, Kami was having problems seeing. He couldn't seem to keep his eyewear from fogging up and freezing.

It's hard enough to climb up when you're having a hard time seeing your feet. It's even more difficult to climb down. The only way Kami could see was to position his glasses at the level of his eyebrows and squint as best he could against the intense ultraviolet rays. Tashi had the same problem, but to a lesser degree. In a true display of chivalry, he offered to swap glasses with Kami. Nothing seemed to work. The heat, combined with the exertion, was hurting all of us.

One might think that Sherpas as experienced as ours would be fully equipped for a summit day on Everest. The reality is that most of the income the Sherpas earn from expeditions goes straight to their extended families. They use very little of it to buy personal climbing equipment. Thus, they rely on expeditions to supply them with everything from boots and crampons to glasses. Expeditions have an option to supply them with a cash advance with which to purchase this gear. This is the route our expedition had gone. Almost without exception, however, the Sherpas choose to save this money for their families. The result is that many of them show up on the mountain with less than adequate equipment and on days such as summit day, you find out where those inadequacies lie. By then, of course, it's too late to do anything about it. Even meetings prior to summit day fail to reveal these problems. The Sherpas are intensely proud, somewhat shy and are often not forthcoming about shortcomings in their equipment. They resolve to make due.

In 1994, Jamie and I had tried to circumvent this problem by providing the Sherpas with thousands of dollars in custom-made clothing and equipment. As it turned out, the Sherpas rarely wore or used it either, electing instead to keep it in mint condition for resale after the expedition. The bottom line? It's very difficult to properly equip a Sherpa. You must rely on them to rely on themselves. They do, but it often means they suffer because of it.

So there we were with me approaching exhaustion and Kami and Tashi having a hard time seeing. In spite of their challenges, they were still doing everything in their power to keep me from falling. Tashi led the way closely in front and Kami pulled up the rear tightly behind. We were not roped together, however, having elected to save the weight of carrying a rope.

At one point, I did slip on my backside, but fortunately, I'd taken the time to clip into the safety line anchored in the snow. I only slid about 10 feet before I plowed to a stop. I'm sure it didn't look pretty, and it wasn't, but I didn't care any more. All I wanted to do was get down before a storm hit.

As the hours passed, the temperature rose substantially. The kind of heat you get at high altitude during the day isn't like any other heat I've experienced anywhere in the world. You feel like you're in a frying pan. The reflected light can blind you in a matter of minutes. A furnace seems to build up inside your clothes. It feels like you're being baked alive, and you are. Gradually, the temperature inside your clothing increases until you feel like you're going to explode.

To remove a layer of clothing, however, is out of the question. It takes too much energy. To do so, you have to sit down, take off your pack and harness and sometimes even your boots. When you're really tired, you just can't be bothered. So, you persevere.

While the temperature was increasing, I was watching the clouds over Tibet build from below. Within an hour, they were starting to lick their way almost to the level of the "Balcony." From there down to the Col, there was no anchored rope. If we had to descend the triangular face below in a storm, I knew one of us might easily fall. I had a pretty good idea who it was most likely to be. So, I approached the "Balcony" with increasing anxiety, searching for some way to bypass the steep, snow-covered face. Unfortunately, it was futile.

"Is there a safer way down from the 'Balcony,'" I asked Kami, "one that might be less steep?"

"No," he said quietly. "Slowly, slowly. No hurry."

If there was a message that transcended my growing concern, fatigue, and fear, it was that, "slowly, slowly. No hurry."

Kami and Tashi's calmness did wonders for me. They didn't seem the least bit perturbed by my struggles, or theirs, not to mention the potential of an approaching storm that could kill all of us. There was a serenity to them, a special peace. It telegraphed beyond words that I didn't need to worry. Whatever was going to happen, was going to happen. Nothing I could do could alter that outcome. We had done and were doing everything in our power to maximize our chances of getting safely back down to Camp 4. Now, we were to await our destiny in peace.

> "Slowly, slowly. No hurry."
>
> – KAMI TSHERING SHERPA

I don't know where this kind of strength comes from. It wasn't just experience, I sensed. It was something else. The stories I'd heard about the legendary Sherpas were true. They were connected — to Everest and to the cosmos, as esoteric, unrealistic, and detached as that may sound. They not only communed and communicated with the mountain. They listened to her and, most importantly, they heard her.

So it was that I came to know Kami and Tashi in a way few people have. I came to see not only their unimaginable physical strength, but their spiritual peace. They are a people like none other. They are the Sherpas of Nepal, the Tigers of the Snow. They exist in harmony with the mountain because they are Everest incarnate, strong metaphysically as well as physically.

We reached the "Balcony" about noon, three hours after leaving the summit. Here, I discovered that the Sherpas never use the term, "Balcony." If I'd used the term, "ridge" that morning when talking to Kami, he would have instantly understood me.

Now, I tried to reassure myself by thinking that, in the heat, the snow on the triangular face below would provide extra purchase for our boots. If we were lucky, our steps would plunge more deeply into the pack than they had on the way up, affording us a greater degree of safety on the 45-degree slope.

Thankfully, that's exactly what happened. As I took my first anxious steps down the face, I was relieved beyond measure to see that my boots penetrated deeper than they had on the way up.

About this time, I could hear Jamie and Jason calling me on the radio. When you're exhausted, it can take a Herculean effort just to figure out where something as obvious as a radio is, find it, and lift it to your mouth. So, I stopped, sat down in the snow, found the radio and tried to speak.

"I'm pretty fried," I said slowly to Jason. "We're just trying to do this right."

Doug came on the radio.

"Al," he said. "Don't mess with this. You're bound to be baked. Take a tablet of dexamethasone and see if that helps."

I explained that I had already taken one earlier. He said that taking a second dose should not be any problem.

"Okay," I said. "Thanks."

I swallowed the pill and my pride for the umpteenth time. Everest was compromising ground, a place where an ego was useless.

Then, it was Jamie's turn to talk. It was great to hear his voice.

"Okay pal," he said. "You'll be all right. Just take your time. I'm looking up for you from Camp 4, but I can't see you yet. There's too much cloud. Stand by."

Over my radio, I could hear something going on in Camp 4. It was Jamie talking to Calgary. I could hear the voices of Karen Harris and other members of our staff back home, as well as friends, but unfortunately, I had no way of replying to them. They seemed to be celebrating.

"Christ," I thought to myself. "What the hell's going on? I'm fighting for my life and they're celebrating. This is hardly a *fait accompli*. I could buy it here in a millisecond, no problem."

The reality was that they were trying to reach me to encourage me too, but they couldn't. For technical reasons, we couldn't make the connection work. I didn't know that one of the reasons they were celebrating was because Jamie had just proposed by radio to his girlfriend, Barb, from Camp 4, and she had accepted! She had been in Nepal leading two of our corporate trekking groups to and from base camp. In one of the most amazing moments on the trip, he apparently tracked her down in her hotel room in Kathmandu and, by satellite from the highest pass on Earth, he had popped the question. He joked later that he had been hypoxic at the time and not responsible for his actions, but the reality was, they were highly compatible and very much in love.

While this love drama was playing itself out, I was approaching complete exhaustion. I hadn't been able to eat anything of any substance all day and as a result, I was hitting the wall — the black, frozen, windswept wall. About 1,200 feet above Camp 4, I lost bladder control. I didn't have the energy to mess with my clothing. So I went in my climbing suit. It felt

I was hitting the wall — the black, frozen, windswept wall.

good not to have to struggle with zippers. Shortly after that, I became so spent that all I could do was take 30 jerky steps, sit in the snow, take a 60-second nap, get up, take 30 more steps, and repeat the process. This went on for about two and a half hours. They were the longest two and a half hours of my life. Strung out in the rarefied air, my legs at the point where they were almost collapsing underneath me, I literally walked the fine line between life and death with every feeble step.

It seemed like days instead of hours. — TENZING NORGAY, *Man of Everest,* on the descent from the summit

Back in Colorado, Steve awaited news.

"Until I knew everyone was safely back in base camp, I wasn't going to celebrate," he remembers. "I'd been there [on Everest] too many times. Alan's support was fading very quickly behind him. I thought, 'This is not over yet.'"

I have never been so anxious in my life. It was not terror, the kind I had felt crossing the ridge from the South Summit to the base of the Hillary Step. It was instead a pervading and almost overwhelming uneasiness that kept eating at the back of my mind. A part of me just wanted to let go of the struggle, collapse, and fall. That would have been a relief, I thought. At least then my legs would stop burning, if only for a second. Of course, I'd probably bust them in no time cartwheeling down the face, but that would be inconsequential in the end. All I wanted to do was stop hurting. I just wanted to lie down and go to sleep.

I have never in my life experienced this level of exhaustion, and I pray I never will again. It made the fatigue I'd experienced running 26-mile marathons seem like child's play. It was many, many times more difficult. The only thing that kept me vertical and in motion was the thought that I had to make this effort count. I had to make it stick. I didn't want to make a stupid mistake and blow it in the last 1,000 feet. That would be silly. I wasn't stupid. I wanted to do the smart thing. That meant literally taking it one step at a time.

Suddenly, Jason came back on the radio:

"Do you have any rope?" he asked.

I looked over at Kami and Tashi. They shrugged their shoulders.

"No, sorry buddy," I replied.

I knew what he was inferring. He wanted the Sherpas to "short rope" me down. That meant basically that they would tether me down the face. I drew the line at that. Yes, I was tired, but I wasn't a lump of clay, at least not yet. I was a qualified climber, even if there wasn't much of the climber left in me. I guess I still had some pride, even though it had long ago lost its place. I was glad we didn't have any rope. I needed to feel in some way that I'd faced the mountain, and myself, on my own terms. Full credit goes to Jason for looking out for my safety, though. He was paying attention to the details, as always.

It seemed like I'd never get to the bottom. I'd look up from my regularly occurring seat in the snow, and the yellow tento at Camp 4 never seemed to be getting any bigger. It seemed like a cruel joke. In my fatigue, I didn't realize I could now see what color they were. You don't notice that stuff when you're fried. The detail's too small, even though to a normal person, it's as plain as day. For an exhausted man, it's all he can do just to keep moving. All you want is for the war to end. You want peace.

It seemed like a cruel joke — and Everest was laughing.

After a while, Kami and Tashi got my descent strategy down to a science. Kami would go ahead of me, take 30 steps and sit down quietly in the snow. Then, I'd pull in beside him, sit down, and a moment or two later, Tashi would park beside me. There we'd sit for a moment, just the three of us, looking down at Camp 4, watching the clouds roll by. Not a word was spoken. There was no impatience, no pressure, no rush whatsoever. It really was, "slowly, slowly. No hurry." I was allowed to be, to be tired, slow, awkward and even a bit spastic. That was okay, I sensed from the Sherpas. It was perfectly okay. In fact, it was understandable and expected. I was accepted for what I was where I was — high and dog tired.

What special men these were, Kami and Tashi, I thought. If they had been Westerners, they'd have been all over me complaining about our rate of descent, how much we should speed up in case we got caught in a storm, and how slowly I was going. What came over me instead was a profound sense of security. It wasn't a false sense of security either, the kind of complacency created by fatigue. I was acutely aware of how much danger we were all in, especially me. I knew how easily I could die. It would have been as easy as rolling over. I held on.

I remember a particularly touching moment then. It was a touching moment because it was exactly that, touching. We were about 800 feet above camp, and the clouds were whisking their way in and out across the face. For a second, you could see the Col. In the next, you couldn't.

As we sat there speechless in the snow, Kami reached over and put his hand on my knee. He didn't say a word. He just laid it there for a moment.

I was either going to do this, or I was going to die.

We do these things not because we have to, but because we want to; in the spirit not of servants, but of good companions.
— TENZING NORGAY,
Man of Everest,
on the Sherpa way

He might just as well have hugged me and sent in a marching band. Without words, he was saying, "You know Al, it will be okay." I'd heard those words from Ang Temba during our first trip to the mountain. I knew then that even if I died, there would be no dishonor. I now knew I'd given it *everything* I had. I was either going to do this, or I was going to die. It was that simple. Whatever happened from this point forward, I knew Kami and Tashi would be right there with me to the end, if necessary.

"Just being with the Sherpas, there is that presence and aura," Steve would tell me later, "— peaceful, calm, gracious. In many ways, they are mentors. Their inner strength is way above the rest of us for the most part.... They are little people physically, but emotionally, spiritually, they are huge."

At some deep level, I knew I wasn't going to die. The storm I had feared had not materialized. We were going to make it.

We *were*. If I had to crawl on my goddamn hands and knees, I was going to make it to Camp 4. No one was going to say I was crazy — ever again. No one was going to tell me again I'd failed. I was going to win. I *was*. That realization filtered its way slowly into my consciousness. I settled into the rhythm of my struggle — stand, stagger out some steps, collapse, nod off, force myself awake, up on my feet again and repeat — over and over and over again. I became an automaton, a mechanical man powered not only by the thin threads of his ever-weakening will, but by the collective strength of those around him. Kami and Tashi did carry me down that day, but they did not use a rope or their hands. They used their spirits.

At 2:30 p.m. on May 23, 1997, the picture I had been trying to paint for so many painful hours finally crystallized before my eyes. Through a break in the clouds, I stumbled into the South Col like a drunkard. Kami and Tashi skipped. Pema came running up the hill with a flask of hot tea. He poured me a cup and slowly, I lifted it to my lips. I drank in its warmth, savoring it like fine wine. Then, he handed me some cookies, hugged me warmly, and helped me back to my tent. There, he helped me off with my clothes, stuffed me into a sleeping bag and handed me a can of Pringles. Then, he went to work brewing more tea and prepared a gourmet meal of macaroni and boil-in-a-bag smoked Canadian trout fit for a king. It was the best meal I have ever tasted.

No one was going to tell me again I'd failed. I was going to win.

> *Noyce brought us tea ... as I was drinking it,*
> *it tastes as sweet as buttered milk, because it is*
> *mixed with love and kindness.* — TENZING NORGAY,
> *Man of Everest,*
> on returning to the South Col
> after his climb to the summit

"Hobson to base camp," I somehow managed to force out in a hoarse voice over the radio. "I confirm the safe return of myself, Kami Tshering Sherpa, and Tashi Tsering Sherpa to Camp 4. We're down from the summit. We're back safe. Over."

A big cheer came back at me from base camp like it was from the tent next door. It reverberated out over the Col, down over those cold and empty oxygen cylinders, out over the memories of Hillary and Tenzing, of Chris Bonington and Peter Habeler and across the auras of Bill March, Laurie Skreslet, John Amatt, Peter Spear, Pat Morrow, Sharon Wood, Dwayne Congdon and the rest of my Canadian heroes who had helped fuel my dream. They were there all right. I felt their presence.

Jamie was there too, right next to me in the tent. He rolled over, wrapped me in his arms like a baby and gave me a long hug. Our bodies didn't just meet. Our spirits melted together. He held me for the longest time as I coughed and wheezed and struggled to breathe. I felt his warmth and love. Our souls touched.

"Nice job Al," he said quietly as he held my head. "Nice job."

Within seconds, I drifted off into a semi-doze. But I couldn't sleep. I hurt too much. My throat felt like course sandpaper, my face burned and my body ached.

Almost all our food was frozen like stone, but I managed to heat up some chocolate and pass it round. Then came another night at the last limit of the earth.

— Tenzing Norgay,
Man of Everest,
on his last night on the South Col

Yet I was alive! I was back from the summit, back amongst friends, back in the warm grace of the Sherpas! I was safe, at least for the moment.

"I feel like my bone marrow's tired," Jamie said.

That's what it felt like and that's what it took.

"I feel like my bone marrow's tired," Jamie said.

Deliverance from the Dream

*I seemed to discover the deep significance of
existence of which till then I had been unaware.
I saw that it was better to be true than to be strong.
The marks of my ordeal are apparent on my body. I
was saved and had won my freedom. This freedom,
which I shall never lose, has given me the assurance
and serenity of a man who has fulfilled himself....
A new and splendid life has opened out before me.*

— MAURICE HERZOG,
first man to climb a 26,000-foot peak,
Mt. Annapurna, Nepal, 1951

IT WAS A SHORT NIGHT. I was so tired, yet I slept only fitfully. Before I knew it, a new day had dawned and at the inhumane hour of 6 a.m., I was abruptly awakened by the sound of Lhakpa Tshering outside our tent, opening the tent zipper beside my head.

"Hobson!" he said enthusiastically. "Need mattress."

"Wha, wha, what's going on?" I thought as I struggled to enter a world I was sure had bashed my head in with a hammer during the night.

"My mattress?," I replied. "What for, Lhakpa? It's barely light."

"Must go, Alan," Lhakpa said. "Soon."

I squinted bleary-eyed out the tent door and was amazed to see that the Sherpa tent that had been beside us the night before was in the process of being packed up. Lhakpa, Gyalbu, Kami, and Tashi were already hard at work stuffing gear into packs. In our tent, Pema was preparing breakfast. Clearly, it was time to get off the Col.

I fought to move. My head felt like a brick. My eyelids hung like lead.

"You guys are nuts," I said, "totally nuts. But okay."

I rolled over in my sleeping bag and off my mattress. In a second, Lhakpa's arm came firing through the tent door, swept the mattress out from under me and it disappeared outside.

"You climb Everest and all they want is your sleeping mattress," I thought, chuckling to myself. "Next thing they'll want is the tent and bags and I'll be lying here in only my underwear freezing my butt off."

"The joys of summiting," I thought. "No rest for the wicked."

What a wicked way I was in. My face really hurt. It burned. Unknown to me, I had second-degree burns as a result of having scraped most of the sun block off my face taking my oxygen mask on and off during the descent. Overnight, Kami had developed mild snow blindness, an excruciatingly painful affliction that fortunately heals in a few days. We'd given him painkillers and eye drops. Fortunately, he could still see and we ensured he had the darkest goggles possible to provide maximum protection for his eyes while he descended.

Most of the team was in quite good shape, all things considered. Pema was hard at it, getting grub prepared. I was thankful I didn't have to melt snow. Jamie and I could have done it, but it was wonderful just to sit up, in itself not an easy task given our state, and have someone hand us a steaming cup of hot chocolate.

I was surprised when Jamie gulped down his concoction and immediately left the tent, muttering something about a rescue. Unknown to me, he had been out of the tent much of the night assisting a climber from another expedition. At the same time, he had checked on me periodically and ensured I had had oxygen at the ready in case mine ran out. This I did not learn until well over a year and a half after the expedition.

"What's he talking about?" I asked Pema as I peered out of the tent across the Col.

My head felt like a brick. My eyelids hung like lead.

"Mexican in trouble," he replied.

Quickly, I opened the tent door further, catching sight of Kami outside. His eyes were bloodshot and watering badly. He was clearly in a lot of discomfort, but as usual, he was chipper.

"Is there someone in trouble?" I asked.

"That tent," he replied, motioning across the Col.

As quickly as I could move in my fatigued condition, I made my way over to the other tent. Jamie was already inside, on the radio, talking to Doug in base camp. He had an exhausted climber cradled in his arms. The man looked like he'd just been through a war. He was drawn, sunburned, and disheveled. His eyes were sunken deeply into his weathered face, and his pupils were black and as big as saucers. He was in trouble.

"The frostbite on his hands looks pretty bad," Jamie said. "What medications do we need to administer and how?"

My jaw dropped.

What was Jamie doing? Was he crazy? Where was this man's team? Why was Jamie playing doctor at 26,000 feet the day after his summit bid?

Hugo had returned from the dead.

I found out quickly. Apparently, Hugo Rodriguez had reached the summit many hours after we had, but collapsed from exhaustion on the South Summit on the descent. As we had rested in our bags on the South Col, he had spent the night alone at 28,700 feet without shelter. In the process, he had badly frostbitten his hands, but had miraculously survived the night. Early that very morning, he had dragged himself out of the snow and stumbled his way all the way back down to the Col. Just as Seaborn Beck Weathers of Dallas, Texas, had refused to die in the spring of 1996, Hugo had also somehow hung on, and returned from the dead.

Within minutes of the Mexican's arrival at the Col, it had become obvious to Jamie that Rodriguez's fellow commercial trip members were incapable of helping him. They were too exhausted. So, Jamie had rallied to his aid. To this day, I have no idea where Jamie found the energy. Without question, his bravery and benevolence rank as one of the most amazing things he has done in his ever-growing list of life accomplishments.

If there is a character trait that separates Jamie, it is his compassion for others, especially in a crisis. It is nothing short of astounding. That day, as I fought just to stand and walk, Jamie not only administered first aid to the ailing Rodriguez, but several hours after I had left the Col, he personally shepherded the frostbitten Mexican down to Advanced Base Camp. The rescue took eight hours.

For this remarkable achievement, Jamie earned the status of hero in my eyes, and in the eyes of everyone else on Everest at that time. I recommended he receive the Order of Canada, the highest honor that can be bestowed on a Canadian civilian. He not only ensured Rodriguez received proper medical attention by liaising by radio with Doug in base camp during the long and arduous descent, but he personally short-roped Rodriguez down the Lhotse Face, with the help of two Sherpas. Somehow, they got him all the way down the face later that day, even though Rodriguez had lost almost complete use of his hands.

Focus only on the next step.

Jamie both led and participated in this rescue from the highest pass on Earth only 24 hours after standing on top of the world himself. Having personally witnessed this feat and experienced the level of exhaustion Everest can inflict, I find that completely beyond comprehension.

"At 26,000 feet, to do something for someone else, like Jamie did, is nothing short of heroic," Doug said.

It took everything I had to get my own body safely down the Lhotse Face from Camp 4 to Camp 2 that morning. My energy reserves were too low. That's not a cop out. That's a fact.

By 10 a.m., our camp on the South Col was completely dismantled. As I bid good-bye to Jamie and Hugo, I turned my attention once again to my feet and the formula that had so far been fail-safe for me, focus only on the next step.

"Today," Pema Temba said as we began our descent to Camp 2, "you clip all ropes."

What this meant was that I was to take no chances. I was to clip my harness into every length of anchored rope, no matter how unnecessary it might seem. This strategy would help safeguard my life, as would Pema's presence.

Most adventure stories never talk about the return home or, in this case, the return to the base of the mountain. After the summit, everyone assumes the "high" point has been reached and all the exciting stuff is over. It's just mechanics from there down, a done deal.

Nothing could be further from the truth, especially on Everest. The reality there is that, except for summit day, you are rarely in greater danger. Thrashed from the extended exertions of the previous days and weeks, exhausted from insufficient length and quality of sleep, dehydrated, sunburned, lighter, weaker, and on the verge of sickness yet again, you can die as easily as if you stumbled onto a busy freeway.

Again, I didn't want that to happen to me. What I discovered within about a minute of leaving the Col, however, was that my coordination was simply not what it had been the day before. I found myself weaving toward the Geneva Spur, fighting to maintain balance, light-headed, slightly disoriented and worst of all by far, uncaring. I'd lost a lot of my drive, what little I had left. On one hand, I wanted desperately to stay alive, but on the other, I just wanted the whole painful ordeal to end. It was a contradiction to be sure. In leaving the "Death Zone" I had entered a new zone, the one where complacency can kill.

You can die as easily as if you stumbled onto a busy freeway.

The fact that I did not lose my concentration that day or in the days ahead has as much to do with Pema as it does with my ability to focus. On two occasions, once on the Geneva Spur, and once as far down as the Icefall, I found myself pitching inexplicably toward the bottom and unable to stop my fall. I had been too tired to clip into the anchored rope. Suddenly, the lightning-quick hand of Pema came out of the cold, snatched hold of my backpack and swung me quickly back to safety. I cannot possibly thank him for what he did for me. Without Pema, I doubt I would be alive today. I was simply incapable of stopping myself. I was falling away from Everest.

As I discovered, as strong as the human will is, our physical limits are not something we can necessarily control. It was as if

I was moved by the invisible strings of a marionette player over the next few days. There was an ethereal feel to it, like I was detached from my body, but was in touch with my mission. I knew what I had to do, but I just couldn't seem to connect with the muscles needed to do it. They responded slowly, like they'd been drugged. After a decent night's rest at the Col, I was far from completely spent, but I was probably further from really being in physical control than I have been my whole life.

Slowly, Pema and I made our way down the steep Lhotse Face. As instructed, I tried to clip into all ropes, but in reality, I didn't manage to get all of them. Sometimes, I just couldn't be bothered, a dangerous act. I fought the urge to say, "Oh, to hell with it," but I didn't always win. I battled myself, not the mountain, the whole way down.

Without Pema, I doubt I would be alive today.

Step by uncomfortable step, we made our way slowly downward over the Yellow Band, past Camp 3, now dismantled, and on toward the top of the Cwm. The day was cloudy and the view obscured. In a way, I was glad. I knew what a huge hole there was beneath me. I didn't need to be reminded of it.

About 500 feet above the glacier, near the start of the steepest point on the Lhotse Face, I looked up and to my amazement, I saw none other than our head Sherpa, Ang Temba, waiting for us.

"Oh, Alan," he said proudly as we came towards him, "you have done well."

We hugged. He held me for the longest time. In that instant, time stood still and I felt a magnificent exchange of energy. Ang Temba, after all, had been with us in 1991 when we'd missed the summit by 3,000 feet. We'd invited him to join us in 1994, but he'd been unable to do so because of other commitments. Now, he had helped lead us back up Everest.

At that moment, I felt a karmic return, the completion of a circle, a settling of accounts. It coursed through me with tremendous warmth.

"We did it," I said, as my eyes filled with tears. "Thanks to you, Ang Temba, we did it."

"We did," he said as a smile came across his face. "We did."

Ang Temba bore gifts — hot tea, fresh cheese, cookies, and hot chocolate. He was like Santa Claus. His was the first familiar face I had seen since leaving the Col, and appropriately so. A feeling that I'd had many times in the years leading up to our '97 trip came back to me that this was how it was supposed to be. I could have met anyone on the face that day, any member of our team could have been there to greet us, but it was Ang Temba.

"All we have to do now is get safely through the Icefall," I said. "Perhaps Sagarmatha (the Nepali word for Everest meaning 'Forehead in the Sky') will allow it."

"Perhaps, my friend," Ang Temba replied. "We will see."

After 10 or 15 minutes of filling our faces and filling each other's ears with stories, Pema Temba and I continued down. Ang Temba continued up in the hope of assisting Jamie with the rescue of Rodriguez. By now, they were also on their way down.

Within half an hour, Pema and I were off the Lhotse Face and making our way across the top of the Khumbu Glacier toward Camp 2. A lone figure approached us. In a moment, I realized it was Jason. He was thrilled to see us. Again, there were hugs, more food, and hot liquids, but mostly lots of congratulations. For a guy who'd made a summit bid on Everest, descended to Camp 2 because of difficulty seeing, and climbed up again from Camp 2 to meet us, all in 24 hours, Jason looked remarkably strong.

"How's your eye?" I asked.

"Much better now that I've descended," he said. "It was a little disconcerting for a while yesterday, but I can see pretty well now. The doc says I'll be 100 percent in no time."

I knew it must have been extremely difficult for Jason to turn around on summit day. Aside from the Sherpas, he had probably been our strongest Western climber, and thus it was particularly unlucky that something had thwarted his summit chances. Surprisingly, he seemed at peace.

"I made the best call and really the only wise one I could make," he said. "Other decisions I've made in the mountains

"We did it," I said, as my eyes filled with tears. "Thanks to you, Ang Temba, we did it."

have been more gray. This one wasn't. This one was black and white. Without depth perception, I simply couldn't climb safely any higher. I'm disappointed, but I'm also relieved to know I'll probably make a full recovery. I'd give my eye teeth for this dream, but not my eyes."

We chuckled.

Jason helped me off with every piece of equipment I didn't absolutely need. He offered to carry it. Under normal circumstances, I wouldn't have allowed it, but these were not normal circumstances. You don't come safely down from the summit of Everest every day, so I let him take some of my gear. I felt a bit like a private giving his gear to the general to carry, but he did it willingly. There was a great feeling of solidarity between us, perhaps the greatest of the whole trip.

A moment later, still with my gear, Jason also continued up the slope to assist Jamie. It was truly amazing to watch this steady stream of supporters coming out to ensure we all got down safely and that Jamie and Rodriguez did as well if fortune allowed.

A few minutes after leaving Jason, while descending the glacier, the magnitude of what we had done finally hit me. As Pema plodded steadily along behind me, watching my every step, elation swept over me. I knew Camp 2 was only minutes away. Tears of joy began to stream down my face and inside, I felt an upwelling of pride and relief. It filled me with an almost overwhelming sense of satisfaction and warmth.

"My God," I thought to myself. "We've actually done it. We've actually climbed Everest! Heck, *I've* climbed Everest! I can't believe it, but it's true. It *is*. The dream *has* come true."

Barring a massive avalanche from the Lhotse Face above me, most of the danger, I knew, was now behind us. Now, if we could just squeak safely through the Icefall, the dream would be complete. If she could just afford us that, it would be wonderful.

Wouldn't that be something? Wouldn't that be marvelous, not only to have climbed Everest, but to have climbed it safely, cleanly, not only without loss of life or limb, but not even with any frostbite? Then, we would have lived up to Doug's dream.

> *"I'd give my eye teeth for this dream, but not my eyes."*
>
> – Jason Edwards

Then, we would have fulfilled our mission. No matter what had happened in the spring of 1996 when all those people had died, we'd shown that the mountain could still be climbed safely.

I cannot describe the wonder of that moment. It was like someone had lit a match inside me and ignited something I had suppressed for days. I celebrated. I celebrated in a way I have never celebrated in my life. I didn't jump up and down or scream. In fact, I didn't even say a word. I didn't need to. I just let the peaceful feeling of deep warmth and satisfaction course through every cell of my body. There, it stuck. It does to this day. I can recall it at any moment, no matter how blue I might be, how down or disappointed, or how potentially overwhelmed with despair. I return to that magical moment on the afternoon of May 24, 1997, and a part of me rebuilds, rejuvenates, and regains strength and peace. It was, and is, priceless. It was worth every dark hour of disappointment, every minute of every hour of training, every week of organizational work, every year of fundraising, and every decade of dreaming. I was fulfilled — finally. My hunger for "success" was satiated.

This satisfaction sits securely in my heart, at the center of who I am. It eclipses anything I felt on the summit because I don't have to block it or try to refocus it elsewhere. I just let it flow, over me and through me, channeling its way into my psyche, lodging itself forever in my living memory. For as long as I am fortunate enough to inhabit this body on this Earth, I pray it always will. My intuition tells me it will. It is inner joy. I take it everywhere I go.

Pema and I returned to Camp 2 a few minutes later like a couple of "surviving" heroes. We were greeted by Lhakpa and the rest of the Sherpas who had blasted down from Camp 4 that morning. Shyam was there too. It was great to see him. Before I'd even opened my mouth to say "Namaste" (the Nepali greeting that means, "I salute the god within you"), he shoved a big cup of hot tea into my hand and smiled a huge smile. I don't think he even said a word, and the greatest part of it was, he didn't need to. He knew what it had taken. He'd spent over

I just let the peaceful feeling of deep warmth and satisfaction course through every cell of my body.

40 days in Advanced Base Camp, like an anchor in the Cwm. He was as solid as they come.

I climbed into the kitchen tent and proceeded to eat everything I could get my hands on. I didn't much care what it was. I just wanted to feel full. It was guilt-free gorging. After my feast, I retired to my tent to sleep it off.

A short while later, Jamie appeared with Rodriguez. With Jamie's help, the Mexican had safely descended the entire Lhotse Face without ever having to really use his hands. There was speculation that he might lose all the digits of both hands. As it turned out, he didn't lose any, a miracle considering he'd survived an entire night alone at the top of the world.

In Advanced Base Camp, Jamie, Jason, Ang Temba, and others passed Rodriguez on to the rest of his teammates. Unlike their fellow expedition members in Camp 4, they had not been in position to make summit attempts and were therefore able to safely escort him down through the Icefall to base camp.

That night I slept like a dead man. I don't think I even awakened to pee. I just fell into a bottomless slumber. When I opened my sore and swollen eyes the next morning, it was another rude awakening. Just like they had on the South Col, by 6 a.m., the Sherpas were already flattening tents. Again, I had to haul myself reluctantly out of my warm little cocoon and get ready to depart long before I was psychologically prepared.

"Can rest in base camp," Lhakpa said. "We down today."

That morning, the Sherpas shouldered the biggest and heaviest loads of the entire expedition, as much as 150 pounds (what I weigh). As usual, they bore their packages on only a tump-line running across their forehead. Again, these small men with huge hearts and tremendous physical and spiritual capacities humbled me.

To save having to make multiple trips up and down the mountain to retrieve gear, the Sherpas had elected to carry all the equipment that had been at Camps 4, 3 and 2 down the mountain in one massive, backbreaking wave. This was a collective feat of strength surpassing anything I had seen before. The only possible exceptions were three porters on our

1991 expedition who each had taken turns carrying our 250-pound communications box barefoot up a steep jungle slope in the pouring monsoon rain.

The loads our Sherpas carried that day were up to five feet wide and six feet tall. If you walked behind a five-foot-two inch tall, 110-pound Sherpa, sometimes all you could see was his tiny feet sticking out for a few inches beneath his towering package. Together, the Sherpas carried everything from spent propane tanks to tents, ice axes, crampons, sleeping bags, pots and pans, even stoves. Only a few of them even bothered to use an ice ax as they moved down the Cwm. None used crampons and none uttered a word of complaint. The way they saw it, it only had to hurt for a few more hours. Then, they could go home to their families.

We broke camp about 10 a.m. Within minutes, a huge cloudbank had rolled in, obscuring the entire upper portion of Everest and much of the Cwm. It was like a curtain call from Chomolungma, a closing of the door as our little party serpentined its way down the glacier. Everest was saying good-bye.

Good karma had been returned.

I didn't even bother to look up. I knew her face was veiled.

I didn't carry 150 pounds. I barely carried 50, which for most Westerners is a heavy load, especially at 21,000 feet.

As our little party wound its way down into the cloud, I sensed we were all going to be okay. Somehow, I knew the mountain wished us no malice. We had honored her and in return, she had honored us. Good karma had been returned.

I have no idea how our Sherpas descended and traversed those innumerable ladders in the Icefall with their loads. I couldn't even keep up carrying my backpack, which was featherweight by comparison. Combined with the cloud that eventually produced a light snow, the whole scene took on a quiet calm. I had to keep reminding myself this wasn't a dream. It was like watching an illusion. The Sherpas disappeared into the fog and soon, there was only Pema Temba and me descending together.

Pema became my guardian angel. As I picked my way through the ice blocks, over the crevasses, through the huge holes, and across the ladders of the labyrinth, he followed silently and patiently behind me. Every once in a while, when I'd stop for a rest, he'd turn and say gently, "Slowly, slowly. No hurry."

For a while, I thought I might spend the rest of my life descending through the Icefall, as I had felt descending from the summit, but shortly before 2 p.m., we finally emerged from the cloud and stepped into bright sunshine at base camp. It was like coming through a very long and dark tunnel. It was a deliverance from the dream.

"'And the Lord said,'" I thought, "'Let there be light.'"

There was. I somehow managed to stumble across the last ladder and minutes later, was greeted again by none other than Ang Temba. He had shouldered his huge load from Camp 2, delivered it safely to base camp, and returned to welcome us back.

That was another powerful moment. He welcomed me again with open arms. This time we knew we had done it, safely. At last, we were on the right side of the wrong place.

At last, we were on the right side of the wrong place.

Like a rag doll, I draped myself over him and together, we fell to the snow and rolled around like a couple of school children. Everything I did was in slow motion. My hair was matted to my head, my face was deep red, and my eyes were swollen. But I could laugh and smile. We were down. We were safely off Everest. I was alive!

I WAS ALIVE! I WAS ALIVE! I WAS ALIVE! We had survived. I celebrated that realization, as I have in so many others since. It was beyond joy. It was rapture; rolling, stumbling, staggering rapture.

He conquers twice who conquers himself in victory.

— PUBLIUS SYRUS

Moments later, Bruce appeared with his camera going, as did Dave with the video camera. Together, we all just cried and laughed and cried some more.

I don't have any good pictures of the scene. We were all too busy being festive. We soaked in the sunshine. I was drunk with happiness.

> *Everybody embraced everybody…. Anyone who had seen us then could never have thought about distinctions between sahibs [clients] and Sherpas. We were all mountaineers together, who had climbed our mountain.*
> — TENZING NORGAY,
> *Man of Everest*

One of the most memorable greetings came minutes later from the most unusual of places, from a relative stranger. A climber from another expedition, a potato farmer from England whom I had met on the trek into base camp, came running up to me and gave me the biggest and longest hug of the trip. He said he'd heard how long I'd been working on this dream and that he was just so proud we'd finally done it. That meant a lot.

But the crowning moment came when I finally returned to base camp. There, as promised, Dave pulled me out a bottle of Fanta. I'd had fantasies about it since leaving base camp on my way up and, at last, my moment had arrived. At last, I was going to suck back the sweet taste of success.

Imagine my disappointment when I took a mouthful of the stuff and realized it had gone bad in the heat. I spat it out in disgust, but then I started to laugh.

"That's so like Everest," I said to Dave. "It's never over even when it's over. There's always something to deal with."

"I'm sorry buddy," he said.

"Don't be. It's not worth it."

I settled for a cup of cold water. That was enough. As I put it slowly to my lips, I sat down in a chair, put my feet up on a rock and gazed expectantly into the Icefall. A peaceful feeling washed over me. Now, I thought, if we could just get everyone safely through there, it would be mission accomplished.

It was beyond joy. It was rapture.

I closed my eyes and soaked in the sun. It felt good not to hurt any more. My legs were spent, my feet were blistered, my face and eyes stung, but I had survived.

Then, I felt something touch me on the shoulder. I opened my eyes and looked straight up into the serene face of Ang Dawa, one of the last men to see me disappear into the Icefall. He smiled.

"How's your chest?" he asked quietly.

"Not bad," I replied.

Slowly, I got to my feet. He gave me a big hug.

"Strong man," he whispered under his breath. "Strong man."

I wept in his arms.

Mission Accomplished

He is lucky who, in the full tide of life, has experienced a measure of the active environment that he most desires. In these days of upheaval and violent change, when the basic values of today are the vain and shattered dreams of tomorrow, there is much to be said for a philosophy which aims at living a full life while the opportunity offers. There are few treasures of more lasting worth than the experience of a way of life that in itself is wholly satisfying. Such, after all, are the only possessions of which no fate, no cosmic catastrophe can deprive us; nothing can alter the fact if for one moment in eternity, we have really lived.

— ERIC SHIPTON,
British climber

A FEW HOURS AFTER I had returned to base camp, we received an urgent radio call from Jamie in the Icefall.

"A Sherpa has fallen into a crevasse and we need a full trauma kit *now!*"

Together, Jamie and Jason rallied again for a rescue. Dave and Doug left from base camp to assist. I did not join them, knowing that at that moment, I was more of a liability than an asset. I could barely walk.

A gripping and dramatic high-altitude rescue ensued, during which Jason rappelled a staggering 15 stories (150 feet) into the crevasse into which Tsultrim Kalsang Sherpa, 26, of the village of Namche Bazaar, had fallen.

"Jamie and I came upon a group of six or eight Sherpas peering into a crevasse," Jason remembers of his descent toward base camp that day.

"We could hear moaning from below. At first, I tried lowering a rope to him [Tsultrim], but I just didn't feel right about it. I wasn't sure he could tie into it properly. So, down I went."

Not even Jason, an emergency medical technician, was prepared for what he saw. One side of the Sherpa's face was swinging freely from a thin hinge of skin and tissue. Apparently, his visage had been sliced by his glasses during the plunge. He had plummeted like a stone into the bowels of the crevasse where his body had somehow wedged into the bottom of the dark, dripping hole, still upright. Miraculously, he was still conscious and breathing, although completely disoriented, and in terrible pain.

One side of the Sherpa's face was swinging freely from a thin hinge of skin and tissue.

"The bottom of the crevasse was so cramped my face was only four or five inches from his," Jason recalls. "I knew immediately who he was. We had drunk chang and laughed together on the trek in to base camp. I held him and told him I wasn't going to let him die, but it was pretty ugly. I have no idea how he survived the fall."

There, face to face with the horror, Jason managed to tie the injured climber into a harness and give the signal to others on the surface to hoist the critically injured man from the depths. Jason then yelled commands to Jamie above to immediately arrange a stretcher, bandages, and a helicopter. Jamie, in turn, relayed these instructions by radio to base camp. There, with the hopes that the injured climber might still be alive if the rescue team was able to get him to base camp fast enough, Bruce, Jeff, and his wife, Kellie, rapidly transformed our mess tent into the world's highest operating theater. Together, they prepped for emergency surgery. Meanwhile, Jason climbed up the rope, out of the crevasse and joined Jamie and the others back in the daylight with Tsultrim. He found a small army of climbers from other expeditions hastening to the edge of the abyss to assist.

"You could come up with a place more difficult to mount a rescue," Doug recalls of his first thoughts upon arriving at the scene, "but it would be damn hard."

In the middle of the deadly Khumbu Icefall, as the sun melted away the foundation of their already unstable world, Jason courageously took charge.

"The situation was like the tower of Babel with a confusion of voices and sounds," Doug remembers. "Jason just took the reigns and said, 'Okay boys, here's what we're going to do.'"

"Finally, this was our chance to show the Sherpas how much we appreciated what they had done for us throughout the expedition," Jamie said. "Here was our chance to show how much we cared."

Slowly, the team of several dozen men from all over the world loaded Tsultrim onto a stretcher and began carrying him down the glacier. One by one, they inched their way over the five remaining ladder bridges slowly melting out of the ice beneath their feet. It was a miracle no one else fell into a crevasse that day.

"Jamie did an awesome job," Jason says. "He was really riding on a high after the summit and that adrenaline rush fed him up and down the mountain. He rose to the occasion gloriously. I admire him for that."

"All of the fixed ropes were bullshit by that point," Doug recalls. "It was a huge deal to be carrying a man on a stretcher over that kind of terrain. Without Jamie and Jason, that guy would have died. It took enormous creative genius to mount such a rescue, especially in those conditions. I think Jason is the most amazing and phenomenal mountain leader I have ever seen, period. And, considering the condition Jamie was in, he was nothing short of amazing too. Jamie pulled this thing off!"

Many tense hours later, the rescue party arrived in base camp with the wounded man. He was still alive. There, in the darkness of our mess tent, Dr. Doug stitched his ghastly torn face back together by headlamp.

"I did not do it [the surgery] alone," Doug said. "Jeff and Kellie [Rhoads] were just spectacular. I could not have done it without them."

> *"Finally, this was our chance to show the Sherpas how much we appreciated what they had done for us."*
>
> – JAMIE CLARKE

The operation took three hours. When it was over, Jason went outside and burst into tears.

"I was mentally and physically spent. I broke down for two or three minutes. It was an emotional release and I needed it."

Hours later, by the light of a new day, along with Hugo Rodriguez, Tsultrim was evacuated by emergency helicopter to Kathmandu. Doug accompanied them.

Both patients made complete recoveries without the loss of any body parts. Tsultrim's vision even returned to 20/20 and his facial scar became almost invisible. Doug attributed the success in saving both men's lives not only to medical science, but to prior planning.

"We were hundreds of miles from the nearest serious hospital," he recalls. "But the whole effort bespeaks of work that was done long before we got on the mountain — work by Alan and Jamie in fundraising, and by Steve Matous in creating the infrastructure so I had one of the finest medical kits a physician could hope for in the field. Half the work was done before we even arrived. It just wasn't a bunch of guys with a harebrained idea."

So it was that Jamie helped to save not one, but two lives during the expedition, and Jason led all the way down the mountain as well as up.

> *"It just wasn't a bunch of guys with a hairbrained idea."*
>
> – Dr. Doug Rovira

What we get from this adventure is just sheer joy. And joy is, after all, the end of life. We do not live to eat and make money. We eat and make money to be able to enjoy life. That is what life means and what life is for.
— George Leigh Mallory,
British mountaineer and Everest climber

And the victories continued even after we'd left base camp. In a touching Buddhist ceremony, Barb and Jamie were married by a Nepalese lama days later in Khunde. After the ceremony, which featured everything from chants and gongs, to incense and local beer, everyone danced into the night to a mix of Sherpa songs and blaring Western rock 'n' roll music. East definitely met West that night, as it had throughout our whole expedition, Sherpas became Westerners and Westerners became Sherpas. It was, without question, the highlight of the expedition for me, bar nothing, not even the summit. We were all together, safe, and laughing. You couldn't have written a better ending if you'd scripted it.

But there was someone missing — Doug. He has had to live with the fact that he never really got to say good-bye to any of us. I have not seen him since he jumped into that helicopter with Hugo and Tsultrim and blasted to the rescue down the valley.

"We landed in Lukla on the way back," Doug recalls. "I remember walking through the mud and yak dung and crying when I realized I wouldn't get the chance to walk out with the team. It was like my entire life for two months had been taken away from me. I had the emptiest feeling. We did this thing as a group. Not one of us could have done it without the others."

Eventually, Doug flew back to Kathmandu and on to North America. The rest of the team made its way back to the Nepalese capital a few days after his departure. There, we took care of the sale, storage, and distribution of much of the expedition's remaining equipment, settled accounts with Sonam and his partners at Great Escapes Kathmandu, and tied up many of the loose ends that are always left after a major Himalayan expedition.

Finally, spent but satisfied, we made our way to the airport. There, we came across an old beggar, a woman wailing on her knees for help, her hands outstretched in desperation. Unlike us, I knew she would never leave this place.

"Without hesitation, one of our Sherpas gave her some money," Jason remembers. "But it wasn't an act of charity. It was, 'I'm to look after other people less fortunate than me.' It was like a payment, a redistribution of wealth."

That was the last lesson we learned from the Sherpas.

When the plane finally became airborne, I let out a huge sigh of relief. I was glad to leave. I'd had enough of Kathmandu.

Minutes later, at an altitude of 29,000 feet, I looked out the window. There again, as for all time, stood Everest's unmistakable black peak poking up through the clouds, as proud, majestic, and defiant as ever.

I spread the fingers of one hand and placed them against the window, forming a powerful but peaceful thought in my mind, and trying to make one last connection with her.

"Thank you," I thought. "Thank you Chomolungma for allowing safe passage for me and my friends to and from your inner sanctum."

"Go in peace," I heard her say. "Follow your path."

*   *   *

The final tally of our expedition was six of 13 climbers safely on top, no deaths, no frostbite, thrilled sponsors, relieved families, one marriage made in high heaven, and two lives saved from a frozen hell. Everyone made it safely back home, and we are all still talking to each other. We'd accomplished our mission.

I think Doug would be proud.

Lessons Learned and Prices Paid

The greatest adventure of all ... is any episode
that involves a risking of self, and with it,
a vulnerability that promises to transform us
into someone new and different.   — PICO IYER

MY RETURN TO North America was nothing like my return to base camp. After the long flight from southeast Asia, we were met by a throng of reporters and a small army of well wishers at the airport in Calgary. The welcoming crew included my twin brother, James, his wife, Anne, and their two children, David and Sarah, who had flown all the way from eastern Canada to meet me. Also in attendance were my second eldest brother, Eric, and my two nieces, Laura Elaine and Shannon Louise of Calgary. My parents, Isabel and Peter, had also made a special trip from Ottawa to be there. I was deeply touched.

My mother and father were the first to meet me. They were as thrilled as I was. Everyone cheered, including me. The authorities at the Calgary airport went to great lengths to ensure Jamie and I had a private reception with our parents before we were met by our friends, the public, and the press at another gate.

I am a lucky man. I have had a dream, and it has
come true, and that is not a thing that happens
often to men.   — TENZING NORGAY,
                                        Man of Everest

When we came through that gate, the doors opened and, instantly, I felt like a character in a bizarre, slow-motion movie. A sea of microphones, lights, television and still cameras came at me like a high-tech tsunami. Time and sound slowed down. It was like a time warp.

After a brief press conference during which Jamie and I spoke, as did representatives of our sponsors (Gloria Simpson from Lotus was there too, all the way from Philadelphia), I was taken by my parents to my apartment and from there, to a barbecue and reception in the backyard of Jamie's brother, Leigh's, home. Most of my closest friends and family were there — Dale, Cathy and Georgia Ens, Cal Zaryski and Grant Molyneux, Patti Mayer, Milan Hudec and their daughter, Natalee, as were Jamie's friends and family. Even David Weinkauf, without whom the expedition would never have happened, was present. There were several touching speeches and lots of toasts. It was a special evening I will always remember.

Conspicuous by their absence that night were John McLernon of Colliers; my eldest brother, Daniel, and his family from Vancouver; and most notably, Diane. Unknown to me, she already had her own special welcoming home party planned for me.

"Because Alan's flight came in on a school night," Diane recalls, "rather than fly in for the evening and have to fly back the next morning to teach, I decided it would be best to wait until the weekend and surprise Alan with a visit. I couldn't take any more time off school because I'd used it all up going to and from base camp. So, I sent him flowers and called to welcome him home. I knew he'd be besieged by well wishers and we wouldn't get any time to ourselves. I also began making arrangements for a real party when he came to visit me."

Unfortunately, I didn't know this. All I knew was that when I looked for the woman I loved, she wasn't there. I was deeply disappointed. She did surprise me the next weekend with a visit, but our time together was strained. I'm afraid I did not understand her decision until she explained it to me months later. By then, it was too late. Our already fragile relationship suffered another key blow the day I returned to Canada. A bank account can only survive so many withdrawals.

After the initial excitement of my homecoming, which was at times emotionally overwhelming, things began to change for me. Slowly, I started to fall into an emotional rut from which I could not extricate myself. The combined physical, emotional, and spiritual toll of climbing Everest, and the subsequent loss of my greatest lifelong dream, was too much for me. Although I tried to crawl out of my depression, my usual ability to focus on the positive temporarily alluded me, and it was many months before I was able to unearth it again.

During this time, my already strained relationship with Diane slowly unraveled. In retrospect, I see now that much of the source of our difficulties was my painful readjustment to life back home. I was probably suffering from a form of post-partum depression, just as the Apollo astronauts had experienced a substantial decompression and psychological re-entry into the world's lower atmosphere. I had all the classic symptoms — sleep disruption, inexplicable and unpredictable anxiety, mercurial mood swings, loss of appetite, and above all, a deep feeling of emptiness. My return to the western world of media interviews, meetings, telephones, voice and e-mail messages, rush-hour traffic, receptions, public appearances, and a plethora of new demands and personal expectations left me emotionally drained. It seemed that once again, I had to put out more energy than I was able to put back in.

Given my experience coming home after my two previous Everest expeditions, this readjustment was something for which I was somewhat prepared, but ultimately inadequately equipped. On my previous expeditions, of course, I had not reached the summit. That made a world of difference not only to me, but to many others and, subsequently, how I interacted with them.

What did climbing Everest actually mean? Why did people treat me so differently now? How was I expected to behave, and who was I expected to be now that I'd achieved the summit?

Now I am free, I kept thinking. I have been freed by
Everest. I could not know yet how wrong I was.

— Tenzing Norgay,
Man of Everest

In an attempt to reenergize and rebuild, I arranged to spend time with Diane and her children. I needed to recover, recharge and reflect, time, as Diane said, to just "be."

"Alan needed time to regroup," Diane recalls. "For me, there were swim meets and graduation ceremonies to attend, report cards to write, phones to answer, horns honking in the driveway. Things seemed to upset him. 'His life had been totally different on Everest,' I tried to tell the kids and myself. He was exhausted. I tried to remember that. But he also needed to remember that our lives hadn't stopped for two and a half months, and we hadn't experienced what he had.

"I tried. I limited phone calls, made fewer plans for outings, tried to keep up with everything at home and school with some sense of sanity. We all have our challenges in life. Mine have just never been as high profile as Alan's."

On the mountain, my life had been tightly focused, stay alive and stay together. See if you can get to the summit, but whatever happens, whatever, *survive!* After Everest, no place, except perhaps a secluded beach somewhere in Thailand, could have done the trick.

I had reached the top of Everest. I had come down
from Everest into a different world. I had travelled
half-way across the world, and been cheered.
Everything has changed for me, I thought. And yet
nothing has really changed, because inside I am
still the same old Tenzing. I was going home now.
But home to what? What would I do? What would
happen to me? I had climbed my mountain,
but I must still live my life. — Tenzing Norgay,
Man of Everest

No one knew what I'd been through except Jamie and the rest of the team. It was completely unreasonable of me to expect anyone to understand. I might just as well have returned from the moon.

Then came the breaking point. While I had been away, Diane had committed to participating in a grueling, 72-hour, 120-mile-long team adventure race involving hiking, biking, canoeing, and swimming with two of her closest friends. It was her own Everest and naturally, she had to train long and hard for it.

"Finally, I had the opportunity to do something that was a real challenge for me," she remembers, "something I could really be proud of. I had two dear friends as fellow teammates and they really believed in me and wanted me to be part of the team.

"I thought Alan would be so proud of me. This time, I had to train and sometimes not be with him. I recalled weekends the previous winter when we couldn't get together because of his training cycle. I felt I had always been understanding and supportive of him. Now, I wanted my turn. I guess it was unrealistic for me to want it so soon."

Three months later, we would have easily survived it. But timing can be everything in life and our timing at that moment was off. I needed Diane to be there for me and she needed me to be there (or rather not there while she trained) for her. Suddenly, I found myself alone, experiencing first hand what she must have felt during my long hours of training for Everest. In a classic case of the shoe being on the other foot and a not-so-uncommon illustration of the need for balance in a couple, I failed to pass the test. I found myself asking why I was in her home alone. I'd just spent months isolated on Everest. The last thing I wanted now was more time by myself. In a cold tent at high altitude, it had been difficult enough. Now, sitting in her living room, it was too much.

In frustration and disappointment, after just 10 days at her home, I packed my bags and left. Within 10 days of my departure, I had rebounded straight into another relationship. Within 48 hours of that, I returned to Diane, told her what I had done, but that was the last straw for her. I had broken her trust. For a month, we tried to reconcile, but we couldn't.

Four months to the day that I had stood on the top of Everest, on September 23, 1997, Diane decided she couldn't try any more. In the wee small hours that morning, before I was to go on a national television talk show, the woman I had so dearly wanted to marry slipped through my fingers. As usual, the breakup took place on the long distance telephone with me in yet another hotel room in another city preparing for yet another speaking presentation.

"That night was one of the most difficult of my life," Diane recalls. "I remember several instances during that conversation when I suggested we should finish our discussion the next night or at a later date. The poor timing was not mine."

Diane insists again that I put the words into her mouth, that she would never have chosen that time to end "us." She has more class and sensitivity than that. But I again sensed there was something very wrong and once again, I set about finding out what it was. It didn't take long. It was the end.

I realized then part of the price I had paid to climb Everest. The mountain was certainly not to blame, but my personality and how I reacted to the challenge of Everest definitely contributed significantly to it. It had been a tremendous strain.

> *I realized then part of the price I had paid to climb Everest.*

> *He is paying the price of fame, with no discount.*
> *As he himself puts it, he is an animal in a zoo, a fish*
> *in a bowl. And if the bowl exhibits him brightly it*
> *also holds him prisoner, amid the crowds and clamour*
> *he is lonely. He is paying not only for fame, but for*
> *being the man he is. If he were less intelligent and*
> *less sensitive he would be happier.*
>
> — JAMES RAMSEY ULLMAN,
> author of *Man of Everest*, on Tenzing Norgay

I didn't cry then. That came later. I just felt numb. I hung up the phone and looked around at the hotel room of my life. I was surrounded by all the trappings of success — five-star accommodations, gourmet food, autograph-seekers, applause, and a new and exciting city almost every day. Inside, however, I felt like I really didn't have a life. It was always up in the air, literally, on aircraft, and it was being constantly interrupted by business travel. I desperately wanted somewhere to ground myself. I wanted a home. I had hoped that home would be with Diane.

My relationship with Jamie followed a similar downhill slide. Unknown to me, he silently resented having had to expend important time and energy during the expedition defending my initial position to climb the mountain without bottled oxygen. Because I had been in so much emotional turmoil over Diane during the trip, rather than confront me, he had decided to keep quiet. His bitterness grew. It wasn't until four months after our return home, the following autumn, that I learned how he had deliberately insulated me from internal team pressures on the oxygen debate during the expedition. His anger and frustration had been simmering too long by then and had turned toxic. That situation was also irreparable.

My relationship with Jamie followed a similar downhill slide.

Despite two months of regular counseling, on November 23, 1997, six months to the day that we stood on the top of Everest, and two months to the day Diane announced her decision, Jamie announced his desire to end our business partnership. I felt like I had been delivered a triple wake-up call — the loss of my dream (because, curiously, when you achieve a goal you also lose it), the loss of my love, and now, the loss of my greatest friend. What was it about the 23rd of the month? Was it some kind of preordained change day for me or was I just being superstitious and insecure? I recalled that my ex-wife, Theresa, had left 10 years earlier on March 23, 1987. Coincidence four times?

It was my initial decision to attempt Everest without the use of bottled oxygen, and it was Jamie's decision not only to help me attain my goal, but to quietly defend me from the criticisms of others, while protecting me from more emotional pain. I would rather he had insisted the other expedition members deal directly with me on the oxygen issue rather than trying to work through him, but because he was my friend, he did not. He did what any true friend would have done. He defended me. In reality, the other expedition members did try to work directly with me, but when I would not change my mind, they turned up the heat on Jamie. In the end, I know I made the right decision to use bottled oxygen. Unfortunately, by that time, the damage had been done.

Should I have decided sooner? Probably. Could I have? Yes, but not without being completely sure that I had given my goal everything I had, short of my life. That, of course, was my mission. That was what I absolutely, positively, needed to know from Everest. It was my whole reason for being there.

The failure of my relationships with Diane and Jamie sent my personal life into crisis. What had been depression quickly became darker. I had reasonably serious thoughts of suicide. Why were those closest to me rejecting me? Was I that bad a guy? How come I couldn't get my life back into balance? If I could climb Everest, why couldn't I make my relationships work?

Perhaps you can recall a dark moment like this in your life, a moment when the very essence of who you were was tested to the core. For me, this was one of those moments.

I miss Jamie's smile, lightning-fast wit and hilarious humor. I miss our late-night work sessions in which both of us, together, were locked on our shared target. Those moments cannot ever be replaced. Nor will he ever be. He is now, and will always remain, one of my greatest life companions. My life has been richer because of him.

The biggest risk I took on Everest was not, it turned out, a physical one. It was the risk of losing my relationship with Jamie. I lost big.

Jamie did not run out of oxygen on his summit bid as I did. Nor did he have to shoulder the emotional load I had. His intimate relationship was not in crisis. In fact, it was flourishing and would lead to a proposal for marriage, an engagement, and a marriage ceremony before our team had even left Nepal. Those two factors, and others, I believe, made all the difference in our experiences on Everest and on summit

What had been depression quickly became darker.

FROM EVEREST TO ENLIGHTENMENT

day. If I hadn't run out of oxygen, we probably would have been able to stand on top together. That had always been our dream.

The mountain helped provide the catalyst for change in my relationship with Jamie, but the seeds of that change were sown during our first expedition in 1991. They germinated during our second trip in 1994 and finally grew to insurmountable proportions, in Jamie's eyes at least, in 1997. Three strikes, you're out. You reap what you sow.

I will never meet two people like Diane and Jamie again. They have since gone on to other adventures, Diane to seeing her children into adulthood, and Jamie to successfully crossing the empty quarter of the Saudi Arabian desert on foot and on camel with his brother, Leigh, and his new-found friend, Bruce Kirkby. It is the largest sand desert in the world and has only been crossed once before. To a certain degree, Jamie has done exactly what I did in 1991. He has brought a partner into the fold to share his experience with him the way I chose Jamie to join me in my Everest effort. In that sense, I have passed the torch to Jamie and he to Bruce. Now, Jamie is asserting his independence. He is spreading his wings, distancing himself from me and, to a degree at least, leaving "the nest" that has been our business partnership and friendship for the last 10 years. He is now my direct competitor for speaking presentations. That hurts, but I wish him well. I send him my love.

So, you see, the chain has been broken and rebuilt in a new way. Jamie and Diane have moved on. Eventually, Jamie will probably share the adventure of child rearing with Barb and thus, a new chain will begin to be built. Diane, I suspect, will re-marry soon, if she hasn't already. The world is unfolding as it should.

Like the Buddhist Wheel of Life, my own life had made its great turning.

— Tenzing Norgay,
Man of Everest

My goal for the first year after Everest was not to have a goal, at least not in the physical sense. I had spent the better part of the last 40 years being a human doing and now I wanted to be a human being. I wanted to kick what I call "the achievement addiction." We do not always profit from growth. It depends what kind of growth it is.

> *There is great happiness in not wanting, in not being something, in not going somewhere.*
>
> — J. KRISHNAMURTI
> (1895–1986)

One of the greatest things about reaching the summit of Everest is that physically, at least, I no longer have anything to prove to anyone, least of all, to myself. "The Olympic gold medal you were always seeking as a gymnast," my twin brother, James, wrote after my return from the mountain, "you now hold in your hands. Cherish this moment as long as you live. You are now on the highest podium you always dreamed of as a boy … and you never have to step down."

One year almost to the day after I summited Everest, Jeff Rhoads made it to the top on his fourth expedition. Not only that, but he repeated the feat a week later, guiding the first disabled climber, Tom Whittaker, of Arizona, to the top with him. In doing so, Jeff became the first Westerner to summit Everest twice in a single season, and in a single week!

"I couldn't believe it was happening," Jeff says. "It was pretty amazing. Maybe that was my karma from '97, the fate of Everest. Maybe that's how the gods planned it."

There *is* a plan to our lives, whether we chose to believe it or not. Sometimes it makes no sense, sometimes it hurts, and sometimes it even takes lives. But there is more to life than what we see, as Patti Mayer said. To deny it is to deny "the other Everest."

I will not be going back to Mount Everest, at least not to climb her. I don't need to go back. The mountain gave me what I needed, and it wasn't just the summit. It was a positive sense of closure with Everest and the deep satisfaction of knowing that I had given it everything I had, short of my life. I had fulfilled my mission. The summit was a bonus. Now I can finish a chapter in my life and begin a new one. Now, I don't have to run any more marathons, compete in any triathlons, or participate in any grueling adventure races unless I so choose. Nor do I have to climb any more geographical mountains, but, of course, I will. I love the mountains and in the summer of 1998 I made my third attempt to climb the just under 15,000-foot-tall Matterhorn in the Swiss Alps. The weather cooperated this time and I managed to get safely to and from the summit. The view from the top was fantastic. And the best part was that the entire climb was over in eight hours and I never even got a headache!

> *I have been seven times to Everest. I love Everest,*
> *but seven times is enough.* — Tenzing Norgay,
> *Man of Everest*

There is a plan to our lives

There are so many other mountains to climb too. There is Mt. Blanc, the highest mountain in the Alps; the infamous north face of the Eiger, also in Switzerland; Mt. Robson in the Canadian Rockies, and on and on. They don't have to be 26,000 feet tall to be challenging and fun. And, they don't have to hurt. Recently, I completed a spectacular hike through the Grand Canyon.

> *Do I myself want to climb again? The answer here*
> *is: On other, smaller mountains — yes. On Everest —*
> *no. On such a peak, with two different responsibilities,*
> *is too much for one man, and there will be no more*
> *such ordeals in my life.* — Tenzing Norgay,
> *Man of Everest*

My next mountain is the summit of self-improvement. I want to become my own best friend. To that end, thanks to new-found friend and meditation instructor, Valerie Simonson, of Calgary, I have discovered the power of Raja Yoga. This is a form of open-eye meditation with ancient origins in India. It has nothing to do with tying yourself in knots, practicing advanced breathing techniques, growing a long white beard, chanting mantras, removing yourself from reality, or sleeping on beds of nails. Raja Yoga meditation is offered through a wonderful worldwide group called the Brahma Kumaris, or "BKs," an internationally acclaimed spiritual university with thousands of centers worldwide. It has earned international awards from the United Nations for its many peace-making efforts, and is fast attracting new meditators all over the world. Hindus, Muslims, Buddhists, Christians and Jews, amongst others, are drawn to it because it embraces all faiths, countries, languages, cultures, races, economic and socioeconomic backgrounds. The BKs believe we are all special souls and the only thing that counts is what's inside us, especially what's in our minds.

The philosophy of Raja Yoga ("Raja" meaning "king" and "Yoga" meaning "connection") is simple, but powerful — to be "in meditation" all day with our eyes *open*, and become "The King of Connection" between our soul and the "Supreme Soul." The BKs believe that because we go through life with our eyes open, we should meditate that way too. And, we should learn to concentrate on only one thing at a time, not only when we meditate, but when we are doing anything in our lives, whether it be driving, handling affairs at the office, negotiating a deal, talking to friends, playing with the kids, or shopping for groceries. We can thus learn to discipline and train our minds so we effectively become self-sovereign, or king of our own thoughts, emotions and actions every minute of every day. This permits the most efficient and effective use of mental, physical, and spiritual energy.

Thanks in large part to Raja Yoga, which helps me achieve inner peace anywhere at any time, I am now coming closer to maintaining a depth of serenity and personal contentment I have been longing for my whole life. It was not to be found through external achievement, but through an inner exploration.

I am probably happier now than I have been my whole life. I now meditate regularly and exercise daily, write in a journal of gratitude, and celebrate the diamonds in every day. I speak all over the world, travel less but enjoy it more, and live a life of tremendous abundance, variety, and fulfillment. I have reconnected with most of the friends I have not seen since beginning my Everest odyssey, and I am continuing to reconnect with my family. I adventure everywhere I go, even when I don't go anywhere but inside my own mind. I have struck out on a new path.

As I have been journeying inward, I have also been journeying downward — below the surface of the sea. I recently earned certification as an advanced open-water scuba diver, and I am in the process of exploring the underwater world wherever my speaking presentations, locale, and traveling schedule permit.

Through a series of "coincidences," I recently hooked up with Graham Hawkes, the world's leading designer of submersibles. He placed second in the world engineering *Design News* awards, behind the man who designed the Galileo Probe that went to Jupiter. Graham has pioneered the concept of "underwater flight." Instead of using ballast, his submersibles feature inverted airplane wings that enable his crafts to "fly" underwater. They can do barrel rolls, figure eights, loops, anything an aircraft can do. They can even swim wingtip to wing tip with manta rays.

Graham's goal is to build the first manned submersible to actually *explore* the deepest point in the ocean, the Challenger Deep of the Mariana Trench, about 200 miles southwest of the Pacific Island of Guam, near the Philippines. It is 36,000 feet deep — deeper than Everest is tall. In fact, you could drop the entire Everest massif into the Mariana Trench and there would still be more than a mile of water above its summit!

Twelve people have been to the surface of the moon, a quarter of a million miles up. Only two have ever been to the bottom of the Challenger Deep, seven miles down. In a bold and pioneering effort, American Don Walsh and Swiss engineer Jacques Piccard went there in 1960 in a strange craft designed by the U.S. Navy called *Trieste*. They were on the bottom for only 20 minutes and because of the limitations of *Trieste*, they were not able to actually explore the Trench. They went straight down and straight up. It took them about seven hours round trip. No human beings have been there since. The world's attention shifted to outer space and "inner space," the wonder of the world's oceans, submerged in our collective consciousness, until now.

This expedition will be historic. It is to open up two-thirds of the Earth's surface to human exploration. It could help lead to the discovery of drugs that might eradicate some of our modern-day diseases, spawn new biotechnology, assist in the identification of news species of plants and animals, and on and on.

This expedition will be historic. It is to open up two-thirds of the Earth's surface to human exploration.

Using Graham's submersibles, we should be able to plunge into the permanent darkness of the Challenger Deep in about an hour. Once there, his ships have a range of about 20 miles along the bottom. They can surface in about an hour as well, all at the atmospheric pressure of sea level. There is no decompression required. In our very first dive, we should exponentially increase the visual knowledge of the deepest ocean floor with the naked eye.

This expedition goes far beyond a voyage to the bottom of the sea. I am considering the very first live broadcast of still photographs and voice made in person from the world's deepest ocean point, possibly to the Internet. I hope to accompany Graham on his historic dives. This would make me the first person to have visited the highest and lowest points on the surface of the Earth.

The deepest dive promises to be the marine equivalent of the first moon landing, and perhaps even provide pictures like those that came back from the Mars Pathfinder. Technology, weather, and finances permitting, millions of people around the world could watch as we open up Earth's last physical frontier.

I am putting together an expedition with Graham whereby I attract investors and sponsors to the event and he builds the submersibles, two high-tech ships that look more like F-18 aircraft than heavy, ungamely submarines. He has already built and tested his $1 million prototype, dubbed "Deep Flight I." It was a huge success and received extensive media coverage in *Time, Newsweek, National Geographic* and *Reader's Digest*, as well as NBC-TV's *Dateline* and many other major television network newscasts and shows worldwide. Our series of dives to ever-increasing depths is to culminate with a plunge to the bottom of the Challenger Deep sometime before or during 2003, the 100th anniversary of the first powered aircraft flight by the Wright brothers in Kitty Hawk, North Carolina, in 1903.

This dream should be far safer than trying to climb Everest. Thanks to the courage and inventiveness of Walsh, Piccard and the entire design team of *Trieste*, we already know we can build crafts to survive in the ultimate abyss. Today, we can test potential submersible designs to pressures well beyond what they will have to endure in the Challenger Deep — in pressure chambers on land. Modern-day ceramics, of which the hulls of the submersibles are likely to be shaped, can withstand pressures of 150 to 190 tons per square inch. Graham's crafts will have to withstand 8 tons per square inch at the deepest depth. And, there should be no sudden storms 36,000 feet down.

> *But if adventure has a final and all-embracing motive it is surely this:*
>
> *We go out because it is in our nature to go out to climb mountains and to sail the seas, to fly to the planets and plunder into the depths of the oceans. By doing these things we make touch with something outside or behind, which strangely seems to approve our doing them. We extend our horizon, we expand our being, we revel in the mastery of ourselves which gives an impression, mainly illusory, that we are masters of the world. In a word, we are men and when man ceases to do these things, he is no longer man.*
>
> — WILFRID NOYCE,
> mountaineer

"When you look at a map of the ocean floor," Graham says, "you're not looking at the sea bed. You're looking at the unexplored surface of the Earth. To this point in the history of the world, we've been prisoners on the top one-third of our planet. The term 'Earth' is a misnomer. We live on 'The Ocean.'

"Imagine what's down there? Imagine 60-foot-long giant squid, untold species of plants and animals. Imagine!"

Jules Verne would be proud.

This expedition appeals to me because it's not competitive, it's not physical and it's pure exploration. Thanks to Everest, I can now undertake this next dream secure in what I learned from Chomolungma — that I must enjoy the journey to the destination and be careful to preserve my relationships along the way. I will find no personal peace at the bottom. I must continue to create it within the depths of myself.

I first became aware of Graham's historic odyssey when I read about it in a San Francisco newspaper in June, 1998. I knew instantly I had to join him. I have since learned that for years before I became involved, the project was called: "The Ocean Everest Expedition."

Coincidence?

> "The term 'Earth' is a misnomer. We live on 'The Ocean.'"
>
> – GRAHAM HAWKES,
> SUBMERSIBLE
> DESIGNER

*　　*　　*

Since coming down off Everest, going down into a valley, climbing up the other side and looking out in completely new directions, I have had a chance to reflect on my 40 years as a high achiever. My conclusion is that the key to personal happiness does not lie outside us. We cannot find it achieving financial, material, or lifestyle goals. Nor can we find it pursuing physical feats such as Ironman, or Everest. I will not find it at the bottom of the ocean either. The key to personal happiness is inside us, just as the Sherpas have been showing me all along.

Joy is not in things; it is in us.

— RICHARD WAGNER
(1813–1883)

The more we race around trying to get more and more done in a day, make more and more money, buy more *things*, run faster or jump higher, the more some of us are realizing the folly in our fanaticism. Some, like me, have either grown tired, or are in the process of growing tired of chasing our tails, trying to get more done in less time, make more sales, own more property, or buy more furniture. We are looking for new ways to think, and live, differently. Thus, my life goal is no longer just to improve my relationship with myself. It is to help others climb their own inner, and outer, Everests as well.

> *We've been hurrying too much. We have to let our souls catch up with our bodies.*
>
> — African tribesman in the middle of a hunt, from *Re-Packing Your Bags*, by RICHARD LEIDER

To that end, I was able to secure sponsorship from one of my speaking clients, Merck Pharmaceuticals, for Dave Rodney (of our '97 trip) and Dr. Denis Brown (of our '91 and '94 expeditions) to return to Everest in the spring of '99. Denis, who suffers from exercise-induced asthma, but who is a powerful high-altitude climber, hopes to become the first Canadian to climb Everest without the use of bottled oxygen. Dave also aspires to climb the peak, but with bottled oxygen, and is to document Denis's climb. Merck is involved because it has developed a revolutionary new asthma medication called "Singulair." The climb is called, "Touching the Sky." I was thrilled to help put the sponsor and the climbers together.

The key to personal happiness lies within us.

As this book went to press, I received word that, although Denis had been unable to make it to the summit, Dave had. Both men returned safely. I was thrilled, especially as I believe Chomolungma recognized Dave's invaluable contribution to my summit effort in 1997, and apparently chose to reward it. Again, there was a closing of a circle. I have no doubt Denis will also some day stand on top. It is his karma, as well.

In a society that defines success almost entirely by what we do and not by who we are, I believe many of us have lost, or are losing touch with, what's really important in our lives. Some of us have lost our way. I am one who did. I do not intend to repeat the same mistakes I made in my first 40 years in the next 40.

One climbs, one sees. One descends, one sees no longer, but one has seen. There is an art to conducting oneself in the lower regions by the memory of what one saw higher up. When one can no longer see, one can at least still know.
— RENÉ DAUMAL

* * *

And now, my fellow Sherpa, I pass the torch to you.

A year to the day that I stood on the top of Everest, I got together for a commemorative hike with some of my closest friends and greatest heroes, among them, Laurie Skreslet. We scrambled to the top of a mountain west of Calgary and there, after playing the audio tape of my radio conversation with Dave Rodney from the top of Everest and admiring the view of the Canadian Rockies, I presented each of my friends with one of the summit stones I had been permitted to accept from the Mother Goddess. The group included Dave Rodney.

I saved the largest stone for last. Cradling it in my hand, I told Laurie Skreslet what he meant to me, how he and his expedition had inspired me 16 years before, and how everything I had done since could in some way be linked to his team's courageous effort.

"Whether you knew it or not," I said quietly as the sun poked out from behind a cloud and a Silent Bystander smiled upon the scene, "you passed a torch to me, and now," I said, as I placed the stone gently in his hand, "I pass it back to you."

* * *

And now, my fellow Sherpa, I pass a torch to you. Whatever peak you're climbing, path you're following, or trying to find, I hope you're sharing your journey with someone you love, doing something you love, and coming to a greater love of yourself. If you are, you are wealthy and wise beyond measure, and ... you are worthy of being called a Sherpa.

Now, follow your path. Lighten the load of others along the way. If you do, no matter what path you're on, you will always reach your peak.

CAN ... WILL ... CAN ... WILL ...

Climb on my friend.

Find out more about Raja Yoga and Open-Eye Meditation

In the United States, contact:

The Brahma Kumaris World Spiritual University
Global Harmony House
46 S. Middle Neck Road
Great Neck, NY 11021

Tel: (516) 773-0971
Fax: (516) 773-0976
E-mail: newyork@bkwsu.com

In Canada, contact:

The Brahma Kumaris Meditation Centre
897 College St.
Toronto, Ontario
M6H 1A1

Tel: (416) 537-3034
Fax: (416) 537-1319
E-mail: bktoronto@titan.tcn.net

Worldwide Information:

www.bkwsu.com

Alan Hobson sharing his success with a young Sherpa after the summit

MT. EVEREST CLIMBER, SUMMITEER, and cancer survivor, Alan Hobson, is fast developing into one of North America's most inspirational figures. A former journalist, winner of the prestigious William Randolph Hearst Award for Excellence in News Writing, and the author of six books on adventure and achievement, he touches audiences worldwide with his riveting speaking presentations about life, death, tenacity and triumph. Drawing on his past experiences as a former nine-time "All-American" gymnast, veteran of three expeditions to Mt. Everest, as well as the recent challenge of a massive medical mountain he calls his own "Inner Everest," (see Postscript), Alan builds bridges between Everest, life-threatening illness, and the Everests we all face every day. He has appeared on many national television talk shows, including *The Oprah Winfrey Show.*

In his lifetime, Alan has been a marathon runner, hang glider pilot, white water kayaker, white water rafter, ice climber, rock climber, parachutist, luger and bobsleigh participant. His latest passions are mountain biking and scuba diving. But his greatest achievement to date, he asserts, is surviving leukemia (cancer of the blood). His overriding message is simple: "We CAN overcome, we WILL overcome." In fact, CAN/WILL™ has become his trademark.

"My life mission is to inspire others to go after their dreams," he says, "and in so doing, touch the boundlessness of their true potential."

Alan is a full-time professional speaker who makes between 40 and 60 presentations a year worldwide. His long list of clients and expedition sponsors includes some of the globe's biggest and most successful companies, among them Kodak, Johnson & Johnson, Merrill Lynch, Morgan Stanley Dean Witter, Mobil Oil, Sony and many more Fortune 100 and 500 organizations.

Alan is happily married to his wife and business partner, Cecilia. They live in Canmore, Alberta, Canada, in their favorite playground, the majestic Canadian Rocky Mountains, just east of Banff.

To reach Alan, or to inquire about
booking him as a speaker,
contact Cecilia at:

Inner Everests Inc.
#5 – 100 Prospect Heights
Canmore, Alberta, Canada
T1W 2X8

Tel: (403) 609-9939
Fax: (403) 609-2818
E-mail: info@alanhobson.com
Web: www.alanhobson.com

Postscript

Alan Climbs
A Medical Mountain

On August 10, 2000, three years after Everest, Alan came face to face with an even bigger mountain. At 42, he was diagnosed with acute leukemia (cancer of the blood) and given less than a year to live. He successfully endured three rounds of intensive chemotherapy, and then on November 15, 2000, received a life-saving adult blood stem cell transplant from his donor brother, Eric. Today, Alan has made a complete and miraculous recovery. He is one of less than a dozen people ever to attain an elite level of fitness after receiving a blood transplant for leukemia — one of the most risky and radical medical procedures known. Some are calling him "The Adventure Equivalent of Lance Armstrong," the cyclist who came back from testicular cancer to win the greatest bicycle race in the world, *The Tour de France*, four times (at the time of this writing).

Alan now incorporates some of the lessons he learned on his "Everest of Illnesses" into his speaking presentations worldwide and his new program has been met with rave reviews. "If your presentation was a 10 before," one client remarked, "it's a 12 now. Your cancer experience has made you more human and it's made your story more personal to people."

A riveting new book about Alan's ultimate adventure is currently in the works. It is to be his sixth published book and Alan's wife, Cecilia, is the book's co-author. Together, they show how the psychological skill sets they used to face cancer can be used to overcome any challenge. No release date has been set yet for the book, but look for it to positively affect the lives of many, many people very soon.

Alan's dreams of diving to the North Pole and to the deepest point in the ocean, The Challenger Deep of the Mariana Trench, have now been replaced by an even greater goal.

"Thanks to my cancer experience, I guess I really did get to the bottom of the world after all," he says philosophically. "I'm thrilled to say that I've successfully surfaced to an even bigger reality. My goal now is to continue my comeback from cancer, and take as many other cancer survivors with me as possible."

To this end, Alan is helping spearhead a pioneering new medical study into the effects of mild aerobic exercise (e.g. hiking, biking, swimming, cycling, jogging, etc.) in combating chronic fatigue in cancer survivors. Chronic fatigue is a challenge faced not only by cancer survivors, but by millions of others who suffer from depression, fibromyalgia and many other debilitating conditions.

"Somehow, through my training and recovery, I not only overcame my own fatigue, I completely eliminated it. My hope is that this study will help others experience a similar victory."

The study is being conducted at the University of Calgary in conjunction with Calgary's Tom Baker Cancer Centre.

To learn more about Alan's latest real-life adventures, or book him as a professional speaker, visit his website at www.alanhobson.com